DATE DUE

AP 22 04			

DEMCO 38-296

The Reign of Mubarak al-Sabah, Shaikh of Kuwait

The Reign of

MUBARAK AL-SABAH

Shaikh of Kuwait 1896–1915

Salwa Alghanim

I.B. Tauris *Publishers*

LONDON • NEW YORK

Published in 1998 by
I.B.Tauris & Co Ltd
Victoria House
Bloomsbury Square
London WC1B 4DZ

175 Fifth Avenue
New York NY 10010

In the United States of America
and in Canada distributed by
St Martin's Press
175 Fifth Avenue
New York NY 10010

A full CIP record for this book is available from the British Library
A full CIP record for this book is available from the Library of
Congress

ISBN 1 86064 350 7

Library of Congress catalog card number: available

Typeset in Adobe Minion by Hepton Books, Oxford
Printed and bound in Great Britain by WBC Ltd, Bridgend

Contents

This book is dedicated to the memory of
my brother, Marzuq Alghanim
and that of
my great-uncle, Saqr Alghanim

Acknowledgements

This book is based on a PhD thesis presented to the Department of Political Sciences at the School of Oriental and African Studies, London University in 1990. I would like to take the opportunity to express my gratitude to the late Professor P. J. Vatikiotis for all his help, enthusiasm and patience. I owe a lasting debt of gratitude and appreciation to Mr Michael Armstrong who helped a great deal with my research; without his support this work would not have been finished. I also wish to thank Dr Michael Burell for reading the entire manuscript.

My greatest debt is to my sisters, Najeebah, Qadriya and Amel and my brother Mahmoud whose selfless support, encouragement and understanding made this research possible. I would also like to express my gratitude to my Kuwaiti informants who responded to my inquisitive questions with patience and tolerance. I am grateful for their help, without which this research would have been impossible. However, I am wholly responsible for all opinions, errors and omissions.

Salwa Muhammad Ahmad Alghanim
London 1998

Introduction

This book is a study of the rule of Shaikh Mubarak al-Sabah, widely regarded as the founder of modern Kuwait, from his seizure of power in 1896 to his death in 1915. It is based almost entirely on unpublished material, largely on those records of the British Foreign office, India Office, and Government of India agencies in the Arabian Gulf which survive in United Kingdom archives. While its intention is to see the history of Mubarak's reign from an Arab perspective, nevertheless the political realities of time and region require a consideration of the role of the British government in the developments of the period. Issues discussed include the reasons for the shaikh's seizure of power, the political concerns underlying the Anglo–Kuwait Agreement of 1899, the nature of Mubarak's involvement in tribal politics, and his relation to the protagonists in the great struggle for mastery of Central Arabia between the al-Sa'ud and al-Rashid dynasties, and the impact that these factors had on the development of Kuwait under his rule. While not denying the importance of the shaikh's political skills, it argues that he was essentially an opportunist and his ability to control events was not only limited, but indeed had largely passed beyond his control during the last years of his reign.

In the last twenty to twenty-five years there has been a great expansion in studies of Arabia in general and the Arabian Gulf in particular. This development is a reflection of the increased interest in the region resulting from the rivalries between the Eastern and Western blocs and more particularly within this context the strategic importance of the area as the principal source of the world's oil. Inevitably this has produced a wealth of studies concentrating on contemporary economic, military and political issues in the Arabian Gulf.

There has not, however, been an equivalent outpouring of significant historical scholarship. This is not entirely surprising; the methodology of traditional Western scholarship does not readily adapt itself to a culture which is characterised by an oral rather than a literary historical tradition. Moreover, where written records do exist, language difficulties have prevented all but the most determined from using them.

Indeed it is the nature of the surviving historical records which has gone far to shape historical studies of the Gulf. For over 200 years the British were the principal, and for much of the time, the sole power in the Gulf, and it is largely upon British records which students of the modern history of the area must rely. Inevitably, Western scholars with Western preconceptions and preoccupations have tended to write about the Gulf as an extension of the history of the West.

The consequences of this situation are readily apparent when one looks at the more important work that has been done in the history of the Arabian Gulf. Certainly the most memorable book produced since the end of the Second World War is J. B. Kelly's magisterial *Britain and the Persian Gulf, 1795–1880*. The superiority of the scholarship and quality of writing have made this book a starting point for all students of Gulf affairs, even those working at a much later period. Kelly was followed by B. C. Busch's excellent monographs *Britain and the Persian Gulf, 1894–1914* and *Britain, India and the Arabs, 1914–1921* which, while treating narrower periods, attempt to provide an overview of developments in the Gulf similar to that of Kelly. The only criticism that can be made of these works is instantly evident from their titles, 'Britain and ...', both Kelly and Busch, as well as numerous others, continue to see the Gulf in terms of the concerns of the West, indeed Busch's books are really contributions to the traditional history of European diplomacy.

When attention is turned to more specific aspects of the history of the Arabian Gulf, the dearth of worthwhile scholarship is even more evident: this is particularly the case in regard to the history of Kuwait. The most widely known history of Kuwait is Colonel H. R. P. Dickson's *Kuwait and her Neighbours* (1956), to which should be added his *Arab of the Desert* (1949) which contains valuable Kuwait material. This is hardly surprising as Dickson was for many years British political agent in Kuwait as well as an enthusiastic student of Arab life and culture. However, the result is that his books should perhaps be regarded more as sources for the history of Kuwait than contributions to the secondary literature. Other works, for a variety of reasons, are even more unsatisfactory: *The Modern History of Kuwait 1750–1965* (1983) by A. M. Abu Hakima is largely derivative, and has nothing new to say, while *Tarikh al-Kuwait* (History of Kuwait) by Adbul Aziz al-Rushaid (1978) is poorly researched, the product of one who is little more than a court historian. *Tarikh al-Kuwait al-siyasi* (Political History of Kuwait) (1962) by Husain Kalaf al-Shaikh Kaz'al presents a traditional view of the history of Kuwait without evaluating the historical data. *Kuwait, Prospect and Reality* (1972) by H. V. F. Winstone and Zahra Freeth is a superficial journalistic account of little interest despite the fact that Mrs Freeth is the daughter of Colonel Dickson.

If there are weaknesses in previous studies of the Arabian Gulf in general and Kuwait in particular, the situation with regard to Shaikh Mubarak ibn Sabah al-Sabah, Shaikh of Kuwait from 1896 to 1915, is even more deficient: there is not a single book or article devoted to the shaikh or his reign. This is a serious omission in the historical record. Even for Western history the shaikh's rule is of some significance. For it was in Kuwait under Shaikh Mubarak that the British first abandoned their policy of non-involvement in Arabia. For almost two centuries the British had avoided any active role in the affairs of the Gulf littoral. However, in Kuwait under Shaikh Mubarak, they took the initiative to involve themselves in the affairs of the Arab littoral. The shaikh has far greater significance, however, as a turning point in Britain's Arabian policy, for it was under Shaikh Mubarak, and as a direct consequence of his activities, that the foundations were laid for the modern Kuwait state.

I have attempted to see the reign of Shaikh Mubarak as an Arab event and through Arab eyes; nevertheless, it would be pointless to deny the existence of the British presence and the effect of British policy on both Mubarak and Kuwait.

Unfortunately, as far as I have been able to ascertain, there are no al-Sabah archives, at least not any whose existence will be admitted, so British records inevitably form the sole basis of the primary sources for this study. During the reign of Shaikh Mubarak the British were the pre-eminent power in the Arabian Gulf, and the only outsiders in a position to record events in and about Kuwait. Of course this reliance on British records leaves one open to the dangers of the same Western bias for which previous scholars have already been criticised. However, the fact that it is on British sources that we are forced to rely does not necessarily do as much injustice to the past as one would ordinarily think, at least as far as the reign of Shaikh Mubarak is concerned.

As will be seen, the British factor in Kuwait's history under Shaikh Mubarak is central to the course of events. Chapter One discusses the shaikh's seizure of power in 1896 by the murder of his two brothers, and at the same time assesses the relationship between Kuwait and the Ottoman Empire at that time. This is important for an understanding of the events in Chapter Two, which analyses the factors which led to the conclusion of the Anglo–Kuwait Agreement in 1899 which laid the foundation for all future relations with Great Britain and which was of far greater advantage to the British than to Kuwait. Indeed, the Agreement owes its existence far more to the efforts of Lord Curzon, the Viceroy of India, than to those of the Shaikh of Kuwait. However, British influence did not extend beyond the edge of the sea, and while their support was at times critical, Shaikh Mubarak faced other problems in the interior of Arabia with which the British were neither able nor willing to assist. Najd was both an opportunity and a danger to the shaikh. Mubarak was an ambitious man and there is little doubt that he aspired to a leading role in the affairs of central Arabia. Yet Arabia was already under the domination of the al-Rashids of Jabal Shammar who posed an additional threat to the shaikh when they championed the cause of the sons of his murdered brothers. Chapters Three and Four describe this conflict and how the shaikh's policy evolved from one of expansion to one of conservation. Finally, in Chapter Five, it is shown how the territorial basis of the state of Kuwait was established as a by-product of European diplomacy.

There is a constant theme in the history of Kuwait in the years between 1896 and 1915, and that is the crucial importance to the shaikh of his connection with the British. Speculation on the might-have-beens of the past is not the proper function of the historian, nevertheless British support was crucial to the continued existence of Shaikh Mubarak and the development of Kuwait as an independent state.

Geneological Tree of the al-Sabah Family

Mubarak (1837–1915) Shaikh of Kuwait 1896–1915

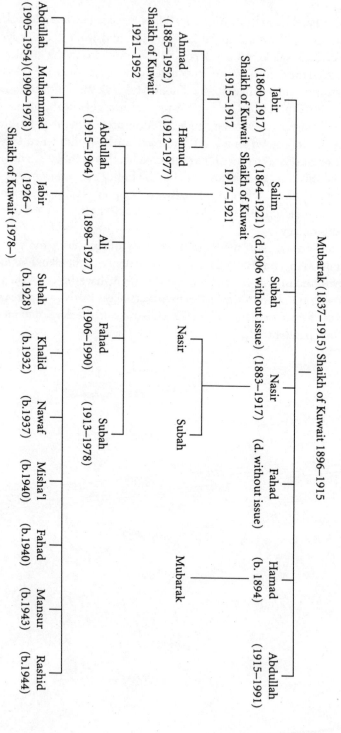

1

Kuwait, the Ottoman Empire and Shaikh Mubarak

Murder by Night: Shaikh Mubarak Seizes Power

On the night of 17 May 1896, Shaikh Mubarak al-Sabah secretly slipped into the town of Kuwait accompanied by his eldest sons, the small group of his personal followers from the Rashayidah of Kuwait and the Ajman tribe. The small band of men quietly crossed the roof-tops to the house of the ruling Shaikh of Kuwait, Mubarak's brother Muhammad. They found Shaikh Muhammad sleeping out of doors, as was common in the hot weather. Shaikh Mubarak shot his brother to death. The noise of the shot was the signal for Jabir to kill his father's oldest brother, Shaikh Jarrah. This was all carried out with great stealth.

Next morning, when other members of the al-Sabah family and leading citizens of Kuwait arrived at the shaikh's palace for the daily council (*majlis*), they were surprised to find Shaikh Mubarak in the place usually occupied by his brother Muhammad. When the hall was full, Shaikh Mubarak announced the death of his two brothers and proclaimed himself Shaikh of Kuwait. Whatever they may have thought of this, the assembly were in no position to object, and accepted the challenge without any protest.

We will probably never know the full story of what happened that night. But we need to understand the origins of the murder in order to make sense of subsequent events, and to correct some misunderstandings about the beginnings of modern Kuwaiti history. The most widely-accepted theory about Mubarak's seizure of power is the interpretation given by H. R. P. Dickson in his book *The Arab of the Desert*, published in 1949. Dickson says that Mubarak acted in May 1896 as a Kuwaiti patriot who was moved to this desperate act by Kuwait's decline under the inept rule of his brothers. Dickson describes Shaikh

Muhammad, who had ruled Kuwait since 1892, as 'lazy and spineless'. He is even ruder about Muhammad's brother and intimate confidant, Shaikh Jarrah, who was murdered by Mubarak's son on that May night, and calls Jarrah 'helpless and slothful'. He claims that Muhammad and Jarrah had come under the evil influence of an 'unscrupulous Iraqi', Yusuf bin Ibrahim, the Shaikh of Dora, whom he alleges to have been pro-Turkish and even a paid Turkish agent who intended to seize Kuwait for himself. Dickson says that Yusuf saw Shaikh Mubarak as the only obstacle to his ambitions in Kuwait, and therefore induced Muhammad to send Mubarak into the desert to keep order among the unruly Bedouin tribes. Having exiled Mubarak from Kuwait itself, Muhammad and Yusuf kept him short of funds in the hope that he would die while carrying out his lonely work. Unfortunately for them, says Dickson, Mubarak learned to survive in the desert and formed ties of friendship and loyalty with the Ajman tribe and with the Rashayidah. Finally, Mubarak despaired of help from his brothers and, conscious of Shaikh Yusuf's designs in Kuwait, decided to take matters into his own hands.

Dickson had a unique position in Kuwait in the middle years of the twentieth century. He served as political agent in Kuwait from 1929 to 1936 and again in 1941. Later in the 1940s he left the Government of India's Political Service for reasons which are not entirely clear. He appears to have been asked to resign, and was almost at once adopted by Ahmad Jabir al-Sabah as a protégé. This enabled Dickson to stay on in Kuwait until he died in 1959. Indeed, his wife Violet lived on in Kuwait until the Iraqi invasion in August 1990 and was evacuated, extremely ill and nearly unconscious, to Britain where she died before the expulsion of Iraqi forces. Dickson and his wife had access to the al-Sabah and everyone else of importance in Kuwait over many years. So his views cannot be set aside lightly. But his very close connection with Mubarak's successors, on whom he depended for his living after he left the British service, means that we must be cautious about accepting his version of events of 1896.

Indeed, some circumstantial evidence contradicts the Dickson version. Firstly, there is no real evidence that the rule of Shaikh Muhammad from 1892 to 1896 was any worse than that of his predecessors, or that Kuwait was suffering any decline. The British records for the years up to 1892 are sparse, but the British officers in Bushire and Basra kept an eye on the northern Gulf. If the condition of Kuwait had deteriorated so badly as to provoke a murder on this scale, we would expect to find some indication of this.[1] Dickson claims that raids on Kuwait by the desert tribes had become chronic, but the surviving records of the British Consulate in Basra and the archives of the British Embassy in Constantinople (to which Basra reported) do not indicate anything out of the ordinary.

As for Dickson's claim that Mubarak seized power so as to make his small country independent of the Ottoman Empire, later chapters will show that Mubarak was not only willing, but anxious to work with the Ottoman authorities in the months after May 1896, at least to the extent that any Arab shaikh of the period was prepared to cooperate with the power which had for centuries been the dominant influence in the Arabian Gulf. Only when he did not get what he wanted from the Ottomans did Mubarak turn to the British for support. As for the claim that Mubarak's opponent, Shaikh Yusuf bin Ibrahim, was some sort of Ottoman agent, the records again suggest a different interpretation. For a start, Shaikh Yusuf was not an 'Iraqi' but came from Najd. Indeed, he came from a long-established Gulf family whose tribal status could be argued to be higher than that of Mubarak's own family, the al-Sabah. Also Shaikh Yusuf was extremely wealthy in his own right and later provided large sums of money to support Shaikh Jasim bin Thani of Qatar and then the Amir of Najd bin Rashid against Mubarak. So it is absurd to see Yusuf as a paid agent of the Ottomans. In fact, Shaikh Yusuf had quite as much difficulty with Ottoman officials after 1896 as did Shaikh Mubarak. Like Mubarak, Yusuf was forced after failing to gain Ottoman support to look for a more reliable partner: first the British and then Mubarak's great enemy, Prince Abdulaziz bin Rashid, the Amir of Najd. By cooperating with the Amir of Najd, Shaikh Yusuf was eventually to become a supporter of a more aggressive Ottoman policy in the region, but all this lay a long time in the future. Interestingly, Shaikh Mubarak himself in all his correspondence with the British never referred to Shaikh Yusuf as an Ottoman agent or supporter: he always described the shaikh as a personal enemy, and in September 1897 the worst thing he could find to say to Mr Gaskin of the British Residency at Bushire was that Shaikh Yusuf had 'caused trouble' between himself and his nephews.[2]

So why did Shaikh Mubarak seize power and commit fratricide? Surely his exile to the desert (if exile it was) cannot have been a significant factor. Mubarak was an experienced desert warrior by 1896 and seems to have been involved in desert warfare for many years. There are hints that he took part in the Kuwaiti contingent which was mobilised during the Ottoman reconquest of al-Hasa in 1871. He certainly led the Kuwaiti contingent on behalf of the Ottomans during the troubles with Shaikh Jasim of Qatar in 1895. The most likely interpretation is that he had been for some years the member of the al-Sabah family responsible for maintaining order in the desert around Kuwait and along the vital caravan routes from Najd and Ottoman Arabia. His tribal and desert links certainly went back a long time, for in 1883 we find that one of his wives was a daughter of Shaikh Thaidan al-Hithlain of the Ajman tribe. If Muhammad did keep Mubarak away from Kuwait in the desert, as Dickson suggests, then he was only sending his brother to an environment which he knew very well and where he had many supporters.

Another explanation of the events of May 1896 was given to the British Consultate in Basra by the sources which first reported these events.[3] This explanation was that Shaikh Muhammad had refused to advance any money to Mubarak. Of course, desert rumours often pointed to arguments over money as the explanation for family disputes. But the rumours were quite likely to be right, as far as can be seen from documentary sources. In the case of the Kuwait murders, even Dickson admits that the immediate cause of the takeover was Mubarak's anger when his brother denied him Rs10,000 for a new wife and a house for her to live in. In March 1897, the British consul in Basra, Captain J. F. Whyte, reported that Mubarak's 'sole object' in killing his two brothers was to take over the wealth of the Shaikhdom which Shaikh Muhammad was thought to have accumulated.[4] Whyte's successor in Basra reported, more than five years later, that Mubarak had hoped when he seized the Shaikhdom in 1896 that he would find several hundred thousand rupees in the treasury. Instead, according to the consul, he only found Rs16,000, and he blamed Shaikh Yusuf of Dora for this very large shortfall.[5]

So the more prosaic picture of a frustrated younger brother seizing control of power and wealth which he was unlikely to obtain by other means now seems closer to the truth than Dickson's 'heroic' version of events. A keen interest in money was certainly to be the dominant motif of much of Mubarak's later life. But, whatever the exact reasons for the seizure of power, British observers at the time considered it to be an unusual event. An official Government of India study of the history of Kuwait, prepared in 1905, observed that there were few political events in the history of Kuwait up to 1896, and that the deaths of Kuwaiti chiefs were normally followed by a smooth transfer of power.[6] The problem in evaluating this judgement is that so little has survived in the way of a documentary record for Kuwait's development up to 1896. But an understanding of Kuwait's relations with other powers in the Gulf region is essential if we are to make sense of Shaikh Mubarak's actions in the early years of his reign. Part of what follows is speculative but it does justice to what is known of Kuwait's early history and it does not contradict any known facts.[7]

The al-Sabah and Kuwait, 1716–1896

The al-Sabah can trace their rule over Kuwait back to the first-ever recorded shaikh in Kuwait, Shaikh Sabah bin Jabir al-Sabah. He assumed the title of Shaikh of Kuwait some time after 1752, and held it until he died in 1762. However, it is unknown how or in what circumstances the al-Sabah became the ruling family of Kuwait as information about the years up to 1752 is extremely scare. We can only say with certainty that the al-Sabah family must have come to Kuwait some time before 1750 as one of a group of families from the great Ana'iza tribal confederation of Najd, who were forced out of Najd by a major drought and food shortage. The group included the al-Sabah, the al-Khalifah (now the rulers of Bahrain), and al-Jalahima and the al-Zayid.[8] Together, they were known as the Utub, deriving from the Arabic word *'ataba*, meaning 'to go'. This name was probably a reference to the long years of wandering which led them to Kuwait. But this is practically all that can be said with certainty.

It is particularly hard to fix the data when the Utub families arrived in Kuwait. In 1817, a British officer, Francis Warden, compiled a 'Historical Sketch of the Ottoobee Tribes' for the British East India Company's Bombay government. He gives the date 1716 for their arrival in Kuwait and the start of a permanent town. But Warden may have been simplifying a complicated process as the Utub seem to have assembled gradually in Kuwait over a period of years, if we are to believe local traditions. For example, the al-Khalifah family tradition is that the al-Khalifah, one of the families in the Utub group, arrived in Kuwait before the al-Sabah, and then found it difficult to accept the rule of the relative newcomers, the al-Sabah. This may explain why the most important section of the al-Khalifah left Kuwait in 1766 on the start of the long journey which eventually brought them to Bahrain.[9] Faced with the proliferation of conflicting accounts, we suggest the following rough chronology:

1. The various Utub families left their original home in the Najd desert towards the end of the seventeenth century. This was probably part of the scattering of the Ana'iza tribe out of Najd because of a long period of drought in the second half of the seventeenth century. When they reached the Gulf coast, the Utub settled in the area of the Qatar peninsula.
2. There are persistent traditions that the Utub stayed in the Qatar region for a considerable period of time, maybe as long as fifty years. They may have spread out during this time from Qatar to neighbouring areas of the Gulf coast. But at some time after 1700, the Utub families assembled (or perhaps reassembled) in Kuwait. It is possible that their maritime traditions as pearl

fishers and traders date back to the time they spent in Qatar, and that they moved from the Qatar region to Kuwait by ship.

If the Utub did arrive in the Kuwait area after 1700, they would have found the region under the control of the powerful Bani Khalid tribe. The Bani Khalid had expelled the Ottomans from the region of al-Hasa in 1670. By 1700, Bani Khalid's power extended from Qatar in the south to Kuwait in the north. Local Kuwaiti historians suggest that Kuwait itself was founded in 1688, before the Utub arrived, by Shaikh Barrak, who was one of the most successful of the Bani Khalid rulers and the 'liberator' of al-Hasa from the Ottomans. But this seems to be a slight error as Barrak died in 1682. The most likely reconciliation of accounts is that the Bani Khalid had some form of residence, perhaps a summer residence, on the site of present-day Kuwait before the Utub began to gather there in the first half of the eighteenth century.

The Bani Khalid continued to be the dominant power in eastern Arabia until well into the eighteenth century. So the al-Sabah and the other Utub families must have accepted Bani Khalid overlordship in their early years in Kuwait. The Bani Khalid suffered their first succession crisis in 1722, on the death of their shaikh, Sa'dun. But the real break-up of the family started in 1752 with the death of the Bani Khalid ruler Sulaiman bin-Muhammad al-Hamid. This may have been the period when the al-Sabah were first able to describe themselves as more or less independent shaikhs of Kuwait. But in any event, the Bani Khalid do not appear to have been oppressive overlords. Indeed, they may have done the early rulers of Kuwait a service by shielding them from any direct contact with the Ottomans, who were kept busy in the first years of the eighteenth century dealing with internal conflicts and war against the Abbasid Empire in Persia. Only when the Bani Khalid disappeared from the Arabian political scene did the al-Sabah have to develop a relationship with the Ottomans.

Above all, the Bani Khalid had no great interest in maritime activities. So the al-Sabah and the other Utub families were left to themselves in pearl-fishing, trading and other forms of fishing. These early years in Kuwait seem to have confirmed the orientation of the al-Sabah and the other Utub families as people who lived essentially by the sea and from the sea. As newcomers to the northern Gulf region, they were cut off from the traditions of desert life, and from the hierarchical and status-conscious pattern of tribal society. As families who had been forced to move far from their original homes, the Utub became a merchant people, with rather a distant and uneasy relationship with the desert which surrounded them on the landward side. Even their most ambitious ruler, Shaikh Mubarak of Kuwait, was to be handicapped in his dealings with the desert tribes by his family's lack of a real power-base in desert society.

Kuwait's relationship with the Ottoman Empire changed after 1800 to one of closer cooperation. Visitors to Kuwait in the middle years of the nineteenth century had to admit that Kuwait gave the impression of being technically in a dependent relationship with the Ottoman Empire, although they also stressed that the Ottoman Empire exercised no real authority over Kuwait.

The documentary evidence for this shift in policy is extremely sparse. But we can be sure that Wahhabi pressure on Kuwait and the Western frontiers of the Basra region played an important role in forcing Kuwait into some form of accommodation with the Ottoman Empire. We know that Kuwait contributed forces to the unsuccessful Ottoman expedition against the Wahhabis in 1798, and may also have participated in the even more disastrous expedition of 1802. For a short time after 1802, Kuwait appears to have paid tribute to the Wahhabis, until a quarrel over this tribute led to an unsuccessful Wahhabi attack on Kuwait in 1808.[10] The invasion of central Arabia by the Ottoman governor of Egypt, Muhammad Ali, removed the Wahhabi threat for a number of years by destroying the Wahhabi capital at Dariya in 1818. But by this time Kuwait seems to have accepted the need for some formal relationship with the Ottoman Empire in order to have at least some security against a resurgence of pressure from its Arabian neighbours.

In 1829, a British visitor, Captain G. B. Brucks, reported that the Kuwait ruling family acknowledged the authority of the Turks, and paid a tribute of rice and dates. In return for this tribute, the Shaikh of Kuwait received an honorary dress from the Turkish government each year.[11]

A few years later, to judge by a report from Kemball in 1858, the payment system was reversed, and the Ottoman authorities in Basra began paying 140 karahs of dates 'in return for the feudal obligation to defend the Turkish possessions on the Euphrates if attacked from the sea'.[12] Kuwait would not have been the only place to receive such a subsidy, as many of the desert tribes took advantage of the ineffective nature of Ottoman authority outside the major urban centres to demand some form of 'protection money' for the safeguarding of caravans and villages.

British observers also make it clear that Kuwait's relationship with the Ottoman Empire was not a simple case of subordination to a superior authority. Kemball, writing in 1856, pointed out the total lack of any Ottoman presence or authority in Kuwait.

In his words: 'Though Koweit has always been acknowledged to be a Turkish dependency, its vessels without exception carrying the Turkish flag, the authority of the sultan over its inhabitants is merely nominal.' He confirmed the shaikh's receipt of an annual allowance in return for the obligation to defend Basra on the Shatt by sea. A few lines later, he spotted the most important point of the arrangement, from the Kuwaiti side: 'No Turkish officer resides on the spot.'[13] As we shall see, it was the Turkish decision to base an official in Kuwait, just over 40 years later, which induced the Shaikh Mubarak to seek the protection of the British as a counter to a Turkish presence which by then was threatening to become actual, instead of being largely symbolic.

Unfortunately for Kuwait and the tribes of eastern/central Arabia, Ottoman policy changed very radically in the late 1850s towards a more effective exercise of control over outlying areas such as the Gulf coast. The new spirit of assertion on the Ottoman side was a consequence of the Crimean War, which had provided the Turkish army with a lot of new equipment, and which had also eased the financial situation of the Empire through the very large loan negotiated on the Empire's behalf by its major allies in the war, Britain and France.

The first indication of the new Ottoman policy came in January 1859, when an Ottoman official Husni Bey arrived in Basra bringing presents for the Shaikh of Kuwait and a bundle of Turkish flags for Arab shaikhs along the Gulf coast as far as Bahrain. The Ottomans were also discussing projects for a railway through Mesopotamia to Basra, as well as a telegraph line. The British consul in Basra suspected that, if either of these projects became a reality, 'stations might be erected on spots which she would claim as an integral part of her Empire.'[14]

While the 1859 mission was a failure, and the official concerned only stayed in Kuwait for less than a month, a follow-up mission in 1860 by another official from Baghdad was more successful. This official, Muhammad Bey, succeeded in obtaining a request from the Shaikh of Bahrain for Ottoman protection. Such a request was exactly what the new assertive policy of the Ottoman Empire required. It also alarmed the British, who regarded Bahrain as falling within their sphere of influence on the Arab side of the Gulf. So in 1861 the British resident in the Gulf persuaded the Shaikh of Bahrain to adhere to the British-backed Trucial System, which had applied throughout the Lower Gulf region since 1820.

By the mid-1860s, the Ottoman pressure on the Arab states of the northern Gulf was becoming insistent. The Ottomans had the great advantage of the divisions between the Arabs, which gave scope for political interference. In particular, the long-standing dispute between Kuwait and Zubair was an excellent opportunity to put pressure on Kuwait.[15] At some time after 1863, a member of Zubair's merchant community, Sulaiman Abdulrazaq Zuhair, had sold an estate on Safiyah Island to Shaikh Jabir al-Sabah of Kuwait. Sulaiman's heirs claimed that Sulaiman had not in fact owned most of the estate, and that the sale was therefore invalid. Late in 1865 or early in 1866, the Qaimaqam of Basra decided to support Sulaiman's heirs in the case. The British consul in Basra was in no doubt that this was a tactical move by the Ottoman *qaimaqam* to inflame relations between Zubair and Kuwait. He suggested that the policy was a risky one for the Ottomans. Either the Kuwaitis would manage to resist, and so would succeed in distancing themselves from all Ottoman authority. Or, if their resistance failed, there was a good chance that the entire settlement would move down the coast to Qatif or Uqair, and 'the Turks will be richer by a depopulated tract.'[16]

There is no doubt that the Ottoman tactic worried the al-Sabah. In May 1866, Shaikh Jabir's brother, Abdullah, went to Basra to try to settle the question on his brother's behalf, but was threatened with imprisonment unless he immediately paid revenues from the disputed estates. He had to be rescued by a Kuwaiti merchant in Basra, who agreed to put up a guarantee for him. Back in Kuwait, the shaikh himself felt it would be safer to request that the British steamers, which often called at Kuwait, should suspend their visits for the time being so as not to provoke the Ottomans.

The dispute over the estate was resolved peacefully when the Governor of Baghdad, Namik Pasha, ruled in favour of the al-Sabah. The governor was apparently influenced by reports that the Shaikh of Kuwait was indeed intending to resist by force. But Namik Pasha demanded a major concession from the al-Sabah in return for his helpful verdict. He told Shaikh Abdullah, who was again acting as an intermediary, that he now wished to establish an Ottoman Customs House in Kuwait. This was of course a very serious blow to the comfortable and distant relations between Kuwait and the Ottoman Empire. The al-Sabah family cannot have been greatly reassured by the governor's assurance that it was only intended to provide 'a tangible display of Turkish sovereignty', and would not limit the shaikh's authority.[17]

The governor followed up this request by ordering the Naqib of Basra to send his brother, Muhammad Sa'id, to Kuwait to make the necessary arrangements. The Kuwaitis stalled as best they could, asking Muhammad Sa'id to postpone the decision until the autumn of 1866, when the leading men of the town would have returned. They also pointed out that the Customs House would serve no practical purpose, as Kuwait produced nothing of value itself, and almost all imports came from Basra, where they had already paid duty.

The issue of the Customs House dragged on inconclusively for some time after the summer of 1866. But bigger threats to Kuwait's status soon appeared on the horizon. In the autumn or early winter of 1866, Shaikh Sabah of Kuwait died and was succeeded by his son, Shaikh Abdullah, who had to face the problem of an immediate request from Namik Pasha that he should go to Baghdad to be invested formally as Shaikh of Kuwait. Abdullah was able to avoid this dangerous and politically-risky trip and to negotiate a compromise under which the *firman* appointing him as Shaikh of Kuwait was delivered to Kuwait by the commander of the Turkish gunboat *Ismir* on 23 January 1867.[18]

But a new danger to Kuwait's delicate relationship with the Ottoman Empire was about to emerge from Central Arabia. The death of Faisal of Najd in December 1865 had been followed by a dispute between Faisal's two sons, Abdullah and Sa'ud, which spilled over from Riyadh and Najd into the northern Gulf region. Indeed, while a unified and strong Sa'udi state in Najd had often caused serious problems for Kuwait and the other Gulf states in the past, the period of instability and strife in Najd after 1865 was to present challenges which were just as serious for smaller neighbours such as Kuwait.

To start with, Prince Abdullah bin Faisal was able to consolidate his position in Riyadh, and to expand the city's defences through the construction of the Masmak fort. On the face of it, this was a positive development for the al-Sabah in Kuwait as Prince Abdullah was apparently a supporter of the al-Sabah in their dispute with the Zuhairs of Zubair.[19] But Prince Abdullah's brother, Sa'ud, weakened Abdullah's position in Najd through intrigues in Riyadh itself and through an alliance with Muscat and Bahrain and some of the desert tribes such as the Ajman. In 1870, Sa'ud moved out of Bahrain and captured Uqair and Hufuf. When Prince Abdullah tried to bring Sa'ud to battle at Jiddah, the result was a decisive victory for Sa'ud. Prince Abdullah left Riyadh and turned to the Ottomans for support against his brother. Unfortunately for Kuwait, Abdullah's appeal for help was well received by the Vali of Baghdad, the reform-minded Midhat Pasha.

The British consul-general in Baghdad was sure that Midhat's positive reply to Prince Abdullah was motivated by the thought that Ottoman intervention in Najd would open the way for a re-establishment of Ottoman control over the entire Gulf region. In the consul-general's words, support for Abdullah would be offered '... with the view of sustaining (the Porte's) nominal suzerainty over those countries, and because he entertains a hope that by so doing the Ottoman government may obtain a more real supremacy over Bahrain, Muscat and the independent tribes of southern Arabia.[20]

Midhat Pasha, with his usual energy and enthusiasm, began to prepare the expedition in support of Prince Abdullah, which would also re-establish Ottoman control over what is now the Eastern Province of Sa'udi Arabia. The British consul-general in Baghdad remarked that Midhat Pasha seemed to under-estimate the warlike nature of the people against whom he would be fighting, and also to be unaware of the difficulties of the terrain. In Colonel Herbert's words, 'the pasha makes light of the undertaking he is commencing.'

Midhat Pasha planned the expedition as a twin operation. A land force of Muntafiq tribesmen and contingents from Zubair and Kuwait would go overland, and there would also be a seaborne element, carried in part by 300 boats supplied by the Shaikh of Kuwait. Kuwait's participation in the expedition alarmed both Sa'ud bin Faisal in Riyadh and Shaikh Isa of Bahrain. They appealed to Britain's resident in the Gulf, Lewis Pelly, to stop Kuwait, on the grounds that this was a violation of the maritime peace. Pelly was prepared to consider the request favourably, but the Government of India refused to become involved in the matter, and instructed Pelly to take no action.

Midhat Pasha got off to a bad start in the Spring of 1871. Cholera broke out among the Ottoman troops. Meanwhile, a Kuwaiti force which had been ordered to punish the Mutair tribe for their attacks on Prince Abdullah's messengers met with a disastrous defeat and fled back to Kuwait after abandoning most of its animals. But Shaikh Abdullah of Kuwait was playing a political role in the Ottoman expedition, as well as a purely military role. It is his political activities in support of the Ottoman campaign which provide the main interest of the summer of 1871. In May 1871, agents of Shaikh Abdullah reached Bida in Qatar, and appear to have tried to mobilise Shaikh Muhammad bin Thani of Qatar and his son, Shaikh Jasim, to attack Bahrain. The inducement offered by Shaikh Abdullah was a promise that the Ottomans were preparing to attack Bahrain, and that Pelly himself had been removed from office in Bushire. In Pelly's words: 'The intrigues of Kuwait Shaikh, in the interest of the Turks, had disturbed the minds of Jasim son of the Gutter Chief.'

Meanwhile, Abdullah was also trying to intimidate the ruler of Bahrain through direct threats. Shaikh Abdullah wrote to the ruler of Bahrain, inviting him to come 'in a friendly manner' to Qatif

> to meet the commander of the Ottoman expedition. According to Abdullah, if the ruler of Bahrain declined the invitation, then the Ottomans might well think of another ruler for Bahrain such as Jasim bin Muhammad bin Thani of Qatar. The ruler of Bahrain, however, was confident of British support and declined Shaikh Abdullah's 'invitation'.[22]

On 25 May 1871 the Ottoman expedition landed at Ras Tanurah, and marched on to Qatif. Sa'ud's governor in Qatif first refused to surrender the fort. But he changed his mind following an Ottoman assault by land which was supported by an attack from the sea by the Kuwaiti fleet'.[23]

After this success, most of the Kuwaiti boats returned home, but Shaikh Abdullah stayed with the Ottoman commander, Nafidah Pasha, as the Ottoman forces moved on to capture al-Hasa. In early July, Shaikh Abdullah went off to Bida, in Qatar, taking letters from the Ottoman commander together with a proclamation from the Governor of Basra stating the sultan's intention to extend Ottoman rule all along the Arab coast to Muscat and to distribute a parcel of Ottoman flags. In Bida, Shaikh Abdullah persuaded Shaikh Jasim bin Muhammad bin Thani to hoist one of the Turkish flags over his house: Major Smith believed that Jasim's enthusiasm for using the flag was because he believed that he would be able to attack Bahrain as an agent of the Ottomans. But Jasim's father, Shaikh Muhammad, gave an evasive reply to Shaikh Abdullah, pleading that most of his people were away at the pearl banks.[24]

Indeed, Shaikh Abdullah's activities on behalf of the Ottomans did not stop with the distribution of flags. A secret agent working for the Arab representative in Bahrain of Britain's resident in the Gulf reported from Qatif that Shaikh Abdullah was in August 1871 awaiting orders from the Ottoman Commander before going again to Bida to establish an Ottoman Customs House. In the agent's clear view, 'the Chief of Koweit takes pleasure in carrying out the Turkish Government orders'.[25]

However, Shaikh Abdullah of Kuwait seems to have lost his enthusiasm for political work on behalf of the Ottomans during August and September 1871. This is not surprising. Bedouin tribes loyal to Amir Sa'ud bin Faisal began to attack the Qatar peninsula, and Shaikh Abdullah was careful not to return there in August. After repeated requests to the Ottoman commander for permission to return to Kuwait, he succeeded in getting the authority to go home, and departed for Kuwait at the start of October.[26]

It was soon after his return to Kuwait that Shaikh Abdullah received the Vali of Baghdad himself, Midhat Pasha, who was on his way to al-Hasa to inspect the new Ottoman conquests. During his visit to Kuwait in early November, Midhat Pasha formally installed Shaikh Abdullah as an Ottoman Qaimaqam, and declared Kuwait to be under the protection of the Ottoman Empire—the first time that such an explicit declaration of Ottoman sovereignty had been made in Kuwait itself'.[27]

At about this time, towards the end of November 1871, Lewis Pelly in the British Residency in Bushire heard a report that Midhat Pasha had compelled

Shaikh Abdullah to instal an Ottoman Customs House in Kuwait, in return for the Ottoman recognition and protection given to him. Pelly's report was, in fact, untrue, but the story shows the fine line which the Ruler of Kuwait was now treading in his dealings with the Ottomans. Support for their new and aggressive policy in the Gulf region could bring Kuwait benefits in its rivalries with other Arab entities. But it could also risk the close Ottoman involvement in Kuwaiti affairs which Abdullah's predecessors had always tried to avoid.

In the months after November 1871, Abdullah continued his policy of association with Ottoman plans. In December 1871, we find him back at Bida, in Qatar, assisting with the establishment of an Ottoman garrison. Reports of Arab observers working for the British suggest that Shaikh Muhammad bin Thani of Qatar and the people of Bida were very unhappy about the new Ottoman garrison. This may explain why Shaikh Jasim bin Thani later showed such hostility to the al-Sabah of Kuwait, who had supported the move.[28]

Shaikh Abdullah also worked to support Ottoman ambitions in Bahrain. During December, he worked with Midhat Pasha to persuade a leading Bahrain merchant in Qatif to obtain the signatures of 50 or 60 'substantial' merchants of Bahrain to a petition requesting Ottoman rule over Bahrain. This plan collapsed when Midhat Pasha was suddenly recalled to Baghdad.[29]

Bearing in mind the normal Arab antipathy towards the Turks, and the traditional Kuwaiti policy of avoiding close contact with the Ottomans, we may wonder why the Shaikh of Kuwait was prepared to cooperate unreservedly with the Ottoman expedition. It may be that Shaikh Abdullah calculated that the Ottomans were aiming for a total takeover of the region, in which case he would benefit from being on the side of the strongest power in the Gulf. Pelly seems to have thought that the Ottoman plan was to occupy Bahrain and to extend their direct influence towards Muscat, so that they would be able to offer control over Bahrain as a 'bribe' (in his words) to the al-Sabah.[30] It seems most unlikely that Abdullah would have wanted or expected to be able to become Shaikh of Bahrain as well as Kuwait. Pelly's remark probably reflects British sensitivity over their position on the Island rather than a considered assessment of local politics.

A more likely explanation is that Abdullah of Kuwait saw the entire episode of the Ottoman expedition into eastern Arabia as a chance to stand by Prince Abdullah bin Faisal of Najd, who had been his ally in Central Arabia in the past. When Prince Abdullah bin Faisal finally reached al-Hasa in late August 1871, salutes were fired in Kuwait.

Under this view, Shaikh Abdullah may have reasoned that the Ottoman occupation of eastern Arabia would be merely temporary and that, once Prince

Abdullah was safely installed in Najd, Ottoman troops would withdraw. If this was Shaikh Abdullah's calculation, then it would be easy to understand why he showed a distinct lack of enthusiasm for participating in the Ottoman expedition in the late summer of 1871, as it became clear that the Turks were intending to stay in the area permanently.

Indeed, Shaikh Abdullah gave a clear indication in September 1871 that he was still hoping for the Ottomans to withdraw from Qatif and al-Hasa. In a conversation with a Bahrain merchant, Hamid bin Hudaid, which was reported back to the British resident in Bushire, Abdullah said that the Ottomans would be well-advised to:

> ... make Abdullah bin Faysul Ameer, give him two Regiments and four guns that is quite sufficient for him to maintain himself against all comers. The Ameer to pay Tribute, and all expenses connected with the Troops. It is no use the Turks keeping the country, they would require a large force to keep the people down and the revenue would not cover the outlay.[31]

All reports suggest that during 1872 Shaikh Abdullah's involvement with the Ottomans caused growing problems for him in his own town of Kuwait. In January 1872, a Persian merchant in Basra observed that the people of Kuwait were 'in perplexity and embarrassed, and regret that they ever meddled in this matter at the outset.'[32] This comment came a few weeks after the Turkish commander had called on Shaikh Abdullah's brother, Mubarak, to raise and lead a force of 2,000 men to assist in putting down tribal disturbances in al-Hasa and Najd. Mubarak had stalled on the request, pleading illness. But the strains caused by Kuwait's policy seem to have intensified as the year went on. In August, a report from Bahrain stated that all business in Kuwait was at a standstill, because Muhammad al-Sabah and his brothers were oppressing the people, and their troops were plundering the shops without payment.[33] Another report claimed that '180 houses in Kuwait stood empty, and that Abdullah and his brother each being Governor of Kuwait between them there is no law at all.'[34]

The British news agent in Bahrain also picked up a report, during February 1872, to the effect that the Ottoman military commander in al-Hasa was now deeply hostile to the al-Sabah, whom he considered to be treacherous to the Ottoman government. All in all, the al-Sabah had earned nothing from their pro-Ottoman policy.

In June 1872, the new Vali of Baghdad made another request to the al-Sabah to raise a force of 2,000 men for service in al-Hasa. Shaikh Abdullah made every possible excuse to avoid complying, and a Kuwait force did not in fact ever go to al-Hasa. But Shaikh Abdullah, after his investiture as *qaimaqam*, could not avoid the vali's command entirely. So he turned up in al-Hasa in August 1872 apparently acting as an intermediary in attempts to bring the conflict in Najd to an end.

By 1873, Shaikh Abdullah seems to have decided to disengage from the struggle in Najd, altogether. In the spring of that year, a member of the staff of Lt. Col. E. C. Ross, the British resident in the Gulf, visited Kuwait and reported that neither Prince Abdullah bin Faisal nor Sa'ud bin Faisal were spoken of with respect! At the same time, a British official reported that Shaikh Abdullah's brother, Mubarak, had visited Prince Abdullah in the desert and had, in effect, offered the Sa'udi prince money to stay away from Kuwait. According to the British report, Mubarak told the prince: 'Don't come into Kowait, because if you do, there is no doubt but that the Turkish authorities will write to Abdullah bin Subah to arrest you and send you to Baghdad. This is your best course, take money if you are in need of it and go into Nejd.'[35]

This bleak brush-off to the Sa'udi prince ended Kuwait's involvement with the war in Najd. The war dragged on with varying fortunes (even though Sa'ud bin Faisal died in 1875) until in 1887 the great rivals of the al-Sa'ud, the Ibn Rashid of Hail, besieged Riyadh and captured it for the first time. After a brief period when members of the al-Sa'ud family were allowed to govern, Riyadh suffered its final humiliation in 1891, when Muhammad Ibn Rashid destroyed its walls and palaces and most of its date-groves, and Prince Abdulraham bin Faisal had to flee the city, with his daughter, Nura, and his son, Abdulaziz, (the future King of Sa'udi Arabia) tied into camel bags.

Back in Kuwait, the al-Sabah reverted after 1873 to their traditional policy of correct but rather distant relations with the Ottomans. In retrospect, Shaikh Abdullah's decision to involve himself so closely in the Ottoman plans for Eastern Arabia during 1871–73 looks like an error of judgement. His brother, Mubarak, would be careful to avoid repeating the error when his turn came to govern the little state.

Mubarak's Inheritance: Kuwait in 1896

It is not easy to find reliable and detailed information about the Kuwait which Mubarak took over on the night of 17 May 1896. The northern Gulf was not often visited by European travellers and officials in the nineteenth century, and the archives of the then Ottoman government have not so far yielded much information about the little state. The oral traditions of the Kuwaitis themselves give some evidence for the quality and texture of life in Kuwait, but do not have much to say about facts and figures. So much of the following section is based on information provided by British observers after 1904, when a British political agent was established in Kuwait. We can only do our best to adjust this information to reflect conditions in 1896, bearing in mind that Kuwait had expanded strongly between 1896 and 1904 despite political uncertainties.

One thing can be said with confidence about the Kuwait of 1896. More than practically any other town on the Arabian Gulf shore, Kuwait was a 'city-state' in the classical sense of the word. Of course, Kuwaitis interacted with the desert hinterland in many ways. They relied on the desert tribes as markets for the goods which Kuwait imported from India, Europe and America. Desert bedouins also provided some of the manpower for Kuwait's pearl-fishing fleet. Many Kuwaitis, including Shaikh Mubarak, had family links and links of friendship with the desert. Even so, the British officer, J. G. Lorimer, was right to state in his entry for Kuwait in the *Gazetteer* of 1908, that 'the whole of Kuwait depends for its wealth and prosperity on one town, and the political predominance of the capital is here greater than in almost any country.'

Of the towns of the lower Gulf, only Dubai presents a similar example of a 'city-state' with rather little political spread into the surrounding hinterland. It is no accident that both Dubai and Kuwait were above all centres of commerce, maritime towns which faced the sea rather than the land. In 1912, the Danish traveller, Raunkiaer, described Kuwait as 'just a place of clay between steppe and sea'. He also pointed out the near-total absence of vegetation and surface water in Kuwait town. What little water could be extracted came from deep wells, which were easily exhausted: indeed, by 1912, Kuwait was relying mainly on water shipped in from the Shatt al-Arab in special boats. In 1896, this source of supply was not available and the water for Kuwait's people had to carried by donkey drawn from wells about four miles south of the town.

These harsh facts compelled Kuwait to rely on its commercial skills and on the exciting, but unpredictable, profits of pearl-fishing. The temperament of the town struck most observers as orderly and cautious. The virtues of Kuwait were the commercial ones of getting and spending what money could be extracted from trade and pearling, and life for most Kuwaitis was always tough. This remorseless struggle for economic survival was tempered to some extent by the wild swings from despair to euphoria in the very cyclical pearling industry. The oral tradition of poetry and reminiscence makes the pearl-diver into the hero of the Kuwaiti imagination, the man who struggles against the elements and who might (but how rarely and unpredictably) be catapulted to wealth by a stroke of fortune.

Population and Society

Estimates for the total population of Kuwait during the nineteenth century vary greatly. Hennel in 1841 put the total population at 25,000. Pelly in 1863 gave a lower figure of about 15,000. Lord Curzon, who did not visit Kuwait during his tour of the Gulf in 1888–89, but who amassed a great deal of information in his obsessive way, believed the population was 20,000. Much later, in 1908, Lorimer quoted a figure of 35,000 in his *Gazetteer*, but the town had been expanding fast in the years up to Lorimer's 1904 visit to Kuwait. A figure of between 20,000 and 25,000 is probably right for 1896.

The people of Kuwait were overwhelmingly Arab by descent. The Persian community numbered about 1,000 according to Lorimer, and there were some Jews, a handful of Armenians and perhaps 4,000 negroes; but there were no Indian traders established in Kuwait. Apart from the al-Sabah family themselves, Lorimer described the upper stratum of Kuwait society as made up of about 14 very wealthy trading families (10 Arab, two Persian and two Jewish families). The rest of the Persian community included about 20 lesser merchants, 100 shopkeepers and some poorer labourers. Lorimer estimated the Jewish community at between 100 and 200. They had their own synagogue and, apart from the two major merchant families, were mainly occupied as cloth sellers and goldsmiths.

The fact that the Indians from Shikarpur and Sind, who played such a role in business life in Bahrain and other Gulf ports, had not established themselves in Kuwait surprised Captain Shakespear when he was political agent in Kuwait in the years up to 1914. In 1911, Shakespear reported scathingly on the lack of sophistication of the leading Arab and Persian merchants of Kuwait. He accused them of relying entirely on one or two Arab correspondents in Bombay for all their business dealings, and accepting any goods which these agents sent them. He suggested that Kuwait would benefit from an influx of Hindu and Muslim traders.[36] Two years later, in his trade report for 1913, he went even further. He called the leading Kuwaiti merchants ignorant, with little or no knowledge of conducting large-scale commercial transactions and no knowledge of foreign languages. As a result, he thought that they were completely at the mercy of their 'few correspondents in India, who themselves were inept'.[37] Shakespear was surely mistaken in this scathing condemnation of the Kuwaiti merchants, who were in fact considered as among the most skilful and successful in the Gulf. A few years later, another British official saw the lack of an Indian presence in Kuwait as a positive advantage for Kuwaiti commerce. This official records that the Kuwaiti Arab traders had always been in the forefront of the Arab business world. Instead of Indians coming to Kuwait to seek business, the Kuwaitis went to India themselves. 'This is an old condition of affairs', the report continues, 'but its importance does not lessen. Hardly a business house in Kuwait does not have at least one member of its family either in Bombay or Karachi.'[38] The sheer success of Kuwait's economy during the last years of the nineteenth century must indicate that this view is correct, and that Shakespear had simply misunderstood the situation.

The town of Kuwait had outgrown its original walls by 1896, and continued to expand up to 1914 and beyond. Only in 1920 was the town re-walled. The architecture of the houses was apparently plain and unadorned: mainly one-storey houses of sun-dried clay, with few doors and windows on the outside, looking taller than one-storey in many cases because of high parapets which enclosed the roof area. Lorimer complained of an ever-present smell of sewage in the streets from the many cess-pits, but Pelly in 1863 described Kuwait as unusually clean, and Raunkiaer in 1912 thought that the streets were 'conspicuous for cleanliness' as well as straight. Kuwait also had a reputation as one of the healthiest towns in the Gulf region, with little or no ophthalmia or smallpox.

Kuwait's links with the outside world in 1896 were by Arab sailing boat and camel only. The steamship service from India to Kuwait had been suspended some years earlier, and would not resume until 1901. There was no telegraph office nearer than the British-manned office in Fao. Telegraphs, therefore, had to be sent by boat to Fao, and from there along the undersea cable to Jask and then by overland line across Persia to India. The Ottoman Empire's nearest official presence was in Basra, which was also the location of the nearest European consulates.

The Kuwait Economy: Trade and Pearling

Kuwait has little fresh water and practically no agriculture. So, from the start, it has had to make its living from other resources. Until the discovery of oil, the only resources available to it were the acumen of its merchants and the skill of its pearl divers and boat builders. In 1896, therefore, Kuwait extracted its living in every sense from the sea.

Fortunately, Kuwait's traders were considered to be among the most skilful in the Gulf. They exploited the opportunities for importing goods from India, Africa, Europe and America, and trading them with the desert tribes of the Arabian interior. Meanwhile, most of the poorer classes of Kuwait made their living from the summer pearl-fishing season, and from the more limited pearl diving of the winter months. The result of this dependence on trade and pearl fishing was that the economy of Kuwait was subject to wild fluctuations, caused by the changes in trade and in pearl diving. A drought in Arabia or the breakdown of political security in the desert could disrupt trade very considerably and often without any warning. In pearl diving, the fluctuations were even more severe. In general, the nineteenth century and early twentieth century were periods of rising demand for pearls among the middle-class ladies of Europe and North America, as well as in the traditional customer groups of the European aristocracy. Even so, the pearling industry was chronically subject to patterns of 'boom and bust'. Partly this was because the precise location of the pearl-bearing oysters was largely a matter of instinct and luck, so that the catch varied from year to year, in addition to the disruption sometimes caused by storms in the Gulf, but also the demand pattern in Europe and North America was subject to shifts of fashion or prosperity, and could be influenced by a build-up of stocks causing prices to fall. For this reason, the pearling industry was never a stable source of revenue. In Kuwait, a good year such as the 'golden year' of 1912 was all too often followed by a bad, year such as 1913, when the pearl catch largely failed, and most Kuwaitis were reduced to real hardship, and even to selling their few household possessions on street corners. Economically, Kuwait, like the other towns of the Arabian Gulf, lived on a roller-coaster.

This was despite the fact that the Kuwait economy was generally thought to be more diversified, and therefore more secure, than the economies of other Gulf towns such as Bahrain and Qatar. In Kuwait, the risk and uncertainty of the pearling business caused some of the leading merchants of Kuwait to make a conscious decision not to get involved in pearling at all. Instead, these merchants concentrated on trading with the tribes of central Arabia.[39] The fact that some merchants avoided the pearling sector in this way, and would not even lend money to the pearl-boat captains as a personal favour, meant that Kuwait was less exposed to the risks of pearling than Bahrain and Qatar, which were effectively on-product economies dominated by pearling. Despite this degree of diversification, Kuwait was still a society influenced at every level by pearl fishing, because of the large number of Kuwaitis employed in the industry as pearl divers and haulers, or as suppliers to the industry in the form of boat building or selling food to the boat captains. The harsh rhythms of the pearl-diving calendar, and the struggle to wrest a living from the oyster beds of the Gulf, shaped Kuwait society in ways which seem almost unbelievable today. Most of the poorer male inhabitants of the town had to spend the summer away from Kuwait, working on the pearl banks of the northern Gulf or the much larger banks of Bahrain. They passed these summer months in constant, dangerous work on small boats with inadequate food. Their reward was often a lifetime of debt slavery, which could not even be ended by death, as their sons often had to inherit their financial burdens from them.

We may wonder why Kuwaitis and other Gulf Arabs accepted these hard conditions of life. The answer has to be that the pearling industry had been the mainstay of the precarious economies of the Arabian Gulf for centuries, long before the Utub families settled in Kuwait. Over the centuries, the industry had developed strong traditions and customs, and had come to be seen as the 'way of life' of the region. It also supported a number of vested interests, such as the boat builders who provided the vessels for the pearling fleet, the suppliers of the food to the divers and above all the merchants who bought the pearls from the pearling boats and sold them in the great markets of Bahrain and Bombay. These vested interests simply dominated Gulf society and prevented significant change. The pearl merchants in particular ensured the continuity of the system by providing loans to the boat captains and the divers at high cost. These loans were often impossible to repay and had the effect of maintaining the various participants on the industry in their traditional status.

The strongly traditional and hierarchical nature of the pearl-diving industry is well summarised in an article by L. E. Sweet, written in 1964:

> The Gulf Arabs constituted, in fact, an economically-specialised ethnically-distinct 'caste' of the coastal populations of the Arabian Gulf. All were organised in lineages with genealogical traditions, which linked them to the great tribes of Arabia ... The chiefs and their kinsmen were the marine of the Gulf, owning and controlling not only sailing craft, but also engaging in or controlling exclusively the maritime activities, pearling, fishing, piloting, the coasting-trade and the long-distance carrying trade to India and Africa.[40]

As already mentioned, the strong traditions and systems of the Gulf pearling industry go back many centuries, long before the al-Sabah and their fellow Utub families settled in the northern Gulf. The pearl banks of the Gulf were certainly being exploited in the second millenium BC if we interpret the reference to 'a parcel of fish-eyes from Dilmun' in a cuneiform tablet of 2000 BC, found at Ur, in the obvious sense of a reference to pearls from Bahrain.[41] In the first century AD, the Roman scholar and scientific writer Pliny the Elder (AD 23–79) says in Book 9 of his *Natural History* that 'the most perfect and exquisite pearls of all are the ones obtained from around Arabia, within the Gulf'.

And these early sources confirm that conditions in the industry were harsh. Back in the sixth century AD, the great Jahilliyah poet al-Mukhabbal al-Sa'idi gives a striking picture of the emaciated, undernourished pearl diver, suffering hardships which a Kuwaiti of Mubarak's time would surely have recognised at once:

> Choices of pearls whose light illuminates
> The throne-chamber of the King of Persia,
> Surrendered at a fabled price
> By the wasted arrow-like diver
> Who with his oil-smeared chest plucked it
> Out of the deep, amidst the menace of the devil-fish.[42]

A little later, in the tenth century, al-Mas'udi visited the pearl banks and confirmed that the divers ate practically nothing except for a little fish and a few dates during the season. They had to paint their legs and feet black, to avoid being swallowed by the beasts of the sea.[43]

Another great Arab traveller, the North African Ibn Battutah, gave a celebrated account of the Arabian Gulf pearling industry when he visited the region early in the fourteenth century. The most interesting part of his account is his demonstration that the famous Gulf credit system was already in place, fulfilling its role as a barrier to change and upward mobility in the industry. He points out that the divers were so badly in debt because of past misfortunes that they had to surrender most of their catch to their creditors as soon as they brought it up to the surface. When the pearls were collected, 'the sultan takes his fifth, and the remainder are bought by the merchants who are there in the boats. Most of them (the merchants) are the creditors of the divers, and they take the pearls in quittance of their debt or as much of it as is their due.'[44]

Although Ibn Battutah refers to pearl banks on both the Arab and Persian sides of the Gulf, it was the Arab banks in the northern Gulf and off Bahrain which dominated the Gulf industry by 1896. On the Arab side, the banks were treated as a common Arab resource, open to all Arabs of the Gulf region. This meant that the Kuwaiti ship captains had a choice of bank on which to spend the summer either the 'high' banks near Kuwait or the 'low' banks off Bahrain. The length of the season itself was closely regulated by the weather, which prevented any deep-sea diving in the winter, and also by the setting of dates for the start and end of the main diving season. The main season – the *ghaws al-kabir* – averaged four months from the second half of May or start of June to late August or September. The pearling boats were expected to remain on the banks until the day appointed by the *sirdal* (admiral of the bank) for the fleet to return home. Any *nakhoda* who left the banks to return to Kuwait before the appointed day would be subject to severe punishment.

Although we have seen that the Gulf pearling industry is of great antiquity, some important changes were taking place during the second half of the nineteenth century. The most significant was the great increase in demand for pearls in Western Europe and North America. Pearls had always been a prized form of jewellery and fashion accessory, but until about 1850 they were only bought by aristocrats and extremely wealthy people. The nineteenth-century bourgeois middle class adopted the pearl necklace as a symbol of wealth and social standing. This expansion in demand, coupled with the continuing demand for pearls in India and countries of the Far East, meant that prices were on a strongly rising trend from 1850 onwards. In 1877 Captain Durand, the first assistant political resident in the Gulf, recorded that the real price of pearls bought from the Gulf boats had increased by 50 per cent over the past 25 years.[45] This rise continued until the First World War and even afterwards, until the Japanese cultured pearl industry knocked the market flat in the 1930s. So Kuwait, like other Gulf pearl-diving ports, experienced its best period economically and ended the nineteenth century on a fairly high economic note. Kuwaitis in 1896 would surely have agreed with the Qatari who told Palgrave, during his Arabian travels in 1863, 'we are all, from the highest to the lowest, slaves of one master, pearl.'[46]

We cannot now be sure how many boats and men were involved in the pearling industry in 1896. Lorimer thought that Kuwait sent about 460 pearling boats to the banks in the years around 1905, employing 9,200 men.[47] Al-Qina'i suggests a figure of 812 pearling boats under Mubarak.[48] Dickson thought that there were 700 pearling boats employing between 10,000 and 15,000 men in the years before 1914.[49] The figures for the number of men employed may seem rather high in relation to our earliest estimates of the total population of Kuwait, but it must be remembered that proportion of the men who worked the Kuwait pearling fleet would not have been permanent residents of Kuwait, but would have been Bedouin from the Arabian desert who combined summer work on the pearl banks with their winter activities as herdsmen and fighters. Even so, Kuwait must have been a very quiet town during the summer with so many of its menfolk away on the nearby pearl banks or on the much larger banks near Bahrain, which were regarded as the common resource of all the Gulf Arabs. The return of the pearling fleet to Kuwait at the end of August was the signal for active commercial life to resume in the town as the boat builders and captains began to prepare for the next season.

Pearl fishing imposed a very special kind of organisation on Kuwaiti society based on a fairly rigid division of functions between the various participants. The system was hierarchical and in many ways oppressive to modern eyes. At every stage, the balance of economic advantage was with the traders who bought the pearls from the diving boats and traded them in the markets of Bahrain and Bombay. The people who suffered the most were the people who worked the hardest on the pearl banks: the divers, who plunged time after time into the dangerous waters of the Gulf until their breath was exhausted, and the haulers who pulled them up at the end of each dive. Back in 1835 Colonel Wilson had identified the essential unfairness of the traditional system commenting that 'the man who makes the most fearful exertions in diving hardly has food to eat.'[50] Quite apart from inadequate food, the divers faced some extremely unpleasant occupational illnesses, including deafness, rheumatism, scurvy, ophthalmia and the 'bends' caused by the frequent changes of pressure as they dived, rested and then dived again. Storms and sudden currents took a regular toll of casualties and sharks, devilfish, jellyfish and swordfish added to their risks. Curzon believed that a total of 250 men had died in the pearl banks from one cause or another during the single season of 1885.

A modern view of this harsh environment must be tempered by the recollection that the entire Arabian environment of the nineteenth century was harsh and violent. Although the divers, the haulers and the other boat workers frequently complained in their poetry and songs of the rapacity of their employers and the inadequacy of their rewards, they also accepted these hardships as an inevitable part of life. The need for credit to finance families during the winter months prevented the divers and haulers from trying to change their status. A theme of the oral traditions of Kuwaiti society was the way in which people generally stayed in their particular social 'group' for generations: the ship captains (*nakhodas*) would take their sons on board during the summer to learn the job of a *nakhoda*, but would prevent the boys from learning any other trade. There were cases of 'upward mobility' (such as divers accumulating money to set up as *nakhodas*) but these seem to have been rare.[51]

If we start at the top of the social pyramid, the richest members of the pearl-diving industry were undoubtedly the pearl merchants (*tawwash*, plural *tawawish*). These merchants fulfilled two key functions: they bough the pearls from the pearling boats and sold them on in the markets of India. They also provided the financial credit which most of the ship captains needed in order to fit their boats out for the pearling season. Even within the *tawawish* there were important distinctions. At the very top were about ten very rich merchants, called *tajirs*, who bought on a very large scale from the ship captains and had their own direct commercial dealings with correspondents in Bombay and even in Europe. According to Lorimer, these *tajirs* did not have to travel to the pearl banks during the summer as all the business they needed came to their door in Kuwait.[52] Ranking below these very substantial merchants were the lesser *tawawish*, who did not have their own international banks and bought up pearls as they were fished. We can recognise these figures in the famous account of the Gulf pearling industry back in 1328 by Ibn Battutah who describes merchants of this kind going round the pearl fleet and taking pearls in settlement of the debts previously accumulated by the divers.

Moving down the economic scale, the next major group was the ship captains (*nakhodas*) who recruited the divers and haulers for their boats, and who exercised dictatorial powers over them during the pearling season. The *nakhoda* depended on his skill in navigation, and his ability to locate concentrations of oysters on the banks by experience and instinct. If the *nakhoda* was lucky enough to own his own ship, free of debt, then he was well-placed to profit from the season. The problem was that, at least by Mubarak's time, relatively few *nakhodas* were in this happy position. Most had fallen into debt to the merchants who supplied them with food and equipment for the season. Instead of functioning as independent operators, these had to accept an economically subordinate position within a fleet of pearling boats belonging to one of the richer merchants. These fleets of boats had come to dominate the industry by 1896, and the truly independent *nakhodas* who were able to operate on their own account were a fairly small minority. In 1910, when four of the leading pearl merchants quarrelled with Shaikh Mubarak and considered transferring their allegiance from Kuwait to another Gulf town, it was found that between them they controlled a 'fleet of between 250 and 300 boats, a very substantial part of the total fleet.'[53]

The complement of a Kuwait pearling boat seems to have varied between 10 and 40 men, with an average of 25 to 30 as the norm. The crew included the *nakhoda* and his deputy, the *muqaddami*, who supervised the crew aboard ship, as well as the helmsman. The working crew members were the divers and the haulers who pulled the divers up in response to a tug on the guard-rope, which indicated that the diver had run out of air. Each boat also carried one man of crucial importance for morale and efficiency: the singer, or *nahham*, who provided entertainment with his songs and who also set the rhythm for the tasks which required teamwork, such as rowing and hauling.

As we have hinted, one of the most important factors in maintaining the strict division of functions between the various groups involved in pearling was the credit system, which underpinned all aspects of pearling. Al-Khusri, in his Arabic-language book *Studies in the History of Kuwait*, implies that the various ship captains had at some time in the past been financially independent operators, and that the erosion of their position to the point where they had to relinquish ownership of their boats to pay debts to the pearl merchants was a fairly recent phenomenon.[54] In making this claim, al-Khusri is reflecting the oral traditions of Kuwait, which describe the individual pearling boat as the production unit of the sector, and which regard the role of the *tawawish* in financing and controlling the boats as an anomaly. However, these traditions may be a little misleading. Back in 1833, Colonel Wilson's 'Memorandum on the Gulf Fisheries' described the merchants as advancing money to the fishing boats at 100 per cent, as well as using their dominant supplier position to supply dates, rice and other necessities at prices of their choosing.[55]

The likely truth is that everywhere in the Gulf the uncertainties of pearl fishing soon caused all participants to sink into debt in varying degrees. The divers and haulers generally depended on their *nakhodas* for financial support to carry them through the winter and to provide for their families while they were away on the pearl banks. Most of the *nakhodas* in turn depended on the merchants for finance to enable them to put to sea.

The mechanisms by which this finance was provided to the captains of the Kuwait pearling fleet is one of the hardest subjects to research after so many years. The merchants who lent the money and the *nakhodas* who received it have not left us any written accounts of their complicated dealings, so that we have to rely on observers such as Colonel Wilson in 1833 and Ibn Battutah 500 years before him for an impression of the way in which the system operated.

We can be sure that most of the industry's working capital originated with the rich merchants, the *tawawish*, who numbered about ten in Kuwait according to the Kuwaiti writer Hissah al-Rifa'i. Some of this capital was provided by direct loans from the *tawawish* to the captains of the ships. There are also persistent references to a special group of financial operators, the *musaqqams*, who seem to have made their living by arranging loans from the *tawawish* for the boat captains, as well as investing their own resources in fitting out the boats. Lorimer gives a clue about their role in the following passage of his *Gazetteer*:

> The Musaqqam is generally a man of substance, but some Musaqqams who have not sufficient capital of their own conduct their business by means of loans, which they obtain for the season from wealthy Arab or Indian merchants at 10–25 per cent interest.[56]

Lorimer's account confirms the hints we have already collected that interest rates in the Gulf pearling industry were extraordinarily high. The rates of 10–25 per cent which he quotes for loans from the *tawawish* to the *musaqqams* for money advanced for a single season are, in themselves, fairly steep. In line with human nature everywhere, we can assume that the *musaqqams* would have lent this money to the *nakhodas* at even higher rates. To judge from the bitter tone of much Kuwaiti and Gulf poetry, the *nakhodas* were not too reluctant to squeeze as much interest as possible out of the divers, haulers and other crew members, to whom they lent money, in advance of each season and during the quiet winter months. The credit system, therefore, must have pressed down extraordinarily high on the divers and haulers at the bottom of this complicated pyramid.

Problems appeared at all levels of the credit structure if there was a bad season due to a poor catch or low prices in the market. The divers, haulers and other crew members would not be able to repay the monies advanced to them in the previous winter to support their families, or the monies loaned at the start of the season to support their families and to cover their personal needs during the fishing season. Moving up the scale this default by the divers and the other crew members put the ship captains in the embarrassing position of being unable to repay their debts to the pearl merchants. The result was that the *nakhodas* were forced to commit themselves for years ahead to working on behalf of the pearl merchants to whom they were now obliged. Equally, the crew members would have to accept a long-term form of debt bondage to their *nakhoda*, to enable them to pay off their debts over a number of seasons.

The following poem composed by a diver shows the impact of this debt accumulation on the lowest strata of the pearl diving economy:

> Our merchant creditors, though the winter has ended,
> Seem to ignore us, and our shares they refuse to surrender.
> Is it because they are now under financial strain
> Or just because they want to spite and deprive us?
> What has become of our livelihood, we who were led
> To dive for pearls, even like a throng of donkeys in a herd?
> We suffered cold and bitter hunger, also chilling humiliation
> As, like slaves, we rushed to serve and do their bidding.
> Where are the pearls we collected for them from the deep?[57]

As so often in history, the debt system was strongly defended by exactly those people who suffered the most from it. When Kuwait suffered one of the periodic economic depressions in the pearl market during 1907 and 1908, because of the decline in the demand for pearls, Shaikh Mubarak made an attempt to reform the financial arrangements governing the industry, so as to limit the amounts advanced to pearlers, and to fix schedules for the repayment of money lent to them by their *nakhodas* and in turn the money lent to the *nakhodas* by the pearl merchants. In particular, Mubarak proposed that no pearler would be allowed to receive more than Rs50 during the winter months. However, the divers, haulers and other seamen criticised the plan to limit their debts in this way, and their criticisms were echoed by the *nakhodas* and the pearl merchants. Even though the political agent praised the new rules as salutary, and as freeing the pearlers from an oppressive economic domination, it soon became clear that the pearlers simply did not want to be freed in this way preferring to continue to be allowed to run up very large debts.[58]

At its worst, the credit system which dominated Kuwait's pearling sector, deserves the name of debt slavery. This emotive term should not be used lightly, but can be justified by the following considerations:

The very high rates of interest charged at each stage of the chain of debts. As we have seen, interest rates of up to 100 per cent were charged on the advances made by merchants to *nakhodas*. The sources available to us are silent about the rates charged to the unfortunate pearl divers and haulers, but we can assume that these were also very high.

Once the divers and haulers had fallen into debt, it was extremely hard for them to escape. Local Kuwaiti law prevented a diver from transferring his allegiance to any other *nakhoda* as long as he retained a debt obligation to one particular *nakhoda*. The primitive and undiversified Kuwaiti economy did not offer any alternative to employment in the pearling sector. So the indebted diver had to stay for years in the service of his *nakhoda*, hoping that a run of good seasons would make it possible to pay off the debt.

Kuwaiti customary law also provided that the debts of a diver or other crew member did not terminate on death, but were passed on to the children of the diver. The credit system, therefore, functioned harshly, especially in the case of the people who worked hardest and took the most risk to bring pearls up from the oyster beds of the Gulf. We must also remember that a minority of boat owners and divers managed to stay out of the credit system and therefore enjoyed the chance to control their income to their own benefit. This minority of 'free operatives' seems to have had an importance out of proportion to its numbers, as it provided an ideal and a source of hope for the many who were effectively imprisoned by the credit system.

Firstly, there were always a few *nakhodas* who had avoided falling into debt and, by luck or good management, had preserved their financial independence. Secondly, a number of pearl divers, mainly of Bedouin origin, organised themselves into free cooperatives, hiring their own boat and even choosing their own *nakhoda* under a form of contract called *mutarabi'ahn*. The Bedouin were apparently able to accumulate the money needed to hire the boat and to fit it out because they possessed an advantage denied to most of the townspeople of Kuwait: a small winter income from their herding and semi-agricultural activities. In his account of the Gulf pearling industry in 1878, Geary comments that only a few of the pearling boats were worked by 'Arabs who are not the bond slaves of the pearl merchants' in this way.[59]

Even though few in number, the free Bedouin cooperatives seem to have influenced the way in which Kuwaitis viewed their main industry. It was the free diver, and especially the diver of Bedouin origin, who appeared in traditional Kuwaiti poetry as a kind of heroic archetype of courage and manhood. Although many divers were economically exploited and harshly treated, the work of the diver was always seen in Kuwait as inherently heroic and worthwhile. A sign of this respect was that the divers were always excused from performing non-diving tasks or chores on board ship. They never took part in rowing and were waited on by other crew members.

The respect accorded to pearl divers in traditional Kuwaiti society rather resembles the respect given in European industrial societies to the coal miners, who wrested the main source of fuel and power from underground pits. The coal miners and the pearl fishers shared a life of real hardship and danger, cut off from normal pleasures for long periods at a time. In both cases, qualities such as endurance, courage and strength were at a premium, and the possessors of these qualities became the 'archetypes' of successful human beings. In the case of the Kuwaiti pearl divers, the heroic quality of their lives gained an extra dimension from the obvious linkage with the Bedouin Arab ideal of bravery, as extolled in Arabic poetry. This is not surprising, as a very significant number of pearl divers in Kuwait were in fact desert Bedouin, who used the pearl banks as a source of summer employment to combine with their winter activities. These divers brought with them a tradition of poetry and recitation which was well-suited to the harsh struggle against nature on the Gulf pearl banks.

There were other reasons why the Bedouin ideal fitted in well with the pearling sector. In particular, the Bedouin divers found a ready parallel between the Gulf pearl banks, which were treated as a common resource open to all Arabs on an equal basis, and the free grazing conditions of the Arabian desert. In both environments, it was individual skill and luck which counted in making a living. In the desert, a skilled leader could identify, by looking at the sky, where rain was likely to fall and where a little grazing might become available. He could therefore ensure that his own people got to the grazing area first, just as a successful captain of a pearling boat could position himself by instinct and experience on the best part of the oyster bed.

In consequence, Kuwait developed a sea-inspired folk culture, with poetry and stories, which extolled the skill and solidarity of the divers in the same way that the poetry of the desert glorified the 'survival-virtues' of pastoral nomadic life. In Kuwaiti poetry, we find frequent references to the random cruelty of waves and storms, and also to the value of coordinated and regulated human effort. The essential qualities of the divers, such as endurance, courage and physical strength, were raised to a heroic level. So also were the romantic aspects of wresting a living from the jaws of the sea, with all this meant in terms of fellowship and camaraderie among the divers and haulers, who spent the summer crowded together on the pearling boats, in their mind's eye they sometimes tended to idealise the past in terms of the predominance of charity, compassion and social responsibility, invoking idealistic visions of the rich helping and succouring the poor, omitting to recognise that while charity, solidarity and compassion did indeed exist, it was more often than not the poor succouring the poor, sharing the little they had with their brethren and seeing to it that their children did not starve should misfortune overtake them, and the rich striving to help their own kind in adversity, standing between them and ruin. Examples abound in each individual acts of charity and mercy by *nakhodas* or merchants helped to save and sustain and ensure a fair, just treatment by a human application of discipline; nevertheless, there were those *nakhodas*, as we have shown, who used every ounce of power invested in them to bully and inflict suffering, choosing to disregard the traditional values of kindness, generosity and simplicity of manners. Kuwaitis might be a town people, with little direct involvement in the life of the great Arabian desert on their doorstep, but they had a mythical structure and a rhythm of life of their own. As Mubarak was to discover, any attempt to prevent them from going to the pearling banks during the season would involve a political risk of the highest order, as it would strike at the heart of their life and values.

By contrast with pearling, the profits from Kuwait's import and export trade seem to have been more stable, although a drought in the desert could still cause a slump in the import–export trade by depriving the Bedouin of the means to buy the food, textiles and metal goods, which Kuwait imported for onward sale to the desert tribes. Many of the merchants involved in the import–export trade in Kuwait deliberately avoided any involvement in pearling, on the grounds that pearling was far too risky and speculative. Kuwait certainly benefited from the presence of a large merchant community, which resisted the lure of pearling: most accounts agree that Kuwait enjoyed a much sounder balance than most of the Gulf towns between pearling and general trading activities. The key elements in Kuwait's trading role were its geographical location on the end of many caravan routes from Najd and Jabal Shammar to the Gulf, and its general policy of charging lower tariffs than Ottoman trading centres such as Basra. In 1831, Stocqueler reported that the Kuwait tariff on imports was only two per cent of value. Pelly in 1865 talks of the advantage Kuwait derived from its very low export tariffs on horses exported to India from Jabal Shammar via Kuwait: horses sent from Shammar via Basra faced much higher charges. Although Mubarak, at the end of his reign, put customs duties up to rather high levels as part of his search for extra finance, it is likely that the tariffs in force in 1896 were still very low.

The goods which came into Kuwait for onward sale to the desert tribes included cloth and rice, sugar, timber, spices, cotton and tobacco. The clothes and textiles came from Britain and America as well as India, but most of the other products seem to have originated in India. In the other direction, Kuwait sent products from the desert to the markets of India. Horses from Jabal Shammar were the most valuable of these items, as India relied on constant inputs of Arab blood stock to maintain the quality of its horse population. In 1865, according to Pelly, Kuwait exported 800 horses to India each year. These horses were bought by agents of Kuwaiti merchants who travelled round Jabal Shammar. The other large export to India was a food product: dates from the very large date plantations of the Shatt al-Arab (where Mubarak's family had considerable private estates). On a smaller scale, Kuwait also exported wool, hides and clarified butter (ghee) produced by the desert tribes as a supplement to their subsistence economy.

In addition to the trade in food and textiles, Kuwait profited during the 1890s onwards from the covert trade in arms. Mubarak took 6 rials (dollars) on every rifle that was imported and two rials again if it was exported. For example, in a single week in October 1911, 6,000 rifles were imported and the shaikhs dues on them amounted to £5,000 or Rs75,000.[60] The other beneficiaries were Haji Muhammad Taqi and Haji Muhammad Ali Marafi, both of whom were Persian Kuwaiti. Rifles were shipped from Europe to the Gulf throughout the nineteenth century, and were then infiltrated through the Gulf ports into Najd and into the Ottoman and Persian Empires. Both the Ottomans and the British objected strongly to this traffic; the Ottomans because it was a general policy to ban private firearms in the Empire, and the British because many of the guns smuggled into Persia would pass on to Afghanistan and the north-west frontier of the British Empire in India, where they would be used to kill British soldiers. The policing of the Gulf to prevent the arms trade never seems to have been effective, and the few indications we can glean from British sources suggest that the clandestine shipment of rifles up the Gulf was increasing during the 1890s, partly in response to political disturbances in Persia and on the Indian frontier.

Kuwait also benefited in all its trading activities from the Ottoman occupation of Qatif in 1871. In effect, Kuwait was the only port in the northern Gulf which was free of Ottoman control after 1871, and it must have seen a rise in its share of Najd's trade with the outside world as a result. As the Danish traveller, Raunkiaer, noted in 1912, the Arabs had a deep personal dislike of the Ottomans, so that the tribes and merchants of Najd were much happier dealing with Kuwait than with centres such as Zubair, Basra and Uqair.

The prosperity of the pearling and trading sectors in Kuwait during the 1890s must have also boosted one of the major manufacturing industries of Kuwait: boat building. Kuwait did not, of course, have any timber resources or raw materials such as rope and coir. All the components of the boats had to be imported from India and East Africa. Kuwait did, however, have a reserve of skilled boat builders, and a series of 'yards' along its shore, which Lorimer describes as the major boat-building centre of the Gulf. Britain's trade report for 1910 mentions that between 65 and 70 boats had been built in Kuwait in the previous year. Some of these were for export to other Gulf ports, but it is not clear how many.

So Mubarak took over a small estate, and a state where many people scraped a rather precarious living. Even so, the economy of Kuwait was one of the most dynamic in its region. The interesting thing is that, despite all the disturbances of the early years of his region, with wars in the desert and pressure from the Ottoman Empire, Kuwait was able to attract more people from the desert to come and live in the town. Mubarak's base of revenues and population was rising strongly in 1896. This would enable him to raise very considerably the scale of his political ambitions.

Mubarak's First Phase: Negotiation with the Ottoman Empire

Shaikh Mubarak seized power in Kuwait in May 1896. Nine months later, in February 1897, he began to seek the protection of the British government: a decision which was to change the history of Kuwait and the northern Gulf.

So the first nine months of Mubarak's reign form a separate chapter of which the main theme was his quest for some form of sanction for his takeover from the Ottoman Empire. To obtain this sanction, he was prepared to spend time and to promise a great deal of money in bidding for the title of *qaimaqam* from the Ottoman authorities, and he was also prepared to fly the Turkish flag. Ironically enough, he did finally obtain the title in December 1897, after he had begun his lengthy negotiations with the British authorities in the Gulf.

As we will see, there are reasons to believe that Mubarak did not regard either the acceptance of the title of *qaimaqam* or the use of the Turkish flag as compromising his essential political independence, but he clearly did decide that his independence was under threat when the Ottoman authorities first proposed in early 1897 to station an official in Kuwait to supervise quarantine arrangements. Titles and flags were one thing. A permanent Ottoman official presence in his town was something else. So he put out his first feelers to the British, a decision which represented a very radical change of course from the policies which he and his predecessors had followed. These policies are best seen as striking the best deal which Kuwait could achieve, as a small and not very warlike state in a rather isolated region of the world, with one regional power: the Ottoman Empire.

Looking back over the early history of Kuwait, we have to admire the skill with which successive rulers of Kuwait managed to maintain the independence of their tiny state. To achieve this aim, they had to make numerous protestations of subservience and loyalty to the Ottoman Porte. Tidy-minded officials of the British Empire and of other European powers, who had a strong professional interest in dividing the world into easily-managed power-blocs, tended to see these protestations as representing an abandonment of independence and an acceptance of the Ottoman sovereignty. Through Kuwaiti eyes, they were facets of a continuous political dialogue, which aimed above all at keeping the Ottomans at arm's length.

The Ottoman authorities were prepared to accept this policy simply because, in large areas of their Empire, they did not have the administrative and military resources to control local rulers and leaders on a day-to-day basis. Although the Ottoman Empire appeared to cover a very large area of the map in the nineteenth century, the reality was rather different. As a recent writer has described it: 'the appearance of orderly administration, indeed of effective administration of any sort, was chimerical ... .' There were army garrisons, it is true, scattered about the empire, but otherwise power was diffuse and the centralised authority was more myth than reality. Gertrude Bell in the course of her travels found that, outside the towns Ottoman administration vanished and the local shaikh or headman 'roamed at will'.[61]

In the Gulf region, the Empire's control was particularly weak until well

into the second half of the century, when the appearance of embryonic projects for telegraph lines and rail routes gave the area a higher priority. As a
result of this new concern, the Ottomans mounted their expedition into al-
Hasa, and granted the title of *qaimaqam* to Shaikh Abdullah of Kuwait in 1871
and to his brother, Shaikh Muhammad, in 1892. The grant of this title and the
fact that Kuwait did occasionally cooperate with Ottoman officials gave the
Porte good reason to regard Kuwait as part of the Ottoman Empire, in the
same way as many other outlying parts of the Empire where the Ottomans did
not exert day-to-day control, but where the local rulers had agreed to some
form of Ottoman rank or title. The Kuwaitis were willing to give this tacit
acknowledgement of Ottoman suzerainty as long as the actual independence
of Kuwait was not compromised by any Ottoman attempt to exert real control. Some hint of the way the Kuwaitis saw the relationship is provided by the
British resident in the Gulf, Sir Lewis Pelly, who remarked after visiting Kuwait
in 1863 that the Kuwaitis 'acknowledge the Turks, as we do the 39 Articles,
which all accept and none remember.'[62] At about the same time, the British
consul in Basra rightly warned that the people of Kuwait would probably not
accept a greater assertion of control by the Ottomans, and might be prepared
to take the extreme step of migrating to an area where they would not be subject to direct Ottoman interference. Writing in 1866, the consul described the
possible outcome of Ottoman interference in graphic terms: 'Instead of a
thriving town, the Turks will be the richer by a depopulated tract.'[63]

Later in his reign, Shaikh Mubarak was to fundamentally change the nature
of Kuwait's relationship with the Ottoman Empire, by bringing the British
into the northern Gulf region as a counterweight to the Ottomans. However,
at the start of his reign, in 1896, Mubarak gave no sign of wanting to break
away from the Ottoman relationship. Indeed, he went to great trouble and
expense to gain recognition from the Porte. He presumably calculated that his
position was so weak that he needed the Turkish Government's recognition.
This impression is confirmed by a report which the British senior naval officer
in the Gulf, Commander Baker, submitted after a visit to Kuwait in July 1896.
Baker found the shaikh extremely sensitive about offending the Ottomans by
visiting the British warship. In Baker's words:

> Kuwait is nominally an independent Arab territory, but in reality the Turks exercise
> great influence over it, more especially since the new Chief acceded to power he
> finds it necessary to play into their hands. I paid him a visit, but he would not come
> off to the Ship. I also noticed that he flew the Turkish flag, and taxed him with it,
> but could not get any satisfactory answer from him.[64]

There were good reasons why Mubarak felt insecure. Shortly after Mubarak and his son murdered their fathers, Mubarak's three nephews fled to the desert. The three nephews, who were to be a problem for Mubarak for many years, were Sa'ud and Sabah bin Muhammad and Hamud bin Jarrah. Once in the desert, they found protection from a Bedouin shaikh, who escorted them to the home of their uncle on their maternal side, Shaikh Yusuf al-Ibrahim of Dora. Mubarak acted quickly in response to this news. His first step was to seize control of the al-Sabah date gardens at Fao, in Ottoman territory. These were the chief source of income for the family. By seizing them, Shaikh Mubarak gained the income for himself and also denied it to his opponents. The money he gained allowed him to start an energetic campaign of bribery. His first target was Hamdi Pasha, the Vali of Basra, to whom he reportedly offered a sum of £T10,000 to use his good offices with the Porte to obtain sanction for Mubarak's rule in Kuwait. Unfortunately for Mubarak, Hamdi was the wrong person to choose, as he was a rarity among Ottoman officials: a scrupulously honest administrator. In his previous post as a director of a government-controlled steamship company, he had been dismissed when he earned the hostility of the Ottoman minister of Marine by objecting to misappropriations of the company's funds. He was also a proud and temperamental man, who deeply resented Shaikh Mubarak's attempt to bribe him.[65]

Mubarak also made a direct approach to the Ottoman government during the summer of 1896, claiming that his two brothers had not been assassinated by him, but had been killed by the Bedouin while he was away from Kuwait. Mubarak assured the sultan that he was a loyal subject, and asked to be confirmed as Shaikh of Kuwait. At the same time, his nephews informed the sultan that it was Mubarak who had murdered their fathers. They asked the Porte to punish Mubarak and to return the estates at Fao to them. They pointed out that they held the deeds for the estates. To reinforce their claims, they retained two lawyers, one at Baghdad and one at Basra. They also obtained an order from the Qadi's Court to sequester the date crop from the estates. However, when the court-appointed officials went to Fao armed with the appropriate papers from the *vali*, the Mudir of Fao refused to surrender the date-crop, and sent a message to Shaikh Mubarak via his brother, Shaikh Jabir, who lived nearby. Mubarak reacted promptly by sending 500 armed men who recovered the date-crop and saw it safely into the hands of the contractors.[66]

Mubarak had therefore won the first skirmish with his nephews and Shaikh Yusuf, but there was always the danger that the Porte would use the family's dispute as a pretext to intervene. This made it particularly unfortunate that Mubarak had antagonised the Vali of Basra. When the nephews launched a flood of complaints to Constantinople about Mubarak's seizure of the date-crop, Hamdi Pasha pointed out to the Porte that there would be benefit from positive support for the nephews. Indeed, Hamdi Pasha tried to get the Porte to agree to the establishment of Ottoman government departments at Kuwait, such as customs and sanitary departments, as well as the stationing of a battalion of infantry. According to a note by the dragoman of the British Consulate at Basra, prepared in October 1896, Hamdi assured the Porte that this extension of Ottoman authority into Kuwait could easily be achieved by supporting Mubarak's nephews against Mubarak.

So Mubarak urgently needed allies in the Ottoman administration to counter the hostility of the Vali of Basra. Although evidence is scarce about the tactics he employed in the summer and autumn of 1896, he seems to have gained the important alliance of the Naqib of Basra, the unscrupulous Muhammad Sa'id. This was a natural alliance as, in the words of the British consul, Muhammad Sa'id was 'not a man of high moral principle' and had very poor relations with Hamdi Pasha.[67] As early as July 1896, the consul was reporting that mendacious unsigned telegrams were being sent to the Porte at Constantinople, blaming the coup in Kuwait on Hamdi Pasha's mis-government. The consul, Captain Whyte, claimed on 'reliable authority' that the *naqib* was responsible for this intrigue against Hamdi Pasha, and that the aim was to engineer Hamdi's dismissal. This may be true, but the timing of the telegrams points to some involvement by Shaikh Mubarak: Hamdi Pasha had been *vali* for four years by the summer of 1896, and had been opposed to Muhammad Sa'id practically from the beginning according to the consul. If Muhammad had been acting purely on his own initiative in starting the 'whispering campaign' against Hamdi, we could perhaps have expected him to begin before July 1896.

Another piece of evidence for an alliance between Mubarak and the *naqib* is Mubarak's attempt to influence the Porte by bribing two influential religious figures in Constantinople who were particularly close to the sultan: the shaikh al-Islam and Shaikh Abul Huda. The latter, often referred to as the 'Arab Rasputin', was also the *naqib*'s supporter in Constantinople, and the *naqib* may have helped Mubarak to make this influential contact.

Muhammad Sa'id died during August 1896, and was succeeded by his son, Rajab, who had been acting *naqib* for some time. It was probably Rajab who had been Mubarak's most active partner in the early summer of 1896, and Muhammad's death did not interrupt the conspiracy against Hamdi Pasha. At the end of 1896, Mubarak and the *naqib* obtained the result they wanted: Hamdi Pasha was dismissed as *vali*, and left Basra on 8 December. We will never know exactly what role Mubarak and the *naqib* played in removing Hamdi from office. What is important is that Hamdi firmly believed that Shaikh Mubarak was responsible for his downfall, and acted accordingly when he was reinstated in Basra some years later. The immediate problem facing Shaikh Mubarak and his enemy, Shaikh Yusuf of Dora, was the competition to buy the support of Hamdi's successor as *vali*, Arif Pasha. Much later, in May 1898, the British consul summarised the new vali's terms of office as governed by one principle – 'namely to support those persons, parties or objects which were able to bring him pecuniary or material benefit.'[68] Shaikh Yusuf seems to have opened the bidding at the start of 1897 with an offer of £T1,500 for support for the nephews, but Shaikh Mubarak offered them a much higher bid of £T7,500 as payment to the *vali* if Mubarak was awarded the title of *qaimaqam*.

Before Mubarak's efforts to suborn the *vali* could produce any result, Kuwait's relationship with the Ottoman Empire changed fundamentally as the result of decisions taken far away from Kuwait and the Gulf. Back in 1894, an international conference in Paris had considered the best ways of reforming the sanitary regulations of the Ottoman Empire so as to control the spread of cholera. The conference's recommendations had included the establishment of a lazaret at Fao, and the creation of Ottoman sanitary control stations at various places in the Arabian Gulf, including Kuwait. For two years, the Ottoman authorities did nothing to implement these recommendations, but a major outbreak of plague in Karachi and Bombay at the end of 1896 caused great concern in the Ottoman Empire. The Sanitary Board in Constantinople, therefore, decided to establish a quarantine station in Fao, and to base officers at a number of ports on the Arabian side of the Gulf, including Kuwait. British officials were worried about the implications of such an extension of Ottoman control to places on the Arabian coast of the Gulf, which came under British protection or which had special treaty relations with Britain. However, they were not unduly concerned about Kuwait, where Britain had (in the words of a senior India Office official reacting to the Ottoman proposal) ' ... acted for long as if Turkey was the suzerain power'.[69] Indeed, the Viceroy of India, Lord Elgin, when asked for an opinion on the Ottoman proposal, commented on 12 February 1897 that 'I see no objection to Turkish quarantine at Koweit, but consider Turkish intervention at other places (in the Gulf) quite inadmissible.'[70]

Officials in London were not therefore worried about the Ottoman proposals to base a quarantine official in Kuwait, but Shaikh Mubarak was very worried indeed. We can presume that he was informed by his friends in Basra of the quarantine proposal as soon as the news arrived. This must account for the communication which the British Residency in Bushire received in the middle of February 1897. The British Residency's Arab agent in Bahrain, Muhammad

Rahim Saffar, wrote to the resident on 15 February that he had received a letter from Shaikh Mubarak of Kuwait, an old and personal friend of the agent. In the letter, Shaikh Mubarak expressed a desire for an interview with the resident or with a trusted member of his staff. Although a long time was to elapse before the British made direct contact with Mubarak, the first step had been taken towards a new relationship between Kuwait and Britain, which was to change the politics of the northern Gulf and to ally a small Arab shaikh with the full might of the British Empire of India.

It is a pity that there are no Kuwaiti sources covering the period when Shaikh Mubarak decided to approach the British, but he and other members of the al-Sabah family did give some indications of their thinking, which survive on the British files of the period. The first indication of the Kuwaiti view of affairs comes in the form of a memorandum written by the legal adviser to the British Embassy in Constantinople, Mr Stavrides, on 6 July 1896. The memorandum was written less than two month after Mubarak seized power. Stavrides argued that Kuwait's ruling family:

> … possess large landed property at Bussorah and especially at Fao, which belongs to them. That is why the sheikhs accept their investiture, sanctioned by the sultan, who grants them the rank of kaimakam, with the title of pasha, of which the sheikh does not deign to make use.

Stavrides' argument that the title of *qaimaqam* was something which the al-Sabah only accepted in respect of their gardens at Basra and Fao, and not in respect of Kuwait itself, did not find much sympathy among British officials in the embassy at Constantinople and in London. What had induced Stavrides to interpret the title of *qaimaqam* in this rather special way ?

Stavrides could hardly have got the idea from Ottoman sources, as the Ottoman authorities were quite clear that the title of *qaimaqam* referred to Kuwait itself, which they saw as an administrative unit of the Ottoman Empire. It is also inconceivable that he got the idea from any of his British colleagues, since the general view in the embassy was that Kuwait was 'practically under Turkish influence'. The most likely explanation is that the interpretation of the title of *qaimaqam* as a title relating only to the gardens at Basra and Fao was the interpretation given by Shaikh Abdullah of Kuwait and Shaikh Muhammad of Kuwait to enquiries from foreign visitors following the earlier grants of the title to these rulers in 1871 and 1892. The interpretation must then have filtered back to the British Embassy by one route or another, so as to inspire Stavrides when he came to write his memorandum.

We can also clarify Mubarak's attitude to the other major sign of Ottoman influence in Kuwait in the early part of his reign – the use of the Turkish flag by the al-Sabah. This was a subject on which he had not given 'any satisfactory answer' when he was upbraided by the senior British naval officer in the Persian Gulf in July 1896. However, in 1901 he did given an explanation for his continuing use of the Turkish flag when in the company of the Vali of Basra and when the British resident visited his house. His explanation, in response to a pointed enquiry from another British official in the Gulf, was that the Turkish flag 'was flown by his father and grandfather on such occasions as a Mahommadan flag, and did not indicate that they (his father and grandfather) were under any control of or protection of the Turks.'[71]

Mubarak's answer on the question of the flag did not impress the literal-minded British officials with whom he was dealing. It probably made a lot of sense to Mubarak. Unlike his British interlocutors, Mubarak dealt in the practical realities of a small state, trying to cut the best deal for itself in an unfriendly world. For practical purposes, he undoubtedly regarded himself as a free agent, the master of Kuwait, free to choose whether to deal with the Ottomans or the British (or with both at once if he wished) in order to secure his own total control of Kuwait. If the Ottomans could offer a degree of support in his battles against his relatives, through a title such as the title of *qaimaqam*, then he would take the title and fly the appropriate flag, while arguing strongly to the British (and, no doubt, to anyone else who would listen) that these were minor concessions which he accepted in respect of his properties at Basra and Fao (in the case of the title of *qaimaqam*), or not even a concession at all (in the case of the Turkish flag).

At the beginning of 1897, the Turkish plan to base a permanent official in Kuwait blew away Mubarak's political smoke-screen. Once this official was in place, Mubarak's title of *qaimaqam* and the sight of the Turkish flag flying over Kuwait would be daily confirmation of his subordinate status within the Ottoman Empire. He immediately decided, we can assume, that this was the moment to play his 'British card' in the form of the letter to the British agent in Bahrain. He could not have known that he had chosen almost the ideal moment to make this approach, as the British authorities were now likely to respond favourably to his approach.

2

Shaikh Mubarak and Britain's Interests
in the Gulf

When Shaikh Mubarak's letter arrived on the desk of the British resident in Bushire, in the middle of February 1897, Britain had been the dominant power in the southern Gulf for just under 300 years. From the very start of this British involvement, in the first years of the seventeenth century, the Gulf had been an adjunct of Britain's rapidly-growing commercial interests in India. The initial reason for British ships to enter the Gulf was the quest for markets for British products, which could not all be absorbed in India.

In the middle years of the eighteenth century, often without any very clear plan or strategy, Britain converted its large commercial interests in India into a political presence: the armed forces of the British East India Company and the British regular army spread their control over Bengal, Carnatica and then much of northern and central India. Towards the end of the eighteenth century, the Company began to rely heavily on the Gulf as a fast route for communications from London, which would otherwise take many months by the long sea route from Africa. The Company's correspondence could go up the Gulf and then by the fast cross-desert route to Aleppo, and on to the Mediterranean and Europe. For a time at the start of the nineteenth century, the Gulf route was the official choice for all important correspondence with Britain, because of uncertainties about the alternative route using the Red Sea and Egyptian ports. Later in the nineteenth century, the Gulf lost much of its importance for communications because the telegraph and the opening of the Suez Canal provided other links. But Britain still had very large commercial interests in the Gulf. Indian manufacturers needed markets in Persia and the Ottoman Empire, for which the Gulf provided the best access. Britain itself benefited from access to these markets for its own industrial products.

Commerce was not the only reason for interest in the Gulf. There was also a major strategic benefit to Britain from its ability to project naval and military force in the Gulf. One example will suffice. In 1837–38, Britain and Russia were in effect fighting a war-by-proxy for influence over Persia and Afghanistan. The war centred on Herat, in Afghanistan, where the Persian Army, which was for practical purposes commanded by its Russian 'advisers', was besieging the town. Herat was defended by Afghans, who were 'advised', bullied and sometimes kicked into action by one British officer, Lieutenant Eldred Pottinger of the political service of the East India Company. In June 1838, Britain compelled the Shah of Persia to call off the siege of Herat by landing British troops on the Persian side of the Gulf, at Kharj Island. This rapid projection of British forces into the Gulf had the desired effect on events at Herat, at the opposite end of the Persian Empire. The shah lifted the siege of Herat, broke with his Russian 'advisers', and gave Britain an extraordinary diplomatic and political success.

On a more mundane level, Britain had a strategic interest in monitoring and sometimes limiting the export of rifles and firearms from Europe to the Gulf region. These rifles had an unpleasant habit of disappearing into Persia. Once in Persia, they could destabilise the Persian Empire or, worse still, filter through to Afghanistan and the north-west frontier of India, where they could be used against British and Indian troops.

Finally, Britain felt a moral incentive during the nineteenth century to act to suppress the slave trade between Africa and the Gulf. Probably no aspect of British involvement in the Gulf was so much resented on the Arab side of the Gulf, where it could certainly be argued that the slave traffic was in no way comparable in horror to the transport of Africans (in British ships) to the southern United States of America and the Caribbean during the eighteenth century. But the anti-slavery interest was strong in Victorian England.

So there were many reasons why Britain took a close interest in the Gulf. One consideration generally dominated British action in the region and throughout its Indian Empire: the need to achieve its political and commercial goals at the lowest possible cost, both in manpower and money. Britain was badly over-stretched throughout the nineteenth century on all frontiers of its Indian Empire, and had to ration its forces extremely carefully. Indeed, we are mistaken if we think in terms of Britain conquering or occupying India by direct military force. In reality a small number of British troops achieved an extraordinary degree of dominance by intelligent use of the political and social divisions within India. As Sir Penderel Moon has put it: 'The Empire was from start to finish far more of a joint Anglo–Indian enterprise and partnership than either party has usually been inclined to admit. As early as 1795, one of the Company's servants, Sir John Shore, wrote: "Our dominion of India has been established and is maintained by the natives themselves."'

To Shaikh Mubarak, sitting in Kuwait, the British Empire in India must have seemed a military giant which could easily extend protection to him; but, as we shall see from the British response to his letter, things looked very different in Simla and in London, where the thin military basis of Britain's Empire was a constant worry. Indeed, Shaikh Mubarak might have been horrified to know that, just 40 years before he sent his letter to Bushire, the British control over India rested on less than 40,000 'white' (i.e. British) troops in the entire Indian subcontinent, working alongside 230,000 soldiers of Indian origin. In that year of 1857, a mutiny among the Indian troops in Bengal came very close to putting an end to British rule altogether. Throughout Bengal, tiny British garrisons were put under siege or massacred. Only some extraordinarily bold action by a few officers, helped by the fact that Indian troops of the Madras and Bombay presidencies refused to join the Bengali rebels, saved the British Empire by a narrow margin. When the blood and dust of the mutiny had settled, Britain wound up its East India Company and made its queen into the 'Queen-Empress' of India. The Royal Commission on the Army of 1859 recommended that the number of 'white' troops in India should be raised to 80,000, and Indian troops should be held at 190,000. In the event, there were about 75,000 'white' troops in India in the first years of the twentieth century: it is not surprising that British officials generally pulled long faces when they were invited to take on new military commitments.

There was a particular reason why the government of India acted with great care in any matters which might lead to conflict with the Ottoman Empire. After the horrifying shock of the Indian Mutiny of 1857, there had been a deliberate policy of reducing the 'Bengali' elements in the Indian Army, and boosting the proportion of soldiers recruited from the 'martial races' of the north-west of India. These soldiers were, of course, mainly Muslim and Sikh. At the back of the British official mind was a fear that the Ottoman Empire might destabilise the Indian Army by using the power of the sultan, as caliph, to declare a *jihad* against Britain. In 1914 when the sultan did proclaim such a *jihad* at the start of the First World War, the gesture fell completely flat. Indian troops of all religions astonished even the most optimistic of the British by their willingness to fight with the Allies against Germany, Austro–Hungary and the Ottoman Empire. At one point during the War, Britain reduced the number of 'white' troops in India to just 15,000 men, but this could not have been foreseen in 1897. The Government of India and the India Office would naturally regard with great suspicion a request from commitment to an Arab leader which risked entanglement with the Ottoman Empire.

How Britain Managed its Gulf Interest: the Trucial System

At the end of the eighteenth century, British commerce was threatened by events in the lower Gulf. Qawasim dhows from Sharjah and Ras al-Khaimah began to raid British, European and Indian ships proceeding up the Gulf to Persian and Ottoman ports. The Qawasim raiders, using their fast and heavily-armed dhows, operated out of a number of secret anchorages in the *khaars* (creeks) of the Musandam peninsula. In the first attack, on 18 May 1797, they captured a small British rig, the *Bassein Snow*, which was carrying dispatches up the Gulf. On this occasion, the British ship and crew were released from Ras al-Khaimah in response to British protests. The Qawasim felt strongly that British ships should pay tolls when passing through Qawasim waters, and continued their raids. In 1807, after a number of small-scale clashes, Qawasim ships from Ras al-Khaimah captured a large British trading ship, the *Minerva*. They killed most of the crew and held the wife of a British officer to ransom. This episode, which was widely reported in Britain and Europe, was followed by nine other attacks on British vessels in a 12-month period.

The rights and wrongs of the Qawasim raids have been fiercely debated ever since. The Qawasim have been presented in extreme terms, as pirates or freedom fighters, depending on the stand point of the historian. Here, we only need to be concerned with the British response, which was bloody and heavy. In November 1809, two large British warships and nine East India Company cruisers accompanied seven troop transports in an attack on Ras al-Khaimah, which destroyed large areas of the town. When this was not enough to discourage raiding, a second British expedition under Sir William Grant Keir occupied Ras al-Khaimah in December 1819.

There was no great enthusiasm in British government circles for stationing large naval forces in the Gulf indefinitely. The solution adopted after the 1819 expedition was the 'General Truce', signed by the Arab rulers of the present-day UAE and Bahrain, in the presence of British naval officers, in January 1820. Under the Truce, the rulers agreed to cease 'all plunder and piracy by land and sea ... not of acknowledged war'. They also agreed to keep registers of their ships, and to adopt a common flag for identification at sea. The General Truce specified that the Arab rulers themselves would have the main responsibility for policing the seas to prevent attacks on Arab and British ships. If the Arab rulers were unable to enforce security for shipping, then they could turn to the British for help. In the words of the 1820 Truce: 'An arrangement for this purpose shall take place between the friendly Arabs and the British at the time when such plunder and piracy appear.' The Truce of 1820 was only the first in a series of truces which Britain persuaded the Arab rulers to accept during the first half of the nineteenth century, in order to regulate all aspects of maritime affairs; safety of shipping, suppression of slavery and control of the arms trade. We do not need to go into the details of these complicated agreements, which culminated in the Perpetual Maritime Truce of 1853, but we do need to remember some important features of the British-inspired 'Trucial System' as it developed in the years up to 1853.

Above all, Britain never wanted to have to station military forces on the Arab side of the Gulf. The aim of the Trucial System, as far as Britain was concerned, was to make the Arab rulers of the lower Gulf responsible for maintaining order among themselves, and for stopping their subjects from attacking British and European ships travelling up the Gulf. Britain could, of course, guarantee peace and security because it could deploy its powerful cruisers from the base at Bushire, on the Persian side of the Gulf, but as far as the Arabs were concerned, this was what we would now call an 'over-the-horizon' force. It was always in the background as a threat and a disincentive to violence, but it only made occasional visits to the Arab side of the Gulf and did not have any permanent base on the Arab coast. For Britain, this method of policing had the beauty of ensuring peace and security at the lowest possible cost. There was a secondary benefit: because there was not any British military presence on the Arab side of the Gulf, Britain did not need to become involved in the affairs of the inland people of the Arab hinterland. Away from the coast, Arab tribes could fight to their hearts' content. Britain was only concerned with security at sea, in the waters of the Gulf. Although this attitude was starting to change at the end of the nineteenth century, Britain realised that it would have to take a closer interest in the Arab side of the Gulf, the Trucial system still influenced the thinking of British officials, inclining them to be suspicious of any new obligations to the Arab rulers which might involve cost or military commitments. Shaikh Mubarak was to be disappointed by this cautious British attitude on many occasions.

The Trucial system was also traditionally confined to the lower (or southern) part of the Arab Gulf coast. North of Bahrain, Britain did not want to play an active role during most of the century, as long as basic security for its shipping could be ensured. There was a brief exception to this rule, however, in 1841, when Kuwait gave the British a unilateral undertaking that it would adhere to the maritime truce for a period of one year from 24 April 1841. This promise, which seems to have resulted from a personal invitation to the ruler of Kuwait by a British naval officer touring the northern Gulf, was not repeated or extended. If it had been repeated, then Kuwait might have become a full partner of the Trucial System, and the entire history of the Gulf would have been very different.

Apart from Kuwait's brief adherence to the British-backed Truce, the question of the application of the Trucial System to the northern Gulf was left to one side until the Ottomans occupied Qatif and al-Hasa in 1871. The Ottoman move of 1871 made the whole question rather urgent for Britain. In the past, British warships had often pursued ships raiding European commerce into the coastal waters north of Qatif, and there had been no power on land able to deny this right of pursuit. Should Britain continue to insist on the right to conduct naval operations in these waters, even though this might lead to a political confrontation with the Ottoman Empire? The evidence suggests that British thinking was not entirely consistent on this point. In January 1879, the British ambassador in Constantinople received instructions to suggest to the Ottoman government a compromise which could resolve the problem: British warships could continue to enter the three-mile limit off the northern Gulf coast around Qatif and al-Hasa, in order to pursue pirates, but they would try to stay outside the three-mile limit as far as possible. In effect, this proposal meant that Britain was ready to recognise Ottoman sovereignty along the northern Gulf coast, at least as far south as al-Udaid.[1] Other files give clues about British thinking at this time, and confirm that the general priority was to avoid any British entanglement in the northern Gulf. One paper of 1879 states that 'wherever the Turkish sovereignty is at the present time firmly established on the (Gulf) coast, they (HMG) are ready to recognise it, and would gladly see it accompanied by a regular and civilised administration.'[2]

In April 1893, Britain went further in the direction of recognising Ottoman sovereignty in the northern Gulf by delivering an official statement to the Ottoman foreign ministry to the effect that the British government recognised Ottoman sovereignty from Basra down to Qatif.

The British documents of 1879 and 1893 dealing with the question of the northern Gulf do not refer specifically to Kuwait, but the implications of their content for Kuwait were, of course, serious. On the British side we can see that a preference developed after 1879 for an effective division of authority along the Arab coast of the Gulf between Britain and the Ottomans, with the dividing line coming somewhere near Qatif. To the south of that approximate limit,

Britain was intensely keen on maintaining its paramount position in Trucial Oman (the present-day United Arab Emirates) and at least as far north as Bahrain. In the north of the Gulf, British officials seem to have assumed that the Ottomans had a general sovereignty, and that the interests of peace and commerce would best be served if the Ottomans enforced this sovereignty. Not much was known in British government circles about the very special position which the al-Sabah had managed to create for themselves in Kuwait, and there was no incentive up to 1897 to research the matter. Indeed, when Kuwait became a live issue in 1896–97, the first reaction of many British officials was to scurry to the files, to see what had been written down about Kuwait in the past. They did not find much material to work on.

The one exception to the general ignorance about Kuwait was Lord Curzon, who was in 1897 the parliamentary under-secretary for foreign affairs, that is the deputy to Britain's foreign secretary. Lord Curzon had travelled widely in the Gulf as part of his research programme for his book, *Persia and the Persian Question*, published in 1892. He had not visited Kuwait itself, but had heard good reports of its prosperity and commercial importance. He had also formed the conviction during his travels that Britain ought to change its policy in the Gulf very drastically, and to extend its influence northwards. This conviction was to lead to a change of policy very much in the interests of Shaikh Mubarak. In early 1897, some months had to elapse before Lord Curzon got the chance to stamp his forceful personality on the Kuwait file first at the Foreign Office, and then as the splendid Viceroy of India.

London Considers Mubarak's Request

Given that there was a general disinclination in London to get involved in any confrontations with the Ottoman Empire, it is not surprising that the British Residency in Bushire reacted very cooly to Mubarak's message of February 1897. A file note within the Residency suggested that it would be 'inadvisable' to have any communication with Shaikh Mubarak, or to encourage any overtures from him.[3]

At the local level, there were strong reasons why the Residency wanted to keep Shaikh Mubarak at a distance. In mid-1896, when news of his violent takeover of Kuwait reached Constantinople, the Sublime Porte had alleged that it was all part of a great British conspiracy to dominate the Gulf. Under this peculiar interpretation of events, the Ottomans suggested that Britain was planning to form an anti-Ottoman confederation which would include Shaikh

Mubarak of Kuwait, the Amir Muhammad Ibn Rashid of Najd and Shaikh Jasim bin Thani of Qatar. Indeed, according to the conspiracy theorists in the Ottoman government, Mubarak had spent a month in early 1896 at the British Residency in Bushire preparing the conspiracy with his British friends.

The British Embassy in Constantinople reported this extraordinary farrago to the Foreign Office in London, and the Government of India asked the British Residency in Bushire for its comments. The political resident in the Persian Gulf, Col. F. A. Wilson, reacted with disbelief, pointing out that the Ottoman allegations were not only untrue but were also inherently unbelievable. As to the truth of the allegations, Wilson could quote the Ottoman vice-consul in Bushire himself as a witness that Shaikh Mubarak had not been in Bushire for 'at least' the last three or four years. As for the probability of the story, the idea that Britain would act in collusion with Shaikh Jasim of Qatar was simply absurd. The British had after all virtually destroyed Shaikh Jasim's fleet in September 1895.[4] The residence concluded that the story must have been put about by a unscrupulous person with the aim of creating mischief between Britain and the Ottoman Empire. Much later, in June 1899, the deputy officer at the Residency, Gaskin, reported his suspicion on mature reflection that the conspiracy story had been put about by Shaikh Mubarak himself, aiming to boost his own status in the region.

The Residency could not simply shelve Mubarak's message of February 1897, however, so it sought guidance from the Government of India, which in turn referred to London. At the India Office in London, the official most closely involved was Sir W. Lee Warner, the secretary of the Political and Secret Department of the India Office. His draft advice to the Foreign Office was that Britain should stand aloof from Kuwait, and that Wilson should be instructed to offer Mubarak a polite excuse to decline an interview. The political committee of the India Office slightly modified this draft, suggesting that Wilson should be given the choice of refusing or granting an interview as he saw fit. At the Foreign Office, the foreign secretary (and prime minister) Lord Salisbury accepted the advice, but did feel it was desirable that Mubarak should be given the interview he had requested.[5] The matter was not given a high priority in London, and papers passed slowly between the various departments of state. Only on 25 March did the Government of India telegraph the Residency in Bushire to tell Wilson that he had discretion to reply as he saw fit to Mubarak's message, while suggesting to Wilson that the interview might 'with advantage be granted'. The delay in replying certainly worried Mubarak, who wrote again to his friend in Bahrain at the end of March reminding him that he was still waiting for an answer to his letter of January.

At the start of April, Captain Whyte, the former British Consul in Basra, had arrived in England. On arrival, he called on Lee Warner at the India Office, and told him that he had received information shortly before leaving Basra that Shaikh Mubarak was planning to ask for a British protectorate over Kuwait at his meeting with the resident. This news was of course alarming for the British officials involved. Thomas Sanderson, the permanent under secretary at the Foreign Office, decided that, in the light of the new information about Mubarak's wish for a protectorate, the idea of an interview 'might as well be discouraged'. Sanderson of course informed the foreign secretary, Lord Salisbury, of the probability that the resident would receive a request for protection, but pointed out that the British commitment to protect Bahrain was already giving Britain a great deal of trouble. Bahrain was an island, of course, so that the scope for involvement in local disputes was relatively small. By contrast, Sanderson pointed out, a protectorate over Kuwait would involve the risk of constant squabbles with the Turks about the coastal tribes in the neighbourhood, unless Britain was prepared to establish a military post in Kuwait.[6]

Lord Salisbury fully appreciated his senior official's unhappiness about the idea of a protectorate over Kuwait. He made an important comment on the margin of Sanderson's note which pointed to the kind of relationship that would in fact be offered to Mubarak nearly two years later: 'I agree we have plenty on our hands ... but might we not obtain from him (Mubarak) a promise not to accept any other protectorate, while only giving him an assurance in return that we will not encroach on his independence, but will treat him in a friendly manner.'[7] The foreign secretary had therefore come out against a simple rejection of Mubarak's approach. So, when the India Office put up a recommendation to the Foreign Office in mid-April (on the basis of the new information supplied by Captain Whyte) that the Government of India should simply be ordered to reject Mubarak's request for an interview, the Foreign Office overruled the recommendation. Instead, the British government decided to wait and see the outcome of any interview that might take place between the resident and Shaikh Mubarak.

The exchanges in Whitehall in the first months of 1897 leave no doubt that there was general opposition in London to the extension of British political involvement to the northern end of the Arab side of the Gulf. As might be expected, given their fear of military entanglement and their particular wish to avoid a straight confrontation with the Ottoman Empire, it was the India Office which was the most strongly opposed. At the Foreign Office, there was also a reluctance to accept new commitments, but Lord Salisbury himself had indicated that he would be prepared to support a more positive response to

Shaikh Mubarak, which would perhaps provide a basis for a political relationship falling short of protection.

Wilson in Bushire was still unaware that Mubarak was likely to ask him for British protection, and continued with attempts to arrange a meeting. In response to Mubarak's second letter, he sent a message via Bahrain that his assistant, J. C. Gaskin, would be in Muhammarah on about 29 April, and would be glad to receive Mubarak there in order to hear what he had to say. Wilson also stressed that Mubarak would be welcome in Bushire, but when Gaskin arrived in Muhammarah, there was no sign of the shaikh. Local enquiries indicated that it was most unlikely that Mubarak would visit the port in the near future. Mubarak was not the only person seeking British support. Late in April 1897, Mubarak's enemy Yusuf ibn Ibrahim himself approached Gaskin, who was visiting Basra. Shaikh Yusuf assured Gaskin that, if he and his al-Sabah allies received British support, and if his al-Sabah allies recovered Kuwait from their uncle, then they would ensure that there was no more piracy against British vessels in the Shatt al-Arab. Shaikh Yusuf would have known that the British authorities were concerned about a number of attacks on British and Indian vessels in the waters near Basra, which were supposed to have been launched from Kuwait. This appeal to British self-interest did not persuade Gaskin, who simply referred Yusuf to the British Consul in Basra.

Both Shaikh Mubarak and his enemy Shaikh Yusuf now faced an uncertain future. Shaikh Yusuf and his nephews had been unable to make any headway through the labyrinthine and corrupt Ottoman administration, a fact which explains Yusuf's approach to Gaskin. On the other side, Shaikh Mubarak seems to have felt that his hold on Kuwait was extremely insecure during the early summer of 1897. This would explain his anxiety to obtain the sanction of the Porte for his rule. On 22 May, Gaskin minuted that he was receiving reports that Mubarak had '... a very limited following and the sympathy of the Arabs is with the sons of the murdered brothers.'[8] Gaskin pointed out that Mubarak had so far been able to retain his hold over Kuwait largely because both factions realised that it was in their common interest to avoid open hostility, which might lead to Turkish interference and the loss of Kuwait's independence.

It may have been at this time that Mubarak made an attempt to come to terms with his adversary. At some stage during the early part of the year he sent his brother, Shaikh Hamud, to see Shaikh Yusuf at Dora, to point out the advantages of reconciliation, and to ask him to return to Kuwait, but the visit achieved nothing. The problem was that Shaikh Yusuf had obtained a copy of a letter which Mubarak had written to the Porte in Constantinople, claiming that it was Shaikh Yusuf, rather than Mubarak, who had arranged the murder of Mubarak's two brothers in 1896. To make the letter more convincing, Mubarak had persuaded most of the leading personalities of Kuwait to sign it, although four men refused to sign: Muhammad al-Farisi, Sayyid Salman al-Sayyid 'Ali, Abdullah al-Rashid and Jabr al-Ghanim. The sight of this letter appears to have convinced Yusuf that there was no scope for reconciliation with Mubarak.[9]

Shaikh Yusuf may have interpreted the approach from Mubarak as a sign of weakness, and this may have encouraged him to try his next move, a military attack on Kuwait itself, or it could be that Yusuf launched the attack out of simple frustration at his failure to gain support from the Ottomans or Britain. In any event, Shaikh Yusuf gathered a large force at Hindyan at the end of June 1897, in preparation for a sea-borne attack on Kuwait. One source at Fao put the size of the force at 10 vessels and 400 men. Yusuf undoubtedly hoped to surprise Kuwait by night, and perhaps to start an internal uprising, for there were rumours of support within the town for him and for the nephews, but if this was the case, he was to be disappointed. As his small fleet approached Kuwait on the night of 30 June 1897, Shaikh Mubarak's supporters were armed and waiting, and Yusuf's fleet withdrew without a shot being fired.[10] It may be that Mubarak's ships pursued him for a short time, as it was later reported that he had been attacked by 'pirates' during his return voyage, but had been able to beat them off.

When news of the attack reached Basra, the Ottoman authorities sent their gunboat *Allus* to Fao, where it seized a vessel believed to have been involved in the attack, and brought it and its crew to Basra. Significantly, the Basra battalion commander, who was conducting the investigation, was recalled from Basra by the Ottoman government due to the belief that he was favouring Shaikh Yusuf against Shaikh Mubarak. At the same time, the Ottomans sent their corvette *Seyad-i Deria* to Kuwait to investigate what was going on.

Shaikh Yusuf's unsuccessful attack on Kuwait caused little interest in London. At the India Office, Lee Warner suggested that British policy should be to continue as 'indifferent spectators' of events in Kuwait, as long as the Gulf rulers under engagements to Britain (i.e. the Trucial rulers and Bahrain) did not intervene, and as long as the peace of the Gulf was not disturbed by this 'naval splutter'.[11] Lord Salisbury agreed that there was no need for any British action or enquiry, as long as the general peace of the Gulf was maintained.

The Ottoman authorities were not prepared to be so indifferent to the attack. Angered by Shaikh Yusuf's disruption of the peace, they ordered him out of Ottoman territory. They also ordered the Vali of Basra to seize all of Shaikh Yusuf's landed property at Dora. Doubtless availing himself of the chance to extract another bribe, the *vali* managed to avoid carrying out this order. Shaikh Yusuf, who must have been seriously worried at the way things were going for him, decided to make another bid for British support for his claims to Kuwait. He set off for Qatar, accompanied by one of the nephews, to see Shaikh Jasim bin Thani. He then went on to Bahrain, where he arrived on 25 July. The news that he was coming to Bahrain had the effect of scaring Shaikh Mubarak's 'confidential delegate', who was also in Bahrain arranging with the British native agent in Bahrain to make a trip to Bushire to see the Resident as part of Mubarak's tortuous and circuitous attempts to follow up his message requesting an interview. The 'confidential delegate', Abdullah ibn Ibrahim, (no relation to Shaikh Yusuf), decided to abandon his mission and return to Kuwait.

However, Shaikh Yusuf's attempts to arrange British support were again unsuccessful. From Bahrain, Yusuf wrote to Lt. Col. M. J. Meade, who had just taken over as Resident in Bushire, and gave his own version of Mubarak's seizure of Kuwait; Yusuf also claimed that he had no personal interest in the matter; as his wealth was independent of Kuwait and he only wanted to help his nephews. Gaskin remarked, 'it appears that he wishes our Government to fight his battles for him.'[12] Unfortunately for Yusuf, Meade had already been informed of London's decision that the conflict between Mubarak and Yusuf did not concern the British government, as long as the peace of the Gulf was maintained. Meade had also been notified of Lord Salisbury's opinion that '... whilst we have not recognised Turkish protection of Kuwait, it is doubtful whether we could deny Turkish influence.'[13]

At this point, one of Meade's subordinates in the Bushire Residency made a suggestion which casts an interesting light on the way Britain viewed events in the Gulf. The subordinate, Gaskin, was inclined to think that the Kuwait situation could be turned to Britain's advantage, by allowing Britain and the Ottoman Empire to divide the Gulf into zones of influence. Gaskin suggested that the British government should get the Turks to accept that Bahrain was under British protection, in return for a British acknowledgement of Ottoman influence in Kuwait. This was a return to the idea of a 'dividing line' which had been put forward in 1879 and 1893, but although Meade passed Gaskin's suggestion in a letter to Sir William Cunningham, the secretary of the Indian government's Foreign Department, the suggestion was not followed up.[14] The main interest of the episode is to confirm the low priority which Britain still attached to Kuwait at this time.

Shaikh Yusuf's servant, Haji Mansur, crossed the Gulf from Bahrain to Bushire and met Colonel Meade on 10 August. He asked Meade if Shaikh Yusuf could come to Bushire in person to plead for British good offices in favour of the nephews. Meade again referred to India, and was told that there was no change in the policy of non-involvement. A week later, Meade sent Gaskin to tell Haji Mansur that the British government would not support Yusuf against Kuwait.

Gaskin thought that a solution might be found to this 'unhappy affair' through private arbitration by a local personality on good terms with both Mubarak and Yusuf. Gaskin suggested Shaikh Isa of Bahrain, who was not only willing to act as arbitrator but who was also distantly related to both Mubarak and Yusuf. Quiet arbitration would be to Britain's advantage, argued Gaskin, since Britain's main priority was peace in the Gulf. Also, while the British government were inclined to see Kuwait as falling within the Turkish sphere of influence, there was no desire to make a public point of this. Private arbitration by Shaikh Isa 'would have the desirable effect of our avoiding the exposure of our policy towards Kuwait and acknowledgement of Turkish claims.'[15]

Mubarak's First Meeting with a British Official

Meanwhile, Shaikh Mubarak had written directly to the resident claiming that he had no delegate of sufficient ability to send to Bushire, and invited the resident to send his own representative to meet him at Kuwait. There is a hint in the letter that Mubarak was feeling insecure in Kuwait, and did not judge it safe to be away. By the time this letter arrived in Bushire, Meade had persuaded the Indian government that Gaskin should be sent to Kuwait to make a preliminary report before proceeding with arbitration. The Government of India had indicated that they approved of Gaskin's idea of arbitration, and that they would like to take the opportunity of a meeting with Mubarak to convey a long-delayed warning about a number of attacks on British Indian ships in the Shatt al-Arab, at least some of which were known to have been made by Kuwaitis.[16]

Gaskin was therefore instructed to go to Kuwait and to 'warn very seriously' that the British government would not tolerate piracy against its vessels and would hold Shaikh Mubarak personally responsible for any such acts by his own people. After conveying the warning, Gaskin was asked to try to establish what it was that the shaikh had been trying to get in touch with Britain about. Finally, he was told to sound Mubarak out about the idea of arbitration by Shaikh Isa.[17]

Gaskin reached Kuwait on 5 September 1897 on RIMS *Lawrence*. He asked that, for the sake of privacy, the shaikh might meet him on the ship, but Mubarak's son Shaikh Jabir told him that there were spies about, and his father '... thought it may bring him trouble with the Turks and begged that I go and see him on shore.' There at a private interview Gaskin gave his government's warning about piracy. The Shaikh 'appeared much concerned' and denied the involvement of any of his subjects. Indeed, he said his own vessels had been attacked so often that he now only allowed them to sail in convoys of three or four; he had complained to the Turks, but never got any satisfaction. He promised to provide the British with any information he could in the future, but asked that the Turks not be told the source.[18]

On the following day there was further discussion of the piracy question, in the course of which Gaskin raised the question of the Shaikh's conflict with his nephews and Shaikh Yusuf bin Ibrahim. Mubarak blamed the whole difficulty on the Shaikh of Dora:

> He declared that after their father's death (*sic*) they were treated like his sons and were at liberty to do what they pleased and had everything they wished for. They would have to come to some understanding with each other sooner or later but unfortunately Yousef bin Ibrahim created mischief. He poisoned the minds of his nephews against him by promises to move the Turkish government to attach the properties from him and hand the same to them. He would be glad to come to an understanding with them and could not wish for a better mediator than Sheikh Issa bin Ali, Chief of Bahrain.[19]

Then Mubarak told Gaskin that he and the people of Kuwait were 'thoroughly disgusted' with the Turks: 'The Turkish officials were every year getting more arrogant in their demands which if are not satisfied they intrigue to get them into trouble and cause them a deal of injury. Though they have to pay heavily for justice they seldom obtain it.'[20]

Because they were a small place they needed the protection of another power and they therefore wished to be brought under British protection on the same basis as the Shaikh of Bahrain and the Trucial shaikhs. He claimed that he had no treaties or other agreements with the Porte, and was at liberty to negotiate with anyone he wished. He added that he was willing to agree to sign any 'reasonable' treaty the British desired and could offer a force of 25,000–30,000 men, 'whenever necessary in the Gulf'. The shaikh asked that his offer be kept 'strictly confidential' since if the British declined his offer and Ottoman officials found out, '... they will cause him a deal of harm and loss through interference with his properties on the Shat-el-Arab.'

Gaskin returned to Bushire to report the result of his meetings with the shaikh to Wilson. Meade was new to the Gulf and all his previous service had been within India. He had never been to Kuwait and knew little of it, other than he had 'heard' that it had a good harbour. At the end of July, he had endorsed Gaskin's idea of using Kuwait as a bargaining counter with the Turks to gain recognition of the British position in Bahrain. While he had thought it would be a 'great pity' to allow the Turks to extend their influence there, he had also admitted that it might not be possible to prevent the Turks from doing this.[21] However, by the time that Gaskin reported on his meeting with the shaikh, Meade's views had become more expansionist and he telegraphed to India that, 'Present seems good opportunity to establish British influence Kuweit which will certainly become a place (*sic*) great importance ... '. He admitted that Mubarak flew the Turkish flag, and his predecessor had accepted the Ottoman title of *qaimaqam*. Nevertheless:

> This ... does not seem insuperable objection to extension our influence as Turks have never exercised sovereign rights at nor have we admitted their protection over Koweit unless therefore we are prepared to allow Turks to absorb Koweit I strongly advise that I may be permitted to proceed further with negotiations.[22]

The new and more vigorous position adopted in Meade's telegram to India seems to have been the result of a chance event. At the time that Gaskin returned from Kuwait Meade had a guest, Major C. G. F. Fagan, who had just completed a brief period as British consul in Basra and was now on his way to take up his position as the new Political Agent at Muscat. Before leaving for the Gulf he had visited Lieutenant-Colonel William Loch, the consul-general in Baghdad, and had been asked to take a message to Meade. Loch believed that in view of recent Turkish activity at the head of the Gulf it was time for the government to decide whether or not they should allow Kuwait to 'pass under the rule of Turkey'. Loch felt that as Britain had never acknowledged Turkish jurisdiction there, nor had the Turks exercised it, there was no reason not to take Kuwait under British protection, '... if the Govt. of India and the Home Govt. can be induced to sanction such a policy.'[23] Among the advantages to be gained by such a step would be the control of the port and town which were of potential importance and a means of suppressing piracy and the slave trade. Loch stressed that any action to secure a British protectorate over Kuwait would probably have to be taken quickly.

In reporting at length on Gaskin's visit, Meade admitted that he suspected the Shaikh of Kuwait's motives; he pointed to the delay that Shaikh Mubarak was experiencing in getting the Turks to recognise him as shaikh despite the fact that he had spent 'considerable sums', and Meade believed that the shaikh's '... advances to us may be made with the object of inducing the Turkish government to hasten their movements.'[24] Nevertheless, using the arguments which had been advanced to him by Loch, he saw that the proclamation of a British protectorate would secure an 'excellent harbour' which could be the sea port of the projected railway through Mesopotamia, it was an important trading centre, and it would extend British control over both the slave and arms trades.[25]

The Government of India were not moved by Meade's arguments; they had already telegraphed Shaikh Mubarak's request for protection to London, but, after consulting the Foreign Office, the secretary of state telegraphed the viceroy on 13 October: 'Her Majesty's Government are not disposed to interfere more than necessary for maintenance of general peace of Persian Gulf or to bring Koweit under protection.'[26] Neither the Indian government, nor the India Office, nor the Foreign Office had any desire to extend British responsibilities to the head of the Gulf.

Meanwhile, the Shaikh of Dora was continuing to exert himself. Before coming to Bahrain in July, Shaikh Yusuf had visited Shaikh Jasim bin Thani of al-Qatar, ostensibly for the purpose of congratulating the shaikh upon his son's return from Mecca. In fact, having just failed in his own attempt at resolving the conflict with Mubarak by force and being spurred by the British, he had gone in search of an ally for a second attempt at invading Kuwait. In Shaikh Jasim he had chosen wisely; the Qatar shaikh had a long-standing grudge against the al-Sabah in general and Shaikh Mubarak in particular.[27] It had been Shaikh Abdullah al-Sabah who had assisted the Turks against al-Hasa in 1871, and indeed had personally induced Shaikh Jasim to raise the Turkish flag over his own house. It had been Shaikh Mubarak who had led a Kuwait force at the request of the *vali* in 1893 when Shaikh Jasim had been in conflict with the Turks. Jasim also believed that Mubarak had expressed to the Amir of Najd satisfaction at the destruction of the Qatar fleet by the British in 1895. Under the circumstances it was unlikely that Shaikh Jasim had counselled caution, and it was probably the summer heat which prevented the Shaikh of Qatar from taking any immediate action against his old enemy. However, with autumn came mild weather and the traditional opening of the rainy season. At the end of September word reached Bahrain that Shaikh Jasim was gathering the Bedouin tribes in order to assist Shaikh Yusuf and his nephews against Kuwait. It appeared that Shaikh Jasim was planning an overland expedition against Kuwait supported by a fleet of 20 vessels; the Bedouin were to gather in the neighbourhood of al-Hasa on 6 November 1897. In preparation for the operation Shaikh Jasim had telegraphed a complaint against Mubarak to the Porte. In addition, he wrote to Shaikh Muhammad Ibn Rashid of Jabal Shammar, the powerful Amir of Najd, requesting his assistance, or at least his good offices, in assuring the neutrality of the Ajman, '... the best fighting men of Shaikh Mubarak'. The support or neutrality of the Amir of Najd was central to Shaikh Jasim's efforts. Britain's Bahrain agent observed: 'In my opinion if Mohammed bin Rashid does not support Jasim neither (*sic*) prevents the Ajman tribe for (*sic*) helping Mobarak of Kowait, he (Jasim) cannot take action against Kowait.'[28]

In the end Shaikh Jasim's attempts to gather Arab support for his expedition were unsuccessful. The Shaikh of Kuwait learnt of Shaikh Jasim's activities and wrote to Sa'id Pasha, the Mutassarif of al-Hasa, asking him to dissuade the Shaikh of Qatar.[29] Sa'id Pasha, who was known for the justice of his rule, was serving his fourth appointment as *mutassarif* and had a natural inclination to maintain the peace of his own territory. Sa'id wrote to Shaikh Jasim and tried to dissuade him.[30] He also wrote to Muhsin Pasha in Basra. The leaders of Basra were all Mubarak's allies and the *naqib*, Sayyid Rajab, and Muhammad 'Ali, the head of the *awqaf* (religious endowments), set out for al-Qatar to try to do their best to stop Shaikh Jasim.[31]

With this powerful opposition building up against the expedition, Shaikh Yusuf himself journeyed to Hail to try to get help from Amir Ibn Rashid of Najd. The amir had already received a request from Constantinople (probably responding to encouragement from Basra) to do what he could to keep the peace in Arabia. So, in mid-October, the amir sent his representatives to Qatar, with a letter suggesting a peaceful reconciliation between Mubarak and Yusuf on the basis that the Shaikh of Qatar should represent Shaikh Yusuf and the nephews, while Ibn Rashid himself spoke for Shaikh Mubarak. As a further incentive to the Shaikh of Qatar to choose the peaceful option, the shaikhs of the Ajman and Murrah tribes wrote to Qatar to the effect that they had taken up the cause of Shaikh Mubarak and were ready to protect Kuwait against Shaikh Jasim.

Faced with this threat of resistance, Shaikh Jasim apparently abandoned his military plans, and decided to attempt reconciliation. At the end of November, the Ottoman Mutassarif of al-Hasa received letters written by two people acting on behalf of Shaikh Jasim, saying that they wanted to go to Kuwait with the aim of achieving a reconciliation, but that they would like the *mutassarif* to obtain Mubarak's prior assent to the visit, and to provide them with a letter of introduction. The British reaction to this news was that Shaikh Jasim probably did not want to humiliate himself by writing directly to the *mutassarif*, but that he needed to find a face-saving alternative to military action now that Ibn Rashid had refused to help him against Mubarak.[32]

In the middle of October, before Shaikh Jasim's change of policy was known, a report was sent from Basra to the British Residency in Bushire. The report stated that a Turkish gunboat had left for the Arab coast, where it was going to 'devote particular attention' to Kuwait. Meade was now keen to take any opportunity to emphasise the importance of Kuwait. He passed on the report to India, with a warning that, if the Turks absorbed Kuwait, this would probably affect British Indian trade passing through the Shatt al-Arab. It is probably not a coincidence that the same argument can be found in a letter from Loch in Baghdad to Meade, which must have reached Bushire at almost the same time as news of the Turkish gunboat. Loch argued that whoever controlled Kuwait was a matter of great importance to India, 'for if the Turks get established there, I understand that it will become a nest of pirates.'[33] Meade's assistant was equally suspicious. He was not impressed by the news that the *mutassarif* was trying to dissuade Shaikh Jasim from attacking Kuwait, as he considered that the Ottomans would be delighted to see either party annihilated.

Meade's full report of Gaskin's visit to Kuwait had now reached India. The Government of India forwarded it to London on 21 October, with a request for early information so as to be informed quickly if the information in the report gave reason to modify the policy in the secret telegram of 13 October (which had stated that Britain should not interfere more than was necessary to maintain the general peace of the Gulf). Less than a week later, on 27 October, the viceroy informed the India Office of the likelihood of an attack on Kuwait by the Shaikh of Qatar, and the strong probability that the Turks had encouraged the attack. Lee Warner was not impressed by the news and noted his personal belief that Kuwait lay outside the British sphere of interest, but the India Office asked the Foreign Office if they would agree to the despatch of a gunboat to watch over events. A Foreign Office official noted that it was not British policy to interfere in Kuwait more than necessary to maintain peace in the Gulf, but that it 'might be useful' to send a gunboat. Sanderson at the Foreign Office, recalling Yusuf's abortive attack on Kuwait in the summer, also thought there would be no harm in sending a gunboat, provided that the commander had instructions not to interfere unless British interest were directly menaced. Sanderson also admitted that the gunboat's commander might find himself in a difficult position.

HMS *Pigeon* was duly ordered to Kuwait under the command of Lieutenant-Commander Mowbray. The ship arrived in Kuwait on 6 November to find everything peaceful. Mubarak assured Mowbray that there was no need for worry since the most that Shaikh Jasim could bring against him was a force of 3,000 men while he claimed to have 16,000 armed men as well as the Bedouin shaikhs in the area who were his 'warm supporters'. He again stressed that he wanted to be brought under British protection, but when this request was passed on to the India Office in London it met with a cool reception. Horace Walpole minuted: 'Mubarak has evidently tried to put himself under British protection either because he has failed to secure recognition from the Turks, or because he hopes by negotiating with us to put pressure on the Turks.'[34] The India Office also noted that Mubarak flew the Ottoman flag, and that his brother had been a Turkish *qaimaqam*. They advised the Foreign Office that the latest developments did not give any grounds for extending a British protectorate so far north of the existing responsibilities of the Government of India. They did feel, however, that British naval vessels could continue to visit Kuwait if it was necessary to bring pressure to bear on Mubarak over cases of piracy. The Foreign Office concurred, and India was informed that there was to be no change to existing policy.

Events in the region now lent some credibility to the warnings which London had been receiving from local officials about Ottoman designs on the Shaikhdom. In particular, Constantinople made changes to the top levels of officials in Basra which suggested that the Ottoman Empire might intervene in Kuwait to support Shaikh Mubarak against his rivals and so extend Ottoman control over Kuwait. Early in November 1897, the superintendent of the Public Debt Department in Baghdad, Fahmi Bey, went to Basra to collect T£50,000, and was understandably annoyed to be told by the *vali* that there was no money in the Treasury. Shortly before Fahmi's visit, the Mushir of Baghdad, Rajab Pasha, had visited Basra to investigate a dispute between the Naqib of Basra and the local admiral, Emin Pasha, who had been accused in mysterious telegrams sent to Constantinople of being involved in the arms trade. Rajab Pasha was followed early in November by Lieutenant-General Muhsin Pasha from Baghdad. The results of these visits were soon apparent. Early in December, Arif Pasha was removed from his post as Vali of Basra, and was replaced by Muhsin Pasha. The Ottoman government then sent a second telegram directing Arif Pasha and Muhsin Pasha to share the administration of the town. This experiment in dual government was not a success as each of the two spent most of his time cancelling the instructions which the other had given. But there were wider implications to the changes.

Firstly, Rajab Pasha was an old friend of Shaikh Mubarak, and a contemporary Arab source suggests that Mushin Pasha had been bribed by Mubarak.[35] It is surely no coincidence that in early December, at almost exactly the time that Arif Pasha was relieved of his post as *vali*, the Porte finally granted Shaikh Mubarak the title of *qaimaqam* which he had been seeking for so long. Shaikh Mubarak had originally promised Arif Pasha T£7,500 when he received the title, but now he refused to pay the bribe and ensured that Arif Pasha would in future oppose Mubarak 'with vehemence'.

Secondly, Ottoman troops now began to mobilise at Baghdad. The British consul in Baghdad, Loch, warned that there were rumours that they were intended to 'watch events' in Kuwait. Loch had also heard that Shaikh Mubarak had asked Rajab Pasha for help against Shaikh Yusuf bin Ibrahim (the main supporter of his nephews) and against Jasim bin Thani of Qatar. Loch therefore concluded that the troops would be sent to occupy Kuwait under the pretext of supporting Mubarak. He warned that the occupation or protection of Kuwait by Ottoman forces would be a 'standing menace' to British trade interests in Turkish Arabia.[36] In Basra too, it was believed that the troops were coming to Mubarak's aid; it was said that the shaikh had been directed to make preparations for supplies and camping grounds. By the end of December Shaikh Jasim was thought to be two days' march to the south of Kuwait and Shaikh Mubarak had apparently moved his forces out of Jahra, the traditional base for the defence of the town. Forbes understood that part of the Ottoman contingent would join the Shaikh in Kuwait while a second wing would land to the south on the Arabian coast and move north with the intention of catching the Qatar forces between the two wings. In addition, it was rumoured that Shaikh Mubarak had contributed a sum of T£20,000 to the Treasury to help meet the expenses of the expedition.

On 31 December the *naqib* left Basra on the Ottoman gunboat *Zohaf* for Qatar, '... to use his influence over Sheikh Jasim bin Thani to refrain from attacking Koweit.' Forbes described Rajab, the *naqib*, as an enormously venal man, 'There is nothing too low, too vile, or too treacherous to which the Najib will not agree if adequately recompensed.'[37] He raised the possibility that Shaikh Jasim might try to bribe the *naqib* to use his influence to prevent the Turkish troops being used against the Qatar forces, so that Jasim could ' ... carry out his revengeful design against Mubarak bereft of support ... .'[38] Forbes reported that Mubarak was now regretting that he had accepted the assistance of the Turks, as he feared he would be dispossessed. He was even said to be willing to make the Turks a present of the T£20,000 he had paid towards the expense of the expedition. To make matters worse, the Naqib of Basra returned to Basra on 18 January 1898 having concluded that there was no chance of settling the conflict peacefully.

When Meade communicated these developments to India, the government remained unmoved and warned him to take no action to assist the shaikh, without special sanction from the government. But while both India and London remained indifferent to Mubarak's fate another issue was looming on the horizon which was to be a significant factor in changing the attitude of officials both in India and London.

The Russian Threat: Lord Curzon Intervenes

In September 1897, the British consul in Jerusalem informed his Embassy at Constantinople that the Russian consul in Jerusalem was being transferred to the Consulate in Baghdad with special orders to identify a suitable place for a Russian coaling station in the Gulf. Loch, the British consul in Baghdad, was alarmed to hear this news as it seemed to confirm an earlier hint that the Russians were taking an interest in Kuwait as a possible base for warships. That hint had come in 1896 or early 1897, when Loch received a visit one evening from the manager of the Baghdad branch of the Ottoman Bank, whom he believed to be acting on behalf of the Russian Consulate. The Bank Manager had tried to sound Loch out about British intentions in relation to Kuwait.

In the light of the fresh news about the Russian Consulate's instructions, Loch signalled the British Residency in Bushire on 16 November 1897 in the following terms:

> The Turks would of course prefer to allow matters to rest in status quo but if squeezed by Russia would agree to (Kuwait's) occupation by that power, partly because (Kuwait) does not belong to them and would form such an admirable bone of contention between England and Russia and partly 'pour embeter les Anglais', a game which everyone in these parts delights in playing.[39]

A month later, Loch returned to Russian activities in the Gulf in the course of a dispatch daated 22 December on the uneasy partnership between Arif Pasha and Muhsin Pasha in Basra to which we have already referred. Regarding the Russian threat, Loch wrote: 'For some months past, vague rumours have been afloat that Russia and her agents were working in the Gulf ... from hints I have received it is Koweit on which Russia's eyes are fixed.'[40] When Loch's paper arrived at the Foreign Office in London, it came into the hands of George Nathaniel Curzon, the parliamentary under-secretary at the Foreign Office, and the one man in Britain most likely to be interested by the link between Kuwait and Russia.

As far as Curzon was concerned, Loch's supposition confirmed his most pessimistic forecast. In December 1897, Curzon had been in the rather lowly position of parliamentary under-secretary for two and a half years. Just a year later, however, he would move to India to start his memorable and controversial period as viceroy. As viceroy, he would above all be associated with ambitious manoeuvres to counter Russian ambitions on the borders of Britain's Indian Empire, culminating in the Younghusband expedition to Tibet of 1904. But Russia and Russian designs on India had always been a major theme of his professional life. In his last year at Eton, he had arranged a lecture to the Eton Literary Society by the lawyer and historian Sir James Stephen on the subject of India and the British role in Asia. The lecture had affected him profoundly. In Curzon's words: 'Ever since that day, the fascination and sacredness of India have grown upon me.' In the late 1880s, he had travelled extensively in Russian Central Asia and the Middle East. His visit to Russia in 1888 included a trip to Tashkent along the newly-constructed railway linking , Bokhara and Samarkand, and running close to the Persian frontier. He described the railway as a 'sword of Damocles' over the head of the Shah of Persia. Curzon then travelled widely in Persian and the Gulf itself, collecting material for *Persia and the Persian Question* in which he spoke in the strongest terms of the need to keep Russia out of the waters of the Gulf. As Curzon was to play such a central role in changing British policy towards the Gulf in general and Kuwait in particular it is worth quoting his views at some length:

> Are we prepared to surrender the control of the Indian Ocean? Are we prepared to make the construction of the Euphrates Valley Railway, of some kindred scheme of the future, an impossibility for England and an ultimate certainty for Russia?[41]

In the position which he occupied in December 1897, as parliamentary under-secretary for foreign affairs, Lord Curzon was rather seriously under-employed. Most of his time was spent acting as the House of Commons spokesman for Lord Salisbury, who combined the offices of prime minister and foreign secretary. In Harold Nicolson's graphic words, 'he chafed under the vague if masterly inactivity of his chief'.[42] Curzon made up for the lack of responsibility in his job by taking a keen interest in the affairs of India and in Russian designs on India. In this, he has been frequently misunderstood. He has sometimes been presented as an unrealistic scare monger who raised the spectre of a Russian conquest of India, but failed to appreciate the immense practical difficulties which would prevent such an expedition. This is unfair to Curzon. His views on the Russian threat to India were considerably more subtle, and were based on the all-too-real fact that Russia had been stirring up trouble for Britain at selected points along the northern frontiers of India for most of the nineteenth century. A recent writer has summarised Curzon's thinking in the following terms 'he concluded that although neither Russian statesmen nor generals dreamed of the conquest of India, "they do most seriously contemplate the invasion of India, and that with a very definite purpose which many of them are candid enough to avow."' The Russian aim in building up invasion scares was to distract Britain from involvement with the Ottoman Empire. In Curzon's words: 'To keep England quiet in Europe by keeping her employed in Asia ... That, briefly put, is the sum and substance of Russian policy.'[43]

So, rather than expecting Russian armies to sweep into India over the Himalayas or through Afghanistan, Curzon thought in terms of a delicate game of chess between Britain and Russia, played for very high stakes, with most of Asia as the chessboard. And in late 1897, he had plenty of evidence to support his fears. In August 1891, a force of 400 Cossacks had moved into a strategic area of the Pamir mountain range, which gave access to the Punjab and India. When they came across a British officer, they ordered him out of what they claimed to be 'Russian territory', and showed him a map in which large areas of Afghanistan and China were marked as belonging to the Tsar. The British reacted quickly by sending a force of Gurkhas to occupy the mountain Kingdom of Hunza, whose ruler claimed that he would throw the British out with the help of the Russians. The British-led force of Gurkhas and Imperial Service troops from Kashmir moved against Hunza in the winter of 1891–92, launching scarcely credible attacks against mountain fortresses and heavily-defended passes. At minimal cost in casualties (and with an impressive number of British awards for bravery) the Gurkha/Kashmiri force succeeded in occupying Hunza and 'closing the door' in the face of the Russians. It was well known that this episode had been keenly resented by the Russian soldiers and politicians who favoured a 'forward' policy against India.

British officers who came across their Russian opposite numbers during the crisis in the Pamirs were generally left in no doubt that the commanders of the Russian Army looked forward to a full-scale war with Britain on the northern frontiers of India. This belligerence was almost certainly confined to the officers of the Imperial Army, and was probably not shared by the Tsar's government in St Petersburg. The policy of the Tsar's government was often hard to read, and there was good reason for a 'Russophobe' like Lord Curzon to take the aggressive remarks of the Russian officers seriously. We have to remember that we look at Russia with the benefit of considerable hindsight. We have seen two fairly spectacular collapses of Russian Empires in our own century: in 1916–17, and again in 1991–92. Back in the 1890s, however, Russia appeared to the world to be a dynamic and rising power; the Russian Empire suffered of course from an archaic social structure (which had been based on serfdom until 1861), but it was emerging as a formidable exporter of grains and raw materials, and was a highly-regarded military power. British soldiers who came across Russian troops in the frontier regions of India were invariably impressed by the good spirit, toughness and smart bearing of the Cossacks, and the scale of the Russian advance into Central Asia during the nineteenth century was indeed astonishing. All the great cities of Uzbekistan had fallen in the 1860s, followed by Merv and the towns of the Turcomans in the 1880s. Russia did indeed seem to be on the march, and her march led towards India.

So it was not surprising that Lord Curzon immediately drew Lord Salis-bury's attention to Loch's warning about Russian designs on Kuwait. Curzon pointed out that, though Shaikh Mubarak had asked for the extension of Brit-ish protection to Kuwait, Britain had so far declined the request. But 'a time may come … when a Protectorate may be the most useful method of antici-pating acquisition by another power.'[44] He suggested that the India Office's attention should be drawn to this 'contingency'. Sanderson at the Foreign Of-fice was dubious about the existence of a Russian threat to Kuwait, which he considered an unlikely and inconvenient place for the Russians to choose. He consulted the India Office, and also privately asked Admiral Lewis Beaumont, the Admiralty's director of naval intelligence, for his observations. Beaumont replied that Kuwait was 'on the way to nowhere', but admitted that it would make a good coaling station, and could be turned into a fortified naval base at a heavy financial cost. If this was done, then it would be of great importance to Russia. Curzon was not too concerned about the plans for a coaling station, which he saw as a mere pretext for Russia in her plan to gain access to the Gulf; but he was unable to persuade his superiors to take any further action on Ku-wait at this point.

Unofficially, Curzon maintained his interest in Kuwait. At the end of Feb-ruary 1898, he wrote privately to Colonel Meade in Bushire to ask his views. Meade's reply must have been welcome to Curzon, as it supported his own thinking. Meade argued that Kuwait was potentially very important, both as a port and as a possible railway terminus. Meade thought that, even if Britain did not want Kuwait for herself, she should certainly deny it to her opponents, and the time was now right to bring Shaikh Mubarak under British influence, even if it was not immediately possible to offer British protection.[45] Curzon followed this up by writing to Lee Warner at the India Office in June to ask for a chance to talk the matter over before approaching the prime minister again about Kuwait. Warner wrote an interesting memorandum in preparation for this visit, setting out the impartial civil servant's view of the arguments for and against British involvement in Kuwait. One argument against British action was the fact that Britain had in the past given at least implied recognition to Ottoman sovereignty over Kuwait, by recognising that the Ottoman Empire controlled points on the Gulf coast to the south of Kuwait. Moreover, Shaikh Mubarak held the Ottoman title of qaimaqam, and had appealed to the Ottomans for protection against his enemies. On the other hand, Warner pointed out, any Ottoman sovereignty over Kuwait was not effectively maintained, and there was no Ottoman control over piracy, slavery or gun running. If the British were to assume control over Kuwait, they would gain a good harbour, a potential railway terminus and an important centre of trade, and they would deny these same advantages to any foreign power. They would also be able to improve their control over slavery and the trade in weapons in the Gulf as a whole. The extension of a British protectorate would certainly lead to diplomatic complications with the Ottoman Empire.[46]

While Curzon and Lee Warner were discussing Kuwait, a new sign of potential Russian interest in the territory appeared on the horizon. This was, in fact, one of the most bizarre episodes in the Kuwait story, involving a game of bluff between the three European powers most involved in Kuwait: Britain, Germany and the Russian Empire. In June 1898, a Russian nobleman, Count Vladimir Kapnist, submitted a petition to the Ottoman Porte requesting a concession to build a railway through Aleppo, Homs, Najaf and Basra, with a terminus on the Gulf at Kuwait. In the petition, Kapnist asked for a licence to build a port in Kuwait, and to drain the land around the Shatt al-Arab. On the face of it, this was an ambitious plan to create a Russian presence in the region of Iraq and the northern Gulf, with enormous political benefit to Russia but at little economic cost (as the capital for the scheme was variously reported to be coming from French and British private sources). Lord Curzon was away from the Foreign Office in the autumn of 1898, preparing to leave for India as viceroy. But in October he saw the report on the project from the British Embassy in Constantinople, and he at once repeated to Lord Salisbury his arguments in favour of a firm British policy in the Gulf, so as to deny access to the Gulf to other European powers. On the specific question of Kuwait, Curzon noted that '... it is not in Turkish but in independent Arab possession; and that such a step could be guarded against by declaring a British protectorate over Koweit.'[47]

Strangely enough, it now seems that the British may have been wrong to make a connection between the Kapnist proposal and Russia's strategic designs on Kuwait. In the following months, some odd aspects of the Kapnist plan emerged, suggesting that it was not a serious commercial proposal, and that it did not have any real official backing from the Russian government. Indeed, the British commercial attache in Constantinople discovered in April 1899 that many senior figures in the Russian government were opposed to the Kapnist plan, and that Kapnist himself had very little influence at the Russian court. On this basis, Professor J. B. Kelly has argued persuasively that the entire Kapnist scheme may have been no more than an operation of deception designed by the German promoters of the Anatolian Railway Company's rival plan for a rail link from Konya to Baghdad and the Gulf. The aim of the scheme, under this interpretation, would simply have been to divert the attention of the British and Russian governments from the German-backed scheme.[48]

However, the Kapnist plan did place Kuwait and the Russian interest in the Gulf high on the agenda of the British Foreign Office. Lord Salisbury was becoming increasingly concerned about the area, and his worries increased when, in November 1898, the Foreign Office received a report on the Kapnist Plan from the director of military intelligence at the War Office, Major-General Sir John Ardagh. Sir John expressed doubts about the financial basis of the plan, and was of course unaware that the Russian government was not really committed to the project. He concluded that the main aim of the plan was political, and that it would allow Russia to acquire 'predominant influence' in the basin of the Euphrates and Tigris, with a view to an eventual takeover of the area. In his words, the scheme provided for rights to acquire land which could result in '... so vast an accretion of territory to that (Russian) Empire as to disturb most materially the balance of power in Asia.'[49] Indeed, the British general anticipated that, if the concession went ahead, there would be 'the inevitable partition of Turkey, Persia and Afghanistan ... .' He felt it was now highly desirable to foster British influence and a British foothold in the main sea ports of Arabia and the Gulf: Mocha, Hodaida, Jiddah, Yanbu, Bandar Abbas, Bushire, Muhammarah, Baghdad, Basra and Kuwait.

By the time that Sir John Ardagh produced his contribution to the growing file on Kuwait, Lord Curzon was completing his preparations for departure for India. Curzon had found time earlier in November 1898 to prepare a lengthy 'Memorandum Respecting Persian Affairs', which dealt at length with the increasing Russian interest in Persia and also with German ambitions. On the Kapnist railway project, Curzon pointed out that it assumed Ottoman sovereignty over Kuwait, which he did not accept. 'A Russian railway ending at Koweit would be in the highest degree injurious to British interests. A German railway to Koweit would be scarcely less so – even a Turkish railway to Koweit would be unwelcome. Any one of these would challenge our hitherto uncontested supremacy in the Gulf ... .'[50]

Curzon's strong views on Kuwait coincided with some alarming reports of French interest in building a coaling station at Muscat, at the other end of the Gulf. The French consul in Muscat had persuaded the sultan to grant a site for a French coaling station at Bandar Jissa, about five miles from Muscat, in direct contravention of the sultan's 1891 promise to the Government of India that he would be cede any part of this territory to any power other than Britain. Indeed, at the start of 1899, Britain had to compel the sultan to renounce his agreement with France, and to re-state his commitment to the 1891 promise. British officials were also well aware that the kaiser of Germany's visit to Constantinople in the previous month, October 1898, had been intended to signal a closer German involvement in Ottoman affairs. As the European powers seemed to be clustering around the Gulf, and to be threatening Britain's exclusive position in the region, the Foreign Office now began to change its stance on the question of a British protectorate over Kuwait.

The change was signalled in a letter which Sanderson of the Foreign Office wrote to Arthur Godley, the permanent under-secretary at the India Office, on 5 December 1898. Sanderson told Godley that, in Lord Salisbury's opinion,

> ... the question of establishing a Protectorate over Koweit and the responsibilities which such a Protectorate would entail is a matter primarily for the consideration of the Government of India, as on that Government would fall the duty of undertaking the arrangements to be made for the assertion and maintenance of the Protectorate and the control of the Sheikh that would be entailed by it.[51]

The Foreign Office therefore indicated that it was prepared in principle to accept a protectorate. In his next paragraph, Sanderson went further:

> If the Government of India is of opinion that the Protectorate can be undertaken without difficulty or any inconvenient extension of the duties of policy already exercised in the Persian Gulf, Lord Salisbury would approve of such a step, and would be prepared to acquiesce in the establishment of such Protectorate and to support it diplomatically in case the Porte should raise counter-claims.

In other words, the Foreign Office was not prepared to take a lead in declaring a protectorate, and continued to insist that there should be no great additional policing responsibilities as a result of the protectorate. But, if the protectorate were to be established, there was at least the promise of Foreign Office support in countering a hostile Ottoman reaction. At the India Office, Lee Warner of course noted the guarded tone of the Foreign Office letter. He pointed out that the Foreign Office first 'approved' but in the same line 'acquiesced' in the idea of the protectorate. He suspected that 'acquiesce' had been inserted by Lord Salisbury himself to strengthen the Foreign Office position. His suspicion may have been due to a comment which Sanderson had made to Sir Alfred Comyns Lyall, a member of the Council of India, at a party on 6 December. Sanderson had apparently said that '... Lord Salisbury attached little or no importance to the Koweit project, and said it was entirely the affair of India.'[52]

Lee Warner was sufficiently encouraged by Sanderson's letter to suggest that it would be 'an admirable result' if Britain could peacefully establish a protectorate over Kuwait. He thought that the time had now come to send a telegram to India, asking their opinion on the situation in Kuwait and on the prospects for making any protectorate effective. The political committee of the India Office, when presented with Warner's idea, added a sentence to the draft to the effect that any assumption of a protectorate must be on the understanding that responsibility for declaring and maintaining the protectorate (and for controlling Shaikh Mubarak) would devolve on the Government of India.[53] The committee also decided to delay sending the telegram until Lord Curzon had reached India and had taken up his duties as viceroy.

Events were now moving faster than the India Office might have wished. On 17 December 1898, *The Times* carried a long article on the details of the Kapnist scheme. Now that the secret was out, the India Office decided to proceed with its telegram to India. From Constantinople, the new British ambassador, Sir Nicholas O'Conor, urged caution about any protectorate over Kuwait, saying that the declaration of a protectorate at the present time would be seen as 'little short of a hostile act' by Turkey. O'Conor also thought that the declaration would certainly produce very serious diplomatic complications, not only with the Ottoman government but probably also with Russia.[54]

O'Conor's warning about the dangers of a protectorate was passed on to the India Office and the Government of India by the Foreign Office, but the impact of the Ambassador's views was considerably weakened by the fact that the Foreign Office provided no covering letter or comment. The India Office interpreted this silence as evidence that neither the ambassador nor the Foreign Office were unduly concerned to oppose the protectorate. Meanwhile, the Government of India had followed the instructions of the India Office, and had asked Meade in Bushire for his views on the situation in Kuwait and the prospects for a protectorate. Meade replied on 30 December 1898, suggesting that he should go to Kuwait immediately to gather the necessary information, and asking for authority in advance to conclude a secret agreement with Shaikh Mubarak, under which the shaikh would not accept a protectorate from any power other than Britain. In return for such a promise, Meade suggested that Britain should agree to support the shaikh 'against all attacks'.[55] This was, of course, a very wide-ranging commitment for Britain to undertake, but Meade seems to have believed that it would be an easy one to implement, as he thought that Shaikh Mubarak could defend himself from the land side, and that the Royal Navy could cope with any threat from the Ottomans or anyone else on the seaward side. His belief that Shaikh Mubarak was capable of handling any Ottoman attack by land was, as became clear after January 1899, a very serious error of judgment. We have to conclude that Meade was seriously ill-informed of the real strength of Kuwait and the risks which Britain would run in supporting the shaikh to such an extent.

Officials in the Foreign Office in London now began to exhibit a sense of urgency which almost matched that of Meade. The Foreign Office had been stung into action by news from Constantinople that an imperial *irade* (decree) had been issued, granting the Kapnist Concession. Although it was now known that the concession would depend to a large extent on British finance, O'Conor warned that he doubted whether Britain had any real control over the scheme. When O'Conor's telegram reached London, Lee Warner noted a little sadly on the file: 'I wish that we had secured Koweit a year ago.'[56]

Lee Warner was not the only one to react to the news from Constantinople. Lord Salisbury himself asked Sanderson to inform the India Office that, despite warnings from O'Conor about the possible risks from a protectorate, the foreign secretary wanted to take all possible precautions against the establishment of a Russian territorial claim in the area of Kuwait, such as might result from the Kapnist project. Lord Salisbury's particular wish was for steps to be taken to ensure that Shaikh Mubarak promised not to cede, lease, mortgage or otherwise alienate any part of his territory to a government or foreign national without first obtaining British consent. In fact, Lord Salisbury was now so keen to get an immediate agreement that he was willing to offer between £4,000 and £5,000 to Shaikh Mubarak as an inducement to sign. Privately, Sanderson told Lee Warner at the India Office that Lord Salisbury would in fact be prepared to go as high as £10,000 to get Shaikh Mubarak's signature.[57]

The India Office was also eager to move ahead fast. In a telegram to the Government of India on 6 January, the India Office asked if the Indian government would require help from the Admiralty. In a private letter to Lord Curzon, Godley pointed out Lord Salisbury's personal interest in the case, and gave his view of the aims of the negotiations: 'We don't want Koweit, but we don't want anyone else to have it',[58] and Meade, waiting in Bushire for orders to proceed to Kuwait, added his voice to those calling for haste. If a protectorate was the goal, he said, then the necessary steps should be taken without delay, otherwise Britain might be forestalled by one of the great powers. Meade also pointed out, in a message sent on 7 January, that it would be hard to keep his fact-finding mission to Kuwait a secret. He repeated his request of a week before for permission to offer Shaikh Mubarak immediate protection, in return for a pledge not to accept a protectorate from any other power.

Meade's continuing emphasis on the need for immediate authority to proclaim a protectorate reflected his long-standing commitment to the idea, and certainly helps to explain the course which negotiations took when Meade finally arrived in Kuwait two weeks later, but it is interesting that not all officials in the area shared his views. The British consul in Basra, A. C. Wratislaw, warned Meade on 13 January that the Ottomans could hardly ignore the threat to their position in the region from the proposed protectorate. They might well appeal for help to the European signatories of the Treaty of Paris and the 1878 Treaty of Berlin. Then, while the diplomats argued, the Ottomans could well invade Kuwait from the landward side. As Britain would probably not want to fight a European war simply in order to acquire a protectorate over Kuwait, there was a real risk that the British government would be forced into a humiliating climb down.[59]

Meade, however, was not inclined to be receptive to warnings of this kind. In reply to London's request that he should proceed along the lines suggested by Lord Salisbury, in other words that he should obtain an agreement that Shaikh Mubarak would not cede or yield any territory to another government or foreign citizen without British consent, Meade gave an encouraging assessment. He told the Government of India that he was optimistic that he could reach Kuwait discreetly, but he suggested that the agreement should be made binding on Shaikh Mubarak's successors as well as on the shaikh himself. He suggested also that, instead of a lump sum, he should be allowed to offer an annual subsidy of up to £1,000. This very large amount confirms just how anxious Meade was to obtain the agreement. This was not all. Meade also said that it was important that he should be allowed to offer Shaikh Mubarak the 'good offices' of Britain, to strengthen his position in relation to other claimants to Kuwait. Meade suggested that, with British support in the form of 'good offices', Mubarak would probably be able to hold his own against his rivals.

Here Meade was introducing a new element into Britain's relations with Kuwait, by making a connection between British interests in the Gulf and the maintenance of Shaikh Mubarak's rule over Kuwait. Instead of guaranteeing

Kuwait against the Ottomans, Meade was effectively saying, Britain should guarantee Shaikh Mubarak against his enemies, so as to secure British objectives in the region. Once the agreement with Shaikh Mubarak was concluded, the British were indeed to find that they had virtually committed themselves to backing Shaikh Mubarak, no matter what he did in his small state.

Meade Receives his Instructions

Meanwhile, the responsible departments in London were working out the details of the agreement which Britain would offer to Mubarak. There were two recent agreements involving Gulf rulers which could be used as precedents. The first of these was the 'lawful and honourable bond' which the Sultan of Muscat and the British resident in the Gulf had signed on 20 March 1891. Under this agreement, the sultan promised that he and his heirs and successors would never 'cede, sell, mortgage or otherwise give for occupation' any of his territory, except to the British government. The second precedent was the group of six 'exclusive treaties' which the rulers of six of the Trucial States (the present United Arab Emirates) had signed in March 1892, in the presence of the British resident. Under these 'exclusive treaties' the rulers of the Abu Dhabi, Ajman, Dubai, Sharjah, Ras al-Khaimah and Umm al-Qaiwain repeated the promise which the Sultan of Muscat had already given, namely that they would not yield any of their territory except to the British government. But the Trucial rulers added two more undertakings:

1. Not to enter into any agreements or correspondence with any power other than the British government.
2. Not to let any agent of a government other than the British government reside in their territory without British assent.

In British eyes both these agreements had the great merit of being entirely one-sided. Both the ruler of Muscat and the rulers of the six Trucial states promised the British that they would not do certain things, but they got no promises or commitments in return from the British side. Although some were to suggest that the very close political relationship which the 1892 agreements with the Trucial rulers had created implied that Britain had some obligations to protect the vital interests of the Trucial States, the fact remains that neither the 1891 Muscat bond nor the 1892 Trucial agreements were in any way formal agreements to provide protection.

Much later, in July 1957, the sunset of Britain's age of supremacy in the Gulf region, Britain's foreign secretary, Selwyn Lloyd, was to state the official view on Britain's role in the Trucial states in an answer to the House of Commons. He denied that there was any specific treaty obligation on Britain to protect the Trucial states, but admitted that an obligation of protection was implicit in the Perpetual Maritime Truce of 1853, which all the Trucial rulers had signed. He did not refer at all to the 1892 exclusive treaties. So, for the British government, any obligation which Britain might feel to provide protection was not embodied in the 1892 agreements, even despite the very close relations which the 1892 agreements (and to a lesser extent the 1891 agreement with Muscat) had created between Britain and the Arab rulers.

Given that none of the agreements under consideration for Kuwait were seen as protectorate agreements, the question which faced British officials in January 1899 was whether to offer Shaikh Mubarak the Muscat formula or the Trucial states formula. The Government of India at first favoured using the 1892 Trucial states formula, so as to extract from Mubarak a promise not to correspond with any governments other than Britain, as well as a promise not to accept agents of other governments on Kuwaiti territory.[60] Lee Warner at the India Office pointed out that the extra undertakings given by the Trucial rulers, including the undertaking not to correspond with foreign powers, 'go beyond what we want'.[61] He favoured using the 1891 Muscat agreement as a model, so that Mubarak would simply promise not to yield any land to a power other than Britain.[62]

It is easy to understand why Warner preferred the 1891 Muscat agreement. Britain's aim was to block the proposed Russian railway. This could be done by preventing the railway consortium from acquiring any land in Kuwait for a terminus. If the agreement went further, and covered correspondence with foreign powers, Britain could find itself obliged to act to enforce the agreement if Shaikh Mubarak subsequently resumed his dealings with the Ottoman authorities.

So the 1891 Muscat agreement emerged as the India Office's preference as a precedent for Kuwait. The India Office still faced a problem in the shape of the Foreign Office's letter of 5 December 1898, passing on Lord Salisbury's approval for the establishment of a protectorate 'if the Government of India is of the opinion that the protectorate can be undertaken without any difficulty or any inconvenient extension of the duties of policy already exercised in the Gulf.' The India Office was well aware that Sir N. O'Conor in Constantinople had warned during December that any protectorate over Kuwait would be regarded as 'little short of a hostile act by Turkey'.[63] Understandably, the India Office felt a need to limit any costs or responsibilities which might fall on the Government of India as a result of any agreement with Mubarak which might develop into a protectorate. Essentially, the India Office and the Government of India needed an assurance that the Foreign Office would take full responsibility for any trouble with Constantinople which might arise from the agreement.

In mid-January 1899, correspondence moved back and forth between the India Office and the Foreign Office on this matter. The final result was entirely satisfactory from the viewpoint of the India Office. On 18 January 1899, Sanderson of the Foreign Office wrote to Godley at the India Office to confirm that, in Lord Salisbury's view, the non-alienation agreement (the formula of the 1891 Muscat agreement, which was now to be offered to Shaikh Mubarak) 'does not go so far as to constitute a protectorate'. Sanderson also said that the foreign secretary, in his letter of 4 January 1891 calling for rapid action to obtain Mubarak's signature, had only wanted to employ 'for Imperial purposes' the 'superior facilities' which the Government of India possessed in the Gulf, and under these circumstances he 'did not contemplate that by according that assistance the Indian government would in the slightest degree pledge themselves to take any action, or to accept any liability under any circumstances that might arise in the future.'[64]

In the eyes of Lord Hamilton, the secretary of state for India, this letter ruled out any commitment to military action to defend Kuwait. Hamilton wrote with delight to Lord Curzon in India that, due to Sanderson's letter, 'we are practically as free from the defence of Koweit, should it be attacked, as we are from defending Somali land against the Abyssinians.'[65] Lee Warner was less sanguine, and commented: 'I am rather afraid of the consequences at any rate to the sheikh who is pretty sure to be evicted if our intentions are suspected.'[66]

But Warner's misgivings cannot obscure the main feature of the inter-departmental correspondence in London during January 1899. Whatever Warner thought, the Foreign Office and the India Office were clear that the non-alienation formula which they planned to offer to Mubarak, on the lines of the Muscat agreement, *did not* imply an obligation to defend Kuwait and could not be interpreted as a protectorate.

The Foreign Office and the India Office had also settled the way to handle the subsidy question. The India Office preferred an annual subsidy to a lump-sum payment, although they felt the amount suggested by Meade was excessive. The annual subsidy was the usual form for subsidies to Eastern rulers, and had the extra advantage of being 'an annual reminder of the obligation to the successors of the signatory chief'. It also had the merit of economy: 'If we are disappointed in the fulfilment of the treaty, we stop our subsidy.' Salisbury was opposed to the annual subsidy, on the grounds that it was a less permanent transaction: 'Instead of buying the neutrality of the sheikh, we are only hiring it.'[67] He was not inclined to press the point, and left the decision to the Government of India, which now briefed Meade on his mission.

These instructions were contained in a telegram to Bushire dated 18 January 1898.[68] The Government of India asked Meade to proceed to Kuwait and to enter into an agreement with Shaikh Mubarak, modelled on the Muscat non-alienation agreement of 1891, as soon as he was satisfied that Mubarak's position in Kuwait was secure and that there was no immediate danger from the Ottomans or anyone else. It also told Meade that he could assure Mubarak of British good offices, as long as Mubarak adhered to the agreement. The Government of India seems to have imagined that this assurance of 'good offices' would be conveyed orally, rather than being written down: London had certainly not intended that any written guarantee should be given of British good offices, and was alarmed when Meade did in fact offer such a written pledge. On the subsidy question, the Government of India left Meade a free choice between an annual subsidy and a single lump-sum payment, although it did express a preference for the lump sum. If Meade chose an annual payment, the government felt that Rs3,000 (about £200) would probably be enough. Curzon had written to Hamilton on 12 January to say that Meade's original proposal of an annual subsidy of 'up to £1,000' was extravagant. Curzon said that Sir Adalbert Talbot, who had been the political resident in the Gulf from 1891 to 1893 and who knew Kuwait well, had thought that the shaikh would be ready to 'tumble into our arms for nothing.'[69]

When he received his instructions, Meade sent a letter to Sir William Cunningham, the secretary of the Foreign Department of the Government of India. This letter of 19 January took a markedly pessimistic view of the situation in Kuwait, and would probably have alarmed very considerably the officials in London who were anxious to avoid the expense and military commitment of a protectorate over Kuwait, if they had known of its existence. In sharp contrast to his optimistic views expressed as recently as 30 December, when he had argued that it would be fairly easy to protect Kuwait against any attacks, Meade now said that he was no longer certain that Mubarak could defend himself. There were rumours that Mubarak's nephews and Shaikh Jasim bin Thani of Qatar were about to attack Kuwait, and Meade also felt that the Ottomans were a threat. He said that, if the Ottomans became suspicious, they might side with the nephews, and Britain would then be forced to support Mubarak 'unless we are prepared to let any money we give him be wasted and our own prestige lowered.'[70] Meade also expressed worry about a possible direct

Ottoman attack on Kuwait, and said that he was no longer confident of being able to defend Kuwait from an attack from the land side with the gunboat available. Additional forces might be required from India.

Meade's letter points to some of his shortcomings as an official in a region such as the Gulf, where individual initiative and a clear judgment were required. His telegram of 30 December, arguing that Britain could easily assure the defence of Kuwait, must have played a part in reassuring officials in London that they were not risking a major military commitment by offering the agreement to Mubarak. Now Meade was indicating that very large military commitments might indeed be incurred if Britain wanted to defend Mubarak and the considerable political investment which it was about to make in him. Furthermore, Meade's letter of 19 January betrays a marked sense of panic in his own mind about the situation in the northern Gulf. This panic was to surface during his negotiations with Shaikh Mubarak and other members of the al-Sabah family, and was to lead him to offer Mubarak far more in the way of promises of support than he had been authorised to offer. Not surprisingly, there was to be a strong call after the negotiations for Meade to be removed from the Gulf before he did any more damage.

The Negotiations of the Anglo–Kuwaiti Agreement of 1899

On the night of 20 January 1899, Meade left Bushire for Kuwait, using the excuse of a shooting trip to Kharj Island as a cover story. He sailed on RIMS *Lawrence*, accompanied by his assistant, Gaskin, and by Muhammad Rahim, the British Residency's agent in Bahrain. Muhammad Rahim was a close friend of Mubarak, and had been invited to assist in the negotiations. The party arrived in Kuwait on the morning of 21 January, and found that, despite their attempts to keep their visit secret, the Turkish gunboat *Zohaf* was standing in Kuwait harbour when they arrived. However, the *Lawrence* was not flying the resident's flag, and Meade hoped that the Turks would not suspect his presence. He made enquiries on shore which seem to have satisfied him that Mubarak's position in Kuwait was secure, and he therefore decided to conclude the agreement as soon as possible.[71]

As a first step, Meade sent Gaskin and the captain of the *Lawrence* ashore to invite Shaikh Mubarak on board the ship. Shaikh Mubarak was as usual rather nervous about public contact with the British, especially with the *Zohaf* in the bay. So, instead of coming out himself, he sent his brother, Shaikh Humud, to call on Meade on the morning of 22 January. Meade told Shaikh Humud that the British had learned of Shaikh Mubarak's wish to enjoy the advantages of British protection in the same way as other Arab sultans and shaikhs, and that he had come to Kuwait in order to enter into 'certain agreements' with the shaikh. He went on to say that, in view of the friendly relations between Britain and the Ottoman government, it was not considered desirable 'just now' to make an open declaration that Britain would take Kuwait under its protection.[72] The British government did not want Turkish influence to extend any further in Kuwait, and did not want any power other than Britain to obtain a protectorate over Kuwait or to own land there. Therefore, Britain was

> ... ready to enter into a secret agreement with shaikh Mubarak by which he should at once bind himself not to have any relations with the representatives of any other powers or to receive the agent or any power other than Great Britain at Koweit. He should agree not to cede, lease, mortgage or otherwise alienate or give for occupation any portion of his territory to the government or subject of any other power without obtaining the previous consent of Her Majesty's Government.[73]

Meade added that the agreement would have to be binding on Mubarak's successors as well as on Mubarak himself, but in return the British government would be ready to assist the shaikh with money, and to give him their good offices 'should he require help'.

So, even before he met Shaikh Mubarak, we can see that Meade was interpreting his instructions in an extremely liberal manner. He had already added to his brief the idea of a promise that Shaikh Mubarak should not have any dealings with foreign powers other than Britain, a promise which he had specifically been asked not to include in the agreement. He had also implied, by his remarks that a protectorate was not on offer 'just now', that there might be a good chance of such a protectorate in the future. Right from the start, he had set the negotiations off on a course which was to cause real dismay in London when the text of the agreement was communicated back.

In reply to this opening statement, Shaikh Humud pointed out that, while his brother would be happy to accept Meade's terms, the al-Sabah family also owned considerable property in Ottoman territory. He hoped that the British government would promise to help in regard to these estates, which the al-Sabah might lose if they offended the Turks. Meade said that he could not give guarantees on this until he had consulted the Government of India. Shaikh Humud asked Meade to meet Mubarak for a personal discussion, and then returned on shore, followed by Gaskin who had been instructed to sound Mubarak out on the matter of the subsidy.

Gaskin came back that afternoon (by which time the Turkish warship *Zohaf* had left Kuwait harbour) and told Meade that Shaikh Mubarak did indeed want to enter into an agreement with Britain, but that he would not conclude the agreement unless he received a written assurance of British support. Gaskin also reported that the shaikh was willing to accede to the non-alienation bond in return for a lump-sum payment of Rs15,000 (about £1,000). On the night of 22–23 January, Meade drew up his draft agreement for presentation to the shaikh next day. The agreement included the clause promising that Shaikh Mubarak would have no dealings with any other than Britain – the clause which the Foreign Office and the India Office had both wanted to avoid. Meade later excused this breach of instructions by saying that Gaskin had heard from Shaikh Mubarak during his meeting on the afternoon of 22 January that the French had been making overtures to Kuwait, which could be frustrated by the clause in question. This excuse looks thin when we recall that Meade had already included the clause banning relations with foreign powers in his opening statement to Shaikh Humud on the morning of 22 January, before Gaskin had spoken with Shaikh Mubarak.

On the morning of 23 January, Meade showed his draft agreement to Shaikh Mubarak. The shaikh said that, while he held the British in 'the utmost regard', he was worried about the trouble which an agreement with Britain might create for him with the Ottoman authorities. He therefore wanted a written assurance from the British government of 'protection and assistance, *especially* in regard to the property belonging to his family situated in Ottoman territory.' To make matters worse, he wanted this assurance to form part of any agreement which he signed with Meade. Even Meade, who was apparently by now determined to secure an agreement at almost any price, appreciated that such a categorical pledge to back Mubarak against the Ottomans in defence of his personal property would never be accepted by the Government of India or by London. But he did agree to give Mubarak a separate letter assuring him and his successors of the 'good offices' of Her Majesty's Government, as long as the conditions of the agreement were observed by the rulers of Kuwait.[74] Beyond this he refused to go. When Mubarak continued to insist on a written guarantee that Britain would protect the al-Sabah family estates in Ottoman territory, Meade threatened to leave Kuwait without signing any agreement, and to seek further instructions from India. Shaikh Mubarak yielded to this threat, and 'without further discussion' agreed to sign Meade's draft.

Shaikh Mubarak and Meade signed the three copies of the agreement, and Meade's assistants witnessed his signature. Shaikh Mubarak called his brother, Shaikh Humud, to witness his signature. This led to complications, as Shaikh

Humud said that he could not sign the agreement unless there was a specific promise from Britain to protect the al-Sabah family estates. The letter from Meade promising British good offices was not enough to satisfy Shaikh Humud, who was supported by Mubarak's other brother, Shaikh Jabir, in his insistence on a written guarantee for family property. Both Humud and Jabir pointed out that the Ottomans had a law which prohibited aliens from holding land in Turkish territory. If Kuwait passed under British protection, they feared that the family would be dispossessed of its important estates. Mubarak therefore decided to ask Muhammad Rahim to witness his signature, instead of Shaikh Humud. He assured Meade that the agreement would be binding on future Shaikhs of Kuwait, even if the signatures of his brothers did not appear on it.

In his report to India, prepared the next day, Meade pointed out that the question of the al-Sabah estates was more important than he had realised, and asked for authorisation to assure the al-Sabah that Her Majesty's Government would look after their property within Ottoman jurisdiction. Not surprisingly the India Office, which was already unhappy about the agreement in the form in which it had been signed, rejected this request for a specific commitment, and merely said that the British government would 'do what they can' to protect al-Sabah property in Ottoman territory.

The Anglo–Kuwait Agreement of 1899: Winners and Losers

The agreement which Meade and Shaikh Mubarak signed on 23 January 1899 was very different from that which Meade had been instructed to seek. He had been ordered to extract from Mubarak a promise not to yield any territory to a power other than Britain, but he had added, on his own initiative, the promises relating to correspondence with foreign powers and receiving the agents of foreign powers which London had been particularly anxious not to include in the agreement. He had apparently been authorised to give Shaikh Mubarak an oral assurance of British good offices, if necessary; but in fact, he had given a written assurance of good offices, a move which caused some alarm when it was reported back to London. He also gave the al-Sabah at least a reason to hope that the British government would consider favourably a guarantee for their properties in Ottoman territory. Finally, and most dangerously of all, Meade had let the idea of British protection for Kuwait hang in the air throughout the discussions. This was the one thing which London had been most anxious to avoid: the great merit of the 1891 Muscat agreement as a precedent for Kuwait had been, it was agreed, that the Muscat formula involved no obligation to protect the Arab party to the agreement. ('We are practically as free from the defence of Kuwait … as we are from defending Somali land against the Abyssinians,' as Hamilton so graphically put it).

Instead of playing down the idea of protection, Meade seems to have gone out of his way to encourage it. Even on arrival in Kuwait, and before he first met Mubarak, he told Shaikh Humud that 'it is not considered desirable just now to openly declare that the British will take Kuwait under their protection,' a remark which surely hinted that a form of undeclared protection was, in fact, being offered. This is certainly the way that Mubarak subsequently interpreted the agreement. In November 1900, the British news agent in Kuwait was reporting back to the British resident that Shaikh Mubarak 'will not listen to the Sublime Porte, because he is internally confident of (the British government's) support,' and at a low moment in 1901 Mubarak was to tell a rather unhappy British naval officer that 'myself, my children, my subjects and my country are under British (*sic*)'.[75]

It is arguable that Mubarak, following his usual policy of playing his diplomatic hand as hard as he could, would have interpreted *any* agreement with Britain as a form of political protection: he certainly entered the 1899 negotiations with the clear intention of acquiring protection from Britain both for his rule in Kuwait and also for his properties within Ottoman territory at Basra and Fao, but Meade played right into his hands.

How did this extraordinary state of affairs come about?

Much of the blame must attach to Meade himself, who arrived in Kuwait in a state of mind verging on panic. It was Meade who introduced the hint of some form of undeclared protection, without any prompting from Mubarak. It was also Meade who threw the promise not to correspond with foreign powers into the negotiations (and Mubarak may not have realised how important this commitment was in legal terms). So, to a very large extent, Mubarak played a passive role, allowing Meade to be carried away by what he saw as the urgency of the situation.

At the same time we must give Mubarak credit for skilful negotiating. Most importantly, Mubarak held out at his meeting with Gaskin on 22 January 1899 for a written assurance of British support. This insistence, cleverly followed up at subsequent meetings, led Meade to decide on 23 January to offer Mubarak the written guarantee of good offices, a move which was to alarm Lee Warner. Although Mubarak may not have appreciated all the legal niceties, the fact that he had got a written assurance of good offices out of the British did very significantly change the nature of the agreement. We have seen that the 1891 Muscat and 1892 Trucial states agreements had the great advantage for Britain of being entirely one sided: the Arab rulers promised not to do certain things, but received no promises at all from Britain in return. Strictly speaking, therefore, the 1891 and 1892 agreements were not 'agreements' at all, as an agreement or treaty normally involves obligations on both sides. Technically, the 1891 and 1892 agreements are probably best seen as 'exclusive unilateral undertakings' to Britain by the Arab rulers. By contrast, Mubarak had obtained something much more like a truly bilateral agreement: he had promised not to do certain things, and in return the British had promised him their good offices.

Finally, and most importantly, Mubarak's delaying tactics and clever use of his family as supporters in the negotiations had pressured Meade into becoming an advocate on behalf of the al-Sabah with the Government of India in the request for a guarantee for their gardens in Ottoman territory. Indeed, Mubarak and his family managed to move the issue of their gardens at Fao and elsewhere in the Basra *vilayet* to the very top of the agenda. By the end of the negotiations of January 1899, the al-Sabah seemed to be more attached to the question of their gardens than to the issue of their status in Kuwait itself. Meade, who had at first brushed the issue of the gardens aside, had to change his mind rapidly when confronted with this determination.

So, while the broad outlines of the agreement reflected British priorities and a degree of panic on the British side, Shaikh Mubarak and his close relatives also played an important role in modifying the original aims of the British side. From the British record, we see Mubarak and his relatives acting single mindedly to promote the interests of their family, both as rulers of Kuwait and also as landowners in Basra and Fao. By working together as a family group, and focusing on their family agenda, they achieved a great deal of success.

British Reactions to the 1899 Agreement

Lord Curzon, who had been Viceroy of India for just over a month at the time of Kuwait negotiations, reacted very positively to the agreement between Meade and Shaikh Mubarak. Writing to the Secretary of State for India in mid-February 1899, he said that 'a vigilant policy on our part in the Persian Gulf during the next five years may save us untold trouble in the future.'[76] Indeed, he seems to have felt that Meade should have gone even further beyond his original instructions. In Curzon's words '[Meade's work] carries us quite as far as I gather Lord Salisbury wished to go, although not as far as, in my opinion, we might require to go before long ... Meade has, I think, done his work pretty well.'[77]

Again, we can see that Curzon, with his strong commitment to a forward policy in the Gulf and elsewhere on the borders of the Indian Empire, was completely out of step with the very cautious and economical attitudes of most of his London-based colleagues. We have seen that, in this memorandum of 9 November 1898, he had argued in favour of a British protectorate over Kuwait, and he was to return to this theme in 1901. His contributions to the discussions in London during January 1899 had always stressed that an agreement with Shaikh Mubarak would ultimately involve a protectorate relationship.

Curzon's own staff on the Government of India seem to have been more realistic than their viceroy, and to have guessed that their masters in London would now share Curzon's enthusiasm. This is the most obvious explanation why the Government of India did not at once report to London on the detailed outcome of the talks. Instead, the government telegraphed to London on 30 January that an agreement had been concluded, and only sent the text of the agreement to London on 10 February in response to a specific request from London.[78] The Indian government's caution was certainly justified by the blazing reaction to Meade's agreement in Whitehall.

In the India Office, Lee Warner was predictably angry when he saw the text. He said that he had to express surprise and doubt as to whether London should ratify the agreement. He was particularly worried about the inclusion of the clause banning correspondence between Mubarak and foreign powers, as he felt that the clause might invalidate Lord Salisbury's guarantee that the Government of India would be free of political or military liability as a result of the agreement. He also felt – with some justice – that Meade's written promise of good offices could lead to troublesome consequences, and that it would be out of the question to promise the al-Sabah any assistance in connection with their property in the Ottoman Empire. He concluded: 'Altogether, the engagement is not what we authorised or asked for, and it is lucky that we telegraphed first before it was ratified.'[79] Lee Warner's superior, Lord Hamilton, even considered that Meade should be removed from his post because of his failure to keep to his instructions, but admitted that it was hard to get good men to serve in the Gulf, and that the most that could realistically be done would be to issue a very distinct warning to Meade.[80]

The Foreign Office, which was responsible for deciding whether to ratify the agreement, was also extremely unhappy. Sanderson pointed out that the decision to follow the 1892 Trucial states model by including the promise not to deal with other powers meant that 'the next time a Turkish Officer visits Koweit, the Sheikh will be able, if he pleases, to get up a row.'[81] Lord Salisbury himself was reported to be 'a good deal annoyed, and I think justly' at the way that Meade had departed from his instructions.[82]

All departments in London faced the problem that it was now too late to modify the agreement to any significant extent. There were fresh rumours of an imminent Ottoman attack on Kuwait, together with reports that Russian agents were on their way to Kuwait. So the threats which had motivated London to offer the agreement to Mubarak were still very much alive. Also, any rejection of the agreement at this stage would certainly damage Meade's position in the Gulf and so hurt British prestige. The Foreign Office notified the India Office on 14 February that ratification of the agreement had been sanctioned, and that a promise could be given to the shaikh that Her Majesty's Government would 'do what they can' to protect the al-Sabah property in Ottoman territory.[83]

The ratification of the agreement left many questions unanswered, however, and as we have seen there were great differences of opinion between British officials about what the British government was in fact offering to Shaikh Mubarak. Mubarak himself also had an interest in interpreting the agreement as a guarantee of protection (which, technically at least, it was not). Most fundamentally of all, it could be argued that the agreement was not a legal document. There is no doubt that most British officials, rightly or wrongly, regarded Kuwait as a part of the Ottoman Empire. Since the agreement was of a type which could only be signed by a fully sovereign ruler, it was probably therefore invalid from the start, and the validity of at least some of its provisions was to be questioned by both sides later in the year. Diplomatically, much of the rest of Shaikh Mubarak's reign can be seen as defining the true meaning of the agreement of January 1899 under the stress of events.

3

Shaikh Mubarak and Najd: The First Phase

Shaikh Mubarak's seizure of power and the Anglo–Kuwait Agreement of 1899 were relatively parochial events with little significance beyond Kuwait. The actual identity of the shaikh had little importance for the ordinary Kuwaiti, and the agreement with the British meant virtually nothing to Kuwait as a whole and indeed, as we have seen, the British only regarded the Shaikhdom as a bargaining counter to secure a role for British commercial interests in the Baghdad railway project. If matters had remained as they were it is likely that the shaikh and Kuwait would have been left in comparative obscurity. However, a series of developments, some of which were beyond the shaikh's control, were to transform Kuwait into a major factor in Arabian affairs and leave Shaikh Mubarak a significant personage in the politics of the region.

When the British resident and Shaikh Mubarak concluded their agreement in January 1899, the British resident impressed on the shaikh that the agreement was to be kept secret. Most British officials must have hoped devoutly that the agreement would only be invoked in the circumstances in which it was designed to operate: namely, to prevent a foreign railway consortium from building a terminus station in Kuwaiti territory.

Shaikh Mubarak was using his new relationship with Britain within months of the ratification of the agreement, as a foundation for a new policy of resistance to the Ottoman authorities, and expansion of Kuwait's influence among the desert tribes of Arabia. To British alarm, Mubarak was soon boasting quite openly that he could afford to ignore Ottoman threats because the British would always protect him. The problem for Britain was that, when things went wrong for Mubarak, they were virtually compelled to support him by diplomatic and military means, unless they wanted to risk losing all influence in the Northern Gulf. In September 1899 the British ambassador in Constantinople intervened to rescue Mubarak from the designs of the Vali of Basra. In 1901, British warships twice saved Mubarak from the consequences of his ambitions, when he had managed to bring the anger of the Ottomans and of Abdulaziz Ibn Rashid of Najd down on his head.

Mubarak therefore had good reason to feel, after January 1899, that he was in a much stronger position than at the start of his reign. He decided to use this new strength to achieve a fundamental change in the balance of power in Arabia: to make Kuwait the arbiter of the region. In these early years after 1899, he came as close as he ever would be to achieving this ambition. Only with his defeat at the hands of Amir Abdulaziz Ibn Rashid at Sarif in March 1901 were the weaknesses of his hand revealed.

In retrospect, it is easy to argue that Mubarak never had the military and political resources or the strong position in desert tribal society which would have been needed to achieve his great plan. He could raise some military levies from the pearl-fishing population of Kuwait itself, but these forces were of poor military quality, and liable to demand to go home when the pearling season began. Among the desert tribes, his allies were never as numerous or as reliable as the tribes who supported his rivals in Najd, the Ibn Rashid and later the al-Saʿud. In particular, the defection of Shaikh Saʿdun of the Muntafiq tribe from the Kuwait camp some time after 1907 was to be a major blow to Mubarak's position in the desert. Among other tribes such as the Mutair and the Ajman there were frequent splits and changes of allegiance. Also, the tribes could only be relied on to fight if there were opportunities to acquire livestock or other goods from their opponents. Any period of military activity, or a long spell of time on the defensive, would cause Mubarak's desert associates to leave him.

At the start of 1899, however, Mubarak must have felt that he had a number of advantages in pursuing his Arabian ambitions. In 1897, the formidable Prince Muhammad Ibn Rashid of Hail had died after many years as ruler of Jabal Shammar and ten years as master of Riyadh. The Ibn Rashid were still the dominant force in Arabia, but their new ruler Abdulaziz Ibn Rashid seems to have lacked the judgement of his uncle.

Meanwhile, Mubarak himself could build up a useful network of tribal support. He could already count on important elements of the Mutair, most of the Awazem and practically all the Ajman. Some years later, a British report pointed out that Mubarak levied *zakat* on the Ajman, imprisoned their shaikhs in Kuwait when they misbehaved, and personally presided over the selection of the chief shaikh of the tribe. Then, during the summer of 1899, Mubarak achieved an alliance with Shaikh Saʿdun, which ensured the support of an important section of the Muntafiq tribe. Mubarak also had the exiled family of the al-Sa'ud living in Kuwait under his protection: the eleven year old Abdulaziz al-Sa'ud who had left Najd in 1891 tied in a camel bag was growing up fast, and showing signs of the skill and personality of his mature years when it came to tribal politics. Above all, even though Mubarak's tribal allies were generally far inferior to those of the Ibn Rashid, they were well-placed to exert economic pressure on Hail, Riyadh and Arabia as a whole. This was because Mubarak could use the Muntafiq and others to cut the road-links between Central Arabia and the main supply ports at Basra and Zubair, as well as the flow of imports through Kuwait itself. When Mubarak exerted his blockade, the results could be dramatic. In October 1900, he arranged for the trade routes into Arabia to be cut, and the cost of a bag of rice in Riyadh rose from $10 to $25. In June 1901, Mubarak repeated the trick, and supplies of rice, wheat, sugar and coffee in Najd fell to almost zero. This led to talk of a possible general revolt against the Ibn Rashid.

Finally, Mubarak had the weapon of money to raise armies and to bribe the desert tribes for support. This weapon was not as strong as he would have liked: desert fighting quickly exhausted his funds, and his methods of raising more money from the Kuwait pearling industry always carried the risk of throttling business (or even forcing the pearl-fishers to abandon Kuwait altogether). However, with a certain amount of straining, Mubarak could still count in a good year on greater financial resources than his Najd rivals.

Mubarak in the Ascendant: January 1899–March 1901

When the strong and feared Prince Muhammad Ibn Rashid of Najd died in 1897, the more adventurous chiefs of his subordinate tribes followed the normal desert practice of testing the resolve of the new leader. They discovered that Muhammad's nephew, Abdulaziz Ibn Rashid, was brave enough, but lacked the maturity and political sense of his predecessor.

Mubarak of Kuwait may therefore have sensed that this was a good time to bid for the support of some of the tribes. Our evidence is fragmentary, as the affairs of the interior of Arabia seldom reached the notice of British officials. Mubarak, however, was certainly courting alliances among the Mutair and the Muntafiq during the summer of 1899. There are hints that it was this more active involvement in desert politics which brought Mubarak into conflict with Ibn Rashid for the first time. The British political agent in Kuwait was to report in 1906 that problems over the levying of *zakat* taxes from the Bedouin were 'what originally caused the trouble between Sheikh Mobarek and Ibn Rashid.'[1]

The Ibn Rashid themselves also contributed to the tension by deciding to interfere in Mubarak's disputes with members of his family. According to Meade, there had been persistent rumours early in January 1899 that Mubarak's nephews were preparing to attack Kuwait with the help of various Arab tribes. Wratislaw reported from the British consulate in Basra in the same month that the people of Qatar had sworn vengeance of Mubarak, and were trying to get allies from other parts of Arabia, including the Jabal Shammar, homeland of the Ibn Rashid.[2]

The final element in the quarrel between Mubarak and the Ibn Rashid must have been the fact that Mubarak was now sheltering the family of the al-Sa'ud in Kuwait, who were still determined to seize Riyadh back from the Ibn Rashid.[3] Surprisingly enough, we do not know exactly when Abdulrahman Ibn Sa'ud's odyssey brought him and his family to Kuwait. It seems that, after their escape from Najd in 1891, the family first fled to Bahrain. Abdulrahman then returned briefly to Najd, before seeking sanctuary in Kuwait, only to be turned away.[4] Assuming that this unsuccessful visit to Kuwait took place in 1892 or early 1893, the refusal is hardly surprising. Shaikh Abdullah of Kuwait was after all friendly with the Ottomans and his successor, Shaikh Muhammad, was afraid of them and anxious not to be involved with a disruptive element such as the al-Sa'ud. Abdulrahman therefore went to Qatar, where we know he was living in 1893.

It seems most likely that Abdulrahman and his family moved from Qatar to Kuwait at some time after Shaikh Mubarak took control of Kuwait in May 1896. Lorimer claims that the al-Sa'ud arrived in Kuwait in 1897. In the summer of 1900, Britain's Arab news agent in Kuwait reported that Abdulrahman had been living in Kuwait for the past three years.[5]

The al-Sa'ud presumably chose Kuwait in preference to Qatar because it was a better strategic base from which to plan the recapture of their inheritance in Najd. Kuwait was the main trading centre of the region, and was constantly visited by the tribes of Najd, so that the al-Sa'ud were well placed to form friendships and to monitor news from the interior. Mubarak could benefit from having such a distinguished family as his guests. His ancestors, the al-Sabah, had come to Kuwait as a group of settlers from the Ana'iza tribe, and had not brought any large tribal following with them. Even within their own group of families, the status of the al-Sabah was generally considered to be inferior to that of other families such as the al-Badr, the al-Zayid and the Jalahimah. The al-Sabah would therefore have seen the presence of the al-Sa'ud as a valuable sign of status in tribal society, in addition to the alliances and tribal followings which the al-Sa'ud could command, even at this low point in their fortunes.

Mubarak gives a sign of his ambitions in Arabia in the form of an entertaining series of personal letters to Meade, the British resident in Bushire, apparently written as a follow-up to the January 1899 meeting. In these letters, sent during March and April 1899, Mubarak built up a picture of Abdulaziz Ibn Rashid as a lonely and incompetent ruler who enjoyed far less respect in Najd than his late uncle. Mubarak's aim was clearly to persuade the British that, by backing the al-Sabah, they had chosen the rising power in north-east Arabia. The texts of the letters are worth quoting at length for the light which they shed on Mubarak as a diplomatic operator. The first extract paints a picture of Abdulaziz Ibn Rashid pleading for help from Mubarak, while being unable to guarantee security of trade and supply of food for his own people:

> News regarding bin Rashid is that all the tribes are not on good terms with him and there is no respect on the part of the tribes left for him and now they rob his followers and act boldly against him. He has held out to me full friendship and asked me for help and I will not support him except in friendship. Now he is residing about three days' journey to the west of Samai for the purpose of guarding the road of the caravan which conveys food to his parts and this year he has experienced great trouble and loss. Foodstuffs are dear in his district.[6]

In April, Mubarak reported that Abdulaziz Ibn Rashid had been defeated in a fight with a section of the Ana'iza tribe, and added: 'His affairs will not live long, as the news does not reflect credit on him in his Government following the government of his uncle, whose proceedings were prudent.'[7]

Unfortunately for Kuwait, Ibn Rashid was very far from the desperate plight which Mubarak depicted in this letters. The letters, in fact, show the position which Mubarak hoped to bring about through his alliances and manoeuvres, rather than the actual state of affairs. When talking to a member of the staff of the British telegraph station at Fao who actually visited Kuwait in late February 1899, Mubarak gave a very different version of events. He told the telegraph official that Ibn Rashid was only four days away from Kuwait, looting the Bedouin tribes. Mubarak also blamed Ibn Rashid's hostility to Kuwait on the activities of Yusuf Ibn Ibrahim and Ottoman intrigues: this reference to an alliance between Ibn Rashid and Mubarak's nephews and Shaikh Yusuf was to become a frequent element in Mubarak's statements on his involvement in Najd.

In April 1899, Ibn Rashid was again reported to be in the vicinity of Kuwait, and heavy fighting took place between Ibn Rashid's forces and the tribes in the desert nearby, after which the Amir withdrew to Najd.[8] Again, this fighting near Kuwait confirms that Mubarak's presentation of Ibn Rashid as a ruler in the final stages of political decline was wildly optimistic, but with the approach of hot weather, the desert fighting died down for a few months.

During the period of inactivity in the summer, Britain's resident in the gulf began to worry that Mubarak would soon find himself under threat from an alliance of his old enemy Shaikh Yusuf Ibn Ibrahim with Shaikh Jasim Ibn Thani of Qatar and the Amir Ibn Rashid of Najd.[9] Shortly after filing his pessimistic report (which repeated the concerns expressed by Wratislaw in Basra in January 1899), Meade spoke with Mubarak's friend Shaikh Kha'zal of Muhammarah, who raised the additional fear that the Turks would stir up trouble by inciting Ibn Rashid to attack Kuwait, so as to have an excuse for direct Ottoman intervention in the Northern Gulf region. Subsequent events were to confirm that Mubarak did indeed face a powerful group of enemies, but he also had useful allies on his side. During the summer of 1899, he took steps to strengthen his diplomatic position in Arabia even further so as to be able to deal with the threat from Ibn Rashid and the potential threat from the Ottomans.

The best indication of Mubarak's diplomatic activities comes in a report of June 1899 from J. C. Gaskin of the British Residency in Bushire. While Meade was away from Bushire, Gaskin received a visit from Shaikh Abdul Salam the leader of the Sunni community in Bushire. Shaikh Abdul Salam brought messages from Shaikh Mubarak in Kuwait, and from Mubarak's confidential clerk Abdullah Ibn Hamad. The message from Abdullah was that the Sa'dun family of the Muntafiq tribe wanted to free themselves from their allegiance to the Turks. Gaskin interpreted the message as indicating that the important Sa'dun element of the tribe wanted to go and live in Kuwait territory. This astonished him, as it seemed incredible that the tribesmen would want to exchange some of the choicest land in Arabia for 'a desert like the Kuwait district'. His understanding of the message may have been at fault here, or the message may have been garbled when it came to the plans of the Muntafiq to re-locate. The main thrust of the message was, however, correct: Shaikh Sa'dun of the Muntafiq was indeed about to strike an alliance with Mubarak. Gaskin's assessment of Mubarak's plans, written in June 1899, is an excellent analysis which is fully supported by what happened next:

Shaikh Mubarak is very ambitious and it strikes me that possibly since his understanding with our government he is attempting to bring about a union of the great Arab tribes under his authority and have a combination strong enough to oppose Turkish encroachments, and if this is the case he must have given these people sufficient reasons to lead them to believe that he has a force at his back which will repel the Turks, so as to induce them to join him.[10]

We also find a report in June 1899 that Mubarak had married a daughter of the Shaikh of the Mutair. His motive for doing this was apparently to reconcile the Mutair with the Ajman, to whom he was already related.

Shaikh Mubarak's stronger position became evident when fighting between his supporters and Ibn Rashid resumed and intensified as cooler weather set in during September 1899. Abdulaziz Ibn Rashid opened the campaigning season by taking the field against some dissident tribes, but at the same time Ibn Rashid's tribal allies came under attack from Mubarak's friends in the desert, including his new allies of the Muntafiq. Indeed, it was Shaikh Sa'dun and the Muntafiq who did the most damage to Ibn Rashid, according to the reports filed by Britain's news agent in Kuwait during the autumn of 1899. In late September, Shaikh Sa'dun raided the Ana'iza followers of Amir Ibn Rashid, collecting 500 camels and other property. At about the same time, Mubarak's allies among the Ajman captured 1,000 camels belonging to Amir Ibn Rashid. Shaikh Sa'dun then followed up his success against the Ana'iza by raiding a group of the Mutair and carrying off 8,000 sheep.[11] In November, the Muntafiq struck again near Hail, the capital of Amir Ibn Rashid, where a 'fierce' battle was fought. The news agent reported that Mubarak had quietly sent about 1,000 men from his own tribe (sic) to support Sa'dun, and that Kuwaiti support was now Sa'dun's main source of strength, although Ibn Rashid was said to be still unaware of the new alliance. The agent concluded: 'On every victory (of the Muntafiq) a messenger comes to Kuwait, and Sheikh Mobarek gives them presents.'[12]

Mubarak's success in fighting a war-by-proxy against Ibn Rashid in the desert was being offset by troubles closer to home. As Shaikh Kha'zal had wisely predicted, the trouble came mainly from the Ottomans. In April 1899, the Ottoman Government re-appointed the energetic and incorruptible Hamdi Pasha to be Vali of Basra. In his previous term as *vali*, which lasted up to December 1896, Hamdi Pasha had tried to take advantage of Mubarak's insecure position at the start of his reign so as to extend Turkish authority in the area. When Hamdi refused to be bribed, Mubarak was suspected of having spent a large amount of money on bribes in Basra and Constantinople to get him removed from office. Clearly, Hamdi would be no friend to Mubarak now that he was back in Basra. Almost immediately after Hamdi Pasha resumed charge in Basra, Mubarak's nephews came back to Basra from their self-imposed exile in Zubair. The British consul in Basra was sure that, with the support of the new *vali*, the nephews would be able to push their claim to Kuwait with much greater energy. The Consul also pointed out that Meade's trip to Kuwait in January 1899 to conclude the secret agreement with Mubarak had aroused suspicion in the Ottoman administration, and that Mubarak might now find it harder to influence the sultan's court than had been the case in 1896.

There was soon a change in Ottoman policy towards Kuwait. In August 1899, Hamdi Pasha received an order from Constantinople to send a harbour master to Kuwait. The British consul reported to his ambassador in Constantinople that the appointment of a harbour master would emphasise the sultan's claim to Kuwait very considerably.[13] A few days later, he warned the ambassador that the Ottoman authorities were apparently intending once more to try to establish an Ottoman customs house in Kuwait.

Hamdi Pasha lost no time in carrying out his instructions, which accorded entirely with his own ambitions. Late in August, he informed Mubarak that he was sending the harbour master of Basra, Hasan Effendi, to Kuwait on the orders of the Ottoman minister concerned. Mubarak tried to dissuade the *vali*, saying that a harbour master was not needed in Kuwait and that anyway the Porte did not understand Kuwait. When Hasan Effendi arrived in Kuwait on 2 September, accompanied by five soldiers, Mubarak took the drastic step of forcibly removing him.

It soon became clear that Mubarak had only acted in this decisive and provocative way because he was fully confident that the British would support him. As the British news agent in Kuwait reported on 4 September, Shaikh Mubarak's 'many replies' to the Ottomans were entirely due to his confidence in the support of God and the British government. To make things worse from the British point of view, Mubarak twisted matters round to suggest that it was Meade's visit to Kuwait in January 1899 which was the real cause of the new friction between Kuwait and Basra.[14]

This was certainly a serious crisis in relations between Kuwait and the Ottoman Empire. The news agent, himself an Arab, warned the British authorities in the Gulf to be vigilant, 'as it will shortly become a big matter'. Back in Basra, the British consul reported on 7 September that he had heard the military authorities in Basra strongly advocating a military occupation of Kuwait. Whatever reservations British officials may have had about their commitments to Mubarak, their response to the crisis was immediate and effective. It came at the highest level of government, and resulted in diplomatic humiliation for the Ottoman Empire.

Meade, who was on leave in India at this time, requested permission to return to the Gulf, and suggested that his deputy, Prideaux, should be sent to Kuwait on board HMS *Sphinx*. Matters were now moving in London and Lord Salisbury, the prime minister and foreign secretary, instructed his ambassador in Constantinople, O'Conor, to lose no time in warning the Ottoman government that Britain, 'while having no designs on Kuwait', did have friendly relations with Shaikh Mubarak. Lord Salisbury told the ambassador that 'a very inconvenient and disagreeable question would be raised' if the Ottoman Government made any attempt to establish Turkish authority or a Turkish customs control in Kuwait without the previous agreement of the British Government.'[15]

When the British ambassador in Constantinople conveyed this elegantly-phrased warning to the Ottoman foreign minister, the minister yielded at once to the pressure. The Porte, he said, had no intention of establishing a customs house in Kuwait, and no military occupation was being contemplated. The minister even claimed that the harbour master had been sent to Kuwait purely on the initiative of the Ottoman minister of Marine and the Naval commander of Basra.[16] Over in Basra the British consul found that the local Ottoman officials were equally keen to deny any aggressive designs on Kuwait. When the British consul discussed the matter with Hamdi Pasha, the *vali* first denied any knowledge of military plans for Kuwait, and then contradicted himself by admitting that there were such plans, but that he had not been consulted about them and that he had no control whatever over the military authorities. Pressing home his advantage, the British consul warned the *vali* against any such action in the future, pointing out that Britain would view it with great dissatisfaction and it would probably lead to complications. In his report on the conversation to the British Embassy, the consul concluded that the Ottomans were not planning any active steps against Kuwait for the present.[17]

So Mubarak's first call on the British to save him from problems with the Ottomans, just eight months after the January 1899 agreement, led to a highly satisfactory result from Kuwait's point of view. Even better, the collapse of Hamdi Pasha's ambitious policy towards Kuwait, as a direct result of British diplomatic pressure, and the acute embarrassment which this policy had caused to Ottoman officials at the highest level, seems to have undermined Hamdi Pasha's position both in Basra and in Constantinople. This setback was to lead to Hamdi Pasha's dismissal from Basra for the second time within a matter of months.

Indeed, the first signs that the *vali*'s position was weakening came only a few days after the British ambassador delivered his sharp warning to the Turkish foreign minister. Hamdi Pasha admitted to the British consul in Basra in mid-September 1899 that the commander of the Ottoman garrison in the town, Muhsin Pasha, was putting all the blame for the diplomatic debacle on Hamdi, on the grounds that Hamdi had failed to give Shaikh Mubarak adequate notice of the plans for sending the harbour master. The consul also heard that Mubarak had telegraphed directly to the sultan, with the support of the Naqib of Basra and members of his family, to complain about the *vali*'s behaviour. Mubarak apparently told the sultan that, although he was a loyal subject of the Porte, he could no longer obey orders transmitted to him through the *vali*.[18]

As in 1896, when Hamdi Pasha was first removed from office, the Naqib of Basra was a crucially important supporter of Shaikh Mubarak in the campaign against the *vali*. The *naqib*, Rajab Pasha, was connected by marriage with one or two families in Kuwait, and visited Kuwait frequently. The *naqib*'s brother, Ahmad, also played a vital role in the campaign by helping to transmit messages to the Ottoman government via Shaikh Abul Huda at Yeldiz. As far as can be gathered, the *naqib* and Mubarak were the leading players in the anti-Hamdi faction, while Muhsin Pasha played a relatively junior role. The British consul describes Muhsin as a venal man who disliked Hamdi Pasha personally and who also desired his position. Muhsin was said to be under the influence of Ahmad Nakib and to have been heavily bribed by Mubarak.

The message which the *naqib* and Mubarak reiterated to the sultan through their allies in Constantinople was that all the Ottoman government's problems with Kuwait were entirely due to Hamdi Pasha's hostility towards Shaikh Mubarak. If Hamdi was removed from his position, they claimed, then Shaikh Mubarak would gladly submit to the Porte. By battering away on this theme, they helped to persuade the Porte to give Muhsin Pasha a new post in Basra which gave him equal authority with Hamdi Pasha on all matters involving Kuwait.[19] Then, at the end of 1899 or the very beginning of 1900, Hamdi Pasha was dismissed from Basra altogether, and Muhsin succeeded him as *vali*. Muhsin Pasha later suggested that it was the visit of the German Railway Commission which finally led to Hamdi's dismissal. He claimed that, during the commission's visit, he had received an 'important' telegram from Constantinople, and that his reply resulted in the sacking of the *vali* and Muhsin's assumption of the post.

Hamdi Pasha's departure certainly changed the relationship between Kuwait and Basra to the advantage of Shaikh Mubarak. All the projects which had so offended and worried Mubarak were dropped by the middle of 1900, including the quarantine office, the plan for a harbour master in Kuwait, and the telegraph line. In July 1900, the new *vali* was reported to be 'extremely averse from raising in any shape the question of the relations of his Government with the Shaikh.'[20] In early 1900 the shaikh received an Ottoman decoration apparently as a result of reports written by the *vali*, ' ... praising in high terms the general loyalty of the former and the correctness of his attitude ... '[21] On his side, Shaikh Mubarak was said to be showing a certain deference to Muhsin Pasha, at least in minor matters, applying to him for advice and assistance on various occasions.

A major advantage to Shaikh Mubarak from the new relationship with Basra was the opportunity to acquire large quantities of rifles and ammunition during the first six months of 1900 with the connivance of his friends in the Ottoman administration in Basra. This connivance emerged when the Ottoman agent in Bushire, who was not part of the new power-group in Basra, tried to report on a large shipment of rifles which was being sent to Kuwait. Muhsin Pasha and the *naqib's* unloved son, Talib, (Talib Naqib's character could be summed up in three adjectives, 'Extortionate – had his own robber-band, a hired gun and last but not least a highwayman.'[22] He wrote to the over-zealous agent in Bushire ordering him to keep quiet and send no further reports on Kuwait.[23] Mubarak's friends in Basra also ensured that Muhsin Pasha took no action in the spring of 1900, when anti-Mubarak elements in Zubair tried to petition the *vali* to stop the Mutair tribesmen from attacking caravans going to and from Zubair. As Kuwait's caravans were passing across the desert without any problems during this time, the Zubairis drew the obvious conclusion that Mubarak was behind the disorder in the desert.[24]

So, by the summer of 1900, the threat to Mubarak from the Basra side had been well and truly neutralised. New prospects were also opening up for Mubarak in Najd, because the al-Sa'ud were beginning to get results from their efforts to develop support among the tribes. In August 1900, Britain's news agent in Kuwait reported that Abdulrahman Ibn Faisal al-Sa'ud had received 'secret letters' from tribesmen in Najd asking him to return, and promising support. The agent added that Mubarak was secretly pleased that Abdul Aziz should be involved in this fight.[25]

Abdulrahman al-Sa'ud did move into Najd in response to these appeals, and scored some initial success against the Jabal Shammar clans. At the end of August 1900, he asked Mubarak for support. Mubarak responded at once to this request, and as a result his previously veiled enmity towards the Ibn Rashid became public knowledge. By October 1900, Mubarak was successfully exploiting his economic weapon, by cutting off all road communications with Najd.

As a result, it was reported that the price of a bag of rice had gone up in Riyadh from \$10 to \$25.

Faced with the al-Sa'ud raids and this serious economic pressure on Najd, Abdulaziz Ibn Rashid marched against the al-Sa'ud. Mubarak issued a proclamation in Kuwait calling on all able–bodied men to follow his standard, under pain of experiencing his displeasure. The hostility between Mubarak and Ibn Rashid was now very much out in the open, and this inevitably attracted the attention of the two major powers with interests in the region, Britain and the Ottoman Empire. On the Ottoman side, the Vali of Basra sent Talib Nakib, the *naqib*'s son, as an emissary to Kuwait to find out what was really going on. Talib was instructed to advise Mubarak to 'draw in his horns', and to take a more conciliatory attitude towards the amir. The British thought that Muhsin only sent Talib as a way of placating the authorities in Constantinople by appearing to lean on Mubarak, and that in reality the *vali* would continue to back Mubarak as far as possible. As a British official pointed out, there might be limits to the support which the Vali of Basra could provide. 'If the Shaikh gets into a real mess, Mohsin Pasha may find it necessary to look after number one.'[26] On its side, the Indian government ordered Kemball to go to Kuwait in person to find out what was happening and to advise the shaikh to avoid, by all means in his power, any display of activity which might give the Ottomans an excuse for greater interference in Kuwaiti affairs.

In early October 1900, the levies which Mubarak had raised in Kuwait marched out into the desert, commanded by the shaikh's nephew and his son, Salim, to join Abdulrahman al-Sa'ud. But Ibn Rashid did not try to confront either Abdulrahman or the Kuwaiti forces directly. Instead, at the end of October, Amir Ibn Rashid caught up with a rapidly retreating Sa'dun at Khamisiyah, where a short and indecisive skirmish took place. This was enough to persuade Sa'dun to withdraw quickly into Turkish territory and to send messages to Shaikh Mubarak asking for help. Ibn Rashid saw an opportunity to bring the wrath of the Ottomans down on Shaikh Sa'dun and on his main supporter, Shaikh Mubarak. Ibn Rashid went to the nearest telegraph office at Suq al-Shuwaikh, and wired a list of demands to the Vali of Basra. These included the expulsion of Sa'dun from Ottoman territory, the restitution of property which Sa'dun had raided from Ibn Rashid's supporters, recognition of himself as the Amir of Najd, and justice for Mubarak's nephews (the sons of Muhammad and Jarrah al-Sabah). If his demands were not met, Ibn Rashid threatened to move against Kuwait and punish the man he knew was the real source of his difficulties, Shaikh Mubarak.[27]

The Vali of Basra was clearly surprised by the size of the amir's force, the speed with which it had moved up to the Ottoman frontier and the amir's determination to strike at his enemies. Muhsin Pasha ordered that Sa'dun should be arrested, but then reported that he had been unable to apprehend Sa'dun as the Muntafiq leader had retreated into the marshes. In fact, Sa'dun was nowhere near the marshes, and stayed close to the desert road to Kuwait. The *vali* was probably therefore playing for time. The government in Constantinople now intervened, ordering the *vali* to send the *naqib's* son, Talib, to Kuwait by the overland route to bring Mubarak to reason. As an inducement to Ibn Rashid to return home, Constantinople also prepared an imperial pardon for Shaikh Yusuf, which the Naqib's brother was ordered to deliver to Ibn Rashid. Finally, the Ottoman military governor in Baghdad reinforced the garrison at Basra with three battalions of infantry and two batteries of artillery.

When Talib reached Kuwait, he found that Mubarak had already mobilised his forces and gone north from Kuwait to join Shaikh Sa'dun. The *vali*, who very much needed to convince Constantinople that he was implementing his instructions to achieve a reconciliation, wrote to Mubarak to ask for a meeting at Zubair, but Mubarak ignored the invitation. According to the news agent of the British Government in Kuwait, Mubarak's confidence was yet again the result of his belief that Britain would back him against the Ottomans. The agent reported to the British resident: 'Shaikh Mubarak's object is to crush Ibn Rashid, and he will not listen to the Sublime Porte because he is internally confident of your support. I know confidentially that he disregards the Turks on A/C (account) of your support.'[28]

The forces of Mubarak and Sa'dun were now facing the army of Ibn Rashid in the middle of the desert, where British support could not be made effective. The two sides were also fairly evenly matched, at about 10,000 men each, so that the outcome could not be predicted.

Despite the tense situation, Muhsin Pasha was able to carry out his instructions to reconcile Mubarak with the amir before any fighting began. The Pasha's channel of communication was the *mutassarif* of the Muntafiq, who was accompanying Mubarak, and who arranged for Mubarak to meet the *vali* at the *naqib's* residence near Zubair on 17 November 1900. During this meeting, Muhsin Pasha managed to persuade Mubarak to accompany him to Basra. When they arrived in Basra on 18 November, Mubarak and Muhsin Pasha spent several hours in the telegraph office, communicating with Constantinople. In these messages, Mubarak expressed profuse loyalty to the sultan, and promised to cease 'coquetting' with foreign powers. The British consul observed that 'Mubarak is undoubtedly very able, but he appeared to be too much inclined to run with hare and hunt with the hounds.'[29]

This first direct confrontation between Mubarak and Ibn Rashid was therefore indecisive in terms of the battle for supremacy in the desert, but there could be no doubt of the scale of Mubarak's ambitions to become the dominant force in Najd. Mubarak had also shown for the second time that he regarded his agreement with Britain of January 1899 as a licence to ignore Ottoman commands when this suited him. Mubarak, however, had not had much success in achieving his ambitions in the desert. Indeed, the main beneficiary of the events of autumn 1900 was the Vali of Basra, Muhsin Pasha. In the view of the British summary of events, written in October 1901, the conflict had been averted at the cost of a considerable increase of Turkish prestige, and the result was seen as 'a considerable blow to any pretension of Mubarak to being an independent Sheikh'. There were also suspicions that Muhsin had made himself a nice profit in bribes.

Mubarak now tried to minimise the impact of his effusive messages to the sultan by trying to convey his own version of events to the British resident in Bushire as quickly as possible. In late November, he sent the resident's news agent in Kuwait to Bushire, with a letter and a verbal message for Kemball. In the letter, Mubarak blamed the recent troubles entirely on Ibn Rashid and Shaikh Yusuf Ibn Ibrahim. He said that Abdulaziz Ibn Rashid was an ignorant young man, motivated by ill will. Unfortunately for Mubarak, the agent cut the ground from under this convenient version of events by telling Kemball that, when Mubarak was in Basra with Muhsin Pasha, he had blamed all the trouble on Abdulrahman al-Sa'ud and Shaikh Sa'dun. Kemball, a much more perceptive and astute officer than Meade, soon suspected that Mubarak had in fact paid a large bribe to Muhsin Pasha to arrange matters. Kemball very much doubted that the *vali* had believed Mubarak's excuses, although he thought the *vali* had probably communicated them to Constantinople.[30]

Kemball rightly concluded that the brief confrontation of November 1900 had not changed the essential situation. He thought that Mubarak would continue to stir up his proxies in the desert to attack Amir Ibn Rashid. Although Kemball believed that Mubarak was now far too confident of rapid victory against Ibn Rashid to listen to any advice, he thought an attempt should be made to warn Mubarak that the British could not and would not protect him against the amir. On 10 December, Kemball wrote to Mubarak to express alarm that the shaikh apparently intended to continue hostilities against Ibn Rashid: 'It seems to me that you are pursuing a dangerous policy by continuing to provoke the Amir of Najd, and I again counsel you to keep quiet.'[31]

Kemball was of course right but Mubarak was in no mood to stop his war against Ibn Rashid now that things seemed to be going so well. When Mubarak left Zubair with the *vali* on 17 November, his forces had been supposed to return to Kuwait. In fact part of this contingent set out in pursuit of Ibn Rashid. We can guess that the aim was not to offer a full battle, but instead to make small raids which would distract Ibn Rashid while Mubarak prepared for a more extensive campaign. Shaikh Sa'dun had meanwhile given the slip to the Turkish major-general, Muhammad Pasha Daghistani, who had been sent to capture him, and was back in the area of Kuwait. There were rumours that he planned to join forces with the Shaikh of the Dafir and with Abdulrahman al-Sa'ud, who had received promises of support from the Ajman and from other Arabs.

Amir Ibn Rashid had also not returned home, and continued to hover around Najd. In mid-December 1900, Mubarak moved out of Kuwait and headed for the Hafar wells, which had for the past two years been Kuwait's major western outpost in the desert and which gave command of the great Batin depression. Mubarak was accompanied by his brother, Humud, his nephew, Khalifa, and his cousin, Jabir ibn Jaz'a, as well as Abdulrahman al-Sa'ud. Mubarak later told Captain Phillips, the senior British naval officer in the Gulf, that the Kuwait levies amounted to about 10,000 men, and the Muntafiq also fielded 10,000. He claimed that 44,000 men from other tribes were on his side, although this is almost certainly a vast exaggeration. Mubarak's total of 44,000 tribal supporters included 4,000 Mutair, 10,000 Awazim, 7,000 Rashayidiyah, 9,000 Ajman and 6,000 from the Bani Khalid.[32]

Things Go Wrong: the Disaster at Sarif

As Mubarak prepared for the decisive battle against the forces of Ibn Rashid, his political position behind the lines was starting to crumble. Talib, the son of the Naqib of Basra, who had worked so assiduously in Mubarak's interests in 1899, was summoned to Constantinople to explain the continuing disorder in north-east Arabia. The sultan's brother-in-law, Qasim Pasha, the commander-in-chief of the Sixth Army Corps in Baghdad, who had been involved in examining the claims of Mubarak's nephews, was sent from Baghdad to meet Ibn Rashid. Ominously for Mubarak, Qasim Pasha was accompanied by Abdullah Effendi, the lawyer acting for Mubarak's nephews. The sultan had apparently directed Qasim Pasha to compel Mubarak to return to his own territory, as the sultan felt that the shaikh was now carrying on the war 'as if he was, or with the intention of becoming, an independent kingdom'.[33]

As the prospect of battle loomed, rumours flew around Constantinople,

Basra and Bushire. The British ambassador in Constantinople told the consul in Basra that he had reports that an unknown number of squadrons of Turkish cavalry had been sent from Damascus to assist the amir. The vice-consul in Muhammarah reported on 11 March that the three main towns of Qasim (Unaizah, Buraida and Zilfi) had submitted to Mubarak, which would have given Mubarak a wedge between Ibn Rashid's capital at Hail and his occupation force in Riyadh.[34] The Kuwait news agent reported to Bushire that Mubarak's nephews had made their peace with Mubarak. Finally, Mubarak's son, Jabir, received a letter from his father saying that all of Najd had submitted to him, and that he had appointed Abdulaziz, the son of Abdulrahman al-Sa'ud, as governor of Riyadh. In the letter, Mubarak reported that he had refused to accept the submission of his nephews, as they would not agree to his terms. At a meeting in Muhammarah in early March, Shaikh Salman, the cousin and deputy of Shaikh Kha'zal, who was well-acquainted with the leaders involved in the conflict, gave the British vice-consul the impression that Mubarak was ' ... in a fair way to become the ruler of Central Arabia vice ibn Rashid, with ibn Saud as his lieutenant.'[35]

All of this was very far from the truth, but in the atmosphere of wild optimism about Mubarak's success it is not surprising that the first hint of the disaster to befall the Kuwaiti confederation did not cause any great alarm. On 28 March 1901, the consul in Basra reported to Kemball in Bushire that the Amir Ibn Rashid's agent in Basra had received a letter from his master telling him that Mubarak's forces had been defeated near Hail, and that Mubarak had been killed. The following day, the consul noted that the Vali of Basra had also received a letter confirming Mubarak's death, but he warned that the information was not 'absolute', and suggested that a ship should go to Kuwait to make an on-the-spot report.[36] A few days later, Britain's native agent in Bahrain recorded local accounts that Ibn Rashid had been victorious, and that Shaikh Mubarak had been killed, together with his brother, Humud, Salim and Shaikh Sa'dun of the Muntafiq.

Although the truth was certainly bad enough, desert rumours had exaggerated the extent of the disaster for Mubarak's forces. It is impossible now to trace the course of events with great precision, but we can offer a suggestion of the most likely pattern of events, based on the available evidence.

Mubarak moved into Najd towards the end of February 1901, and spent a considerable time seeking the support of various Bedouin tribes previously loyal to Ibn Rashid, while he waited for Sa'dun and his men to arrive. While Mubarak waited, the Amir Ibn Rashid received news of his presence. On 9 March, Mubarak was joined by Sa'dun and his men. Two days later, encouraged or perhaps deceived by his reception in Najd, Mubarak set out in pursuit of the Amir, who was thought to be in the vicinity of Hail accompanied only by the Shammar.

On the morning of 17 March, Mubarak's forces met those of the amir at al-Sarif, near Unaizah. Amir Ibn Rashid had apparently prepared the ground in advance, erecting a series of shelters or barricades to shield his infantry.[37] Impetuously, Mubarak threw his cavalry (probably largely Ajmans and Murrahs) against these barriers. When the rifle fire of the amir's men had thrown Mubarak's cavalry into disorder, the amir launched his own horsemen, and after fierce fighting drove the shaikh's cavalry from the field. In the confusion, the Kuwait tents were plundered, either by defeated members of the force fleeing from the battlefield and hoping to make a quick profit out of the confusion, or as part of a pre-arranged plan of treachery. When they realised that the day was lost, Mubarak's personal followers took him from the battlefield.

Mubarak arrived in Kuwait on 31 March. Abdulrahman and Sa'dun arrived a few days later with about 200 men. For many days, groups of stragglers made their way back to Kuwait in small parties ranging from a few individuals to groups of 10 to 20. There is no surviving record of the number of dead which Kuwait suffered, but Lorimer reported that in 1907 local tradition claimed 700 were killed, including 150 prisoners murdered after the battle.[38] Among the dead were Mubarak's brother, Humud, and his cousin, Khalifa bin Abdullah al-Sabah.

With the amir victorious and Mubarak and his allies defeated, it was natural to assume that the amir, either with or without Ottoman sanction or assistance, would proceed directly to Kuwait and eliminate the source of his difficulties. Indeed, in Kuwait local opinion expected an attack as soon as the pearl fleet went to sea in May. It appears that Mubarak's chief concern was that the amir would attack with Ottoman encouragement and he went to great, if not ridiculous, lengths to disguise the extent of his defeat. Even before he returned from Najd, his sons had taken steps in Kuwait to suppress all discussions of the defeat.[39] Kemball thought that the Shaikh was ' ... anxious that the Turkish authorities should not know the extent of his reverse, as he fears that if they knew it, they would no longer consider him the formidable person he has hitherto been considered.'[40] Indeed, the shaikh tried to hide things even from Kemball, and in an account which Kemball 'found impossible to credit', claimed a great victory in which, despite being heavily outnumbered, his force had killed 320 of the amir's men with the loss of only 36 of their own. Kemball was even more surprised to discover that the shaikh had kept the fact of his brother Humud's death from his own son, Jabir. Mubarak's spirit seemed to be completely shattered: for a week after his return there was no communication with the outside world, and even his allies in Basra were forced to send a Turkish officer to Kuwait to see if he was really still alive.

A poem entitled: 'Cowardice Reproached' written by a Shammari poet describes the Sarif battle saying:

> Even Sabbah ran till his head shook,
> And Sadun! Oh, how he dismissed
> He captured She-Camels?[41]

At first neither Wratislaw nor Kemball greatly feared an attack by the amir unless he was authorised by the Ottomans. However, their view changed with the news that Wasim Pasha was about to arrive in Basra to investigate the outbreak of fighting and the Kuwait situation in general. Kemball had already expressed the fear that the amir would be encouraged to attack Kuwait on the understanding that he would make the place over to Shaikh Mubarak's nephews, who could be expected to be obedient vassals of the Porte. Both men now feared joint Ottoman action with the amir, who was only five days from Basra.

They thought it was now too late to warn the amir and a direct warning to the Porte was necessary; indeed, Wratislaw believed that even such a warning would be 'futile' unless Britain was willing to back up the warning with force. Their fears appeared to be confirmed when, on 25 April, Major-General Muhammad Pasha Daghistani arrived, followed the next day by the first contingent of Ottoman troops from Baghdad.[42] Still worse, Shaikh Mubarak was soon summoned to Basra to be 'reconciled with the Amir'. Wratislaw warned that if the shaikh were ' ... foolish enough to come he will certainly be detained.'[43]

The British government was in the awkward position of not being able to control its client and, at the same time, unable to allow him to be overthrown. From London the secretary of state for foreign affairs observed, 'We could scarcely allow the Sheikh to be crushed or deposed, although he has acted against our advice in attacking the Amir of Nejd.'[44] In Constantinople, O'Conor dropped a hint to the minister of foreign affairs on 29 April that he ' ... trusted that nothing would occur to disturb the *status quo* there.' At the same time, Kemball was instructed to go to Kuwait; the shaikh should 'politely decline' to go to Basra and a gunboat should remain at Kuwait for the shaikh's support.[45] In fact, Mubarak, who was no fool, had already declined the invitation pleading indisposition. Not being deceived by the shaikh's diplomatic illness, Qasim Pasha warned the shaikh's agent that the shaikh ' ... had better hurry up and put in an appearance for his own sake'.[46]

The situation was complicated by the fact that plague had broken out in Basra and General Daghistani was forced to move his troops up the river to undergo the requisite 10 days' isolation at the quarantine station there.[47] Quarantine would be completed on 11 May and after that day he would be free to move, but Qasim Pasha continued to insist on a personal meeting with Mubarak and wrote to the shaikh, 'You know very well that written correspondence is not possible before the matter is personally discussed and the views of each other are ascertained.'[48] The *vali* also wanted to see Mubarak, and was willing to come to Kuwait, but he too was cut off by the plague.[49]

Qasim Pasha was also trying to meet the Ibn Rashid. Indeed it was reported that he had asked Ibn Rashid to meet him 'near' Kuwait with a force of 2,000 men, but the amir, like Mubarak, was unwilling to come too close to the Turks. Instead, he stayed in the desert with a small band of followers, and sent his envoy Fahad ibn Sabhan to Basra to see Qasim Pasha. The amir told the pasha that he would attack Kuwait unless Shaikh Mubarak was expelled and replaced by one of his nephews, who would act as Ottoman Governor of Kuwait.[50]

Fahad ibn Sabhan then went on to see Shaikh Kha'zal of Muhammarah, to ask his advice on resolving the conflict between the Amir and Mubarak. Shaikh Kha'zal warned Fahad against trusting the Turks. According to Kha'zal, though the Turks were pleased with Mubarak's defeat, they did not want Ibn Rashid to become too strong, and would probably intrigue to reduce his power. Indeed, it was likely that they were only asking Ibn Rashid to advance towards Kuwait so as to have an excuse for putting a garrison in Kuwait to protect it. Once the Ottomans occupied Kuwait they would never leave it. Kha'zal asked Fahad if Ibn Rashid would prefer a Turk to an Arab in Kuwait. Put in these terms, Fahad said no. Mubarak, even though an enemy to Ibn Rashid, was preferable to a Turkish governor in Kuwait. Kha'zal pressed home his advantage in the discussion by inviting Ibn Rashid to make peace with Mubarak. As he put it, 'it was always easy to adjust Arab quarrels if foreigners were not called in.' Fahad then gave a clue about Ibn Rashid's real preoccupations by asking Kha'zal if he thought that Shaikh Mubarak was likely to expel the al-Sa'ud from Kuwait. Kha'zal pointed out that Amir Ibn Rashid was harbouring enemies of Mubarak. The fairest solution would be for both Ibn Rashid and Mubarak to turn their guests out.[51]

On 11 May 1901, when the ten-day quarantine period ended, Major-General Daghistani departed with his troops for Amara on the Tigris. The direct Ottoman threat to Kuwait therefore seemed to be over for the time being, and the pearling fleet left Kuwait for the start of the pearl season. But the Ottomans had not abandoned their designs on Kuwait. On 16 May, the Vali of Basra left

Basra with a military escort, on his way to Kuwait on the instructions of the Porte. The *vali* had been given a special *irade* to exempt him and his party from quarantine restrictions. At Jahra, the *vali* was met by Mubarak's son, Jabir, with a force of 400 horsemen. According to the British news agent in Kuwait, this large force was meant to prevent the *vali* from forming an unfavourable opinion of Mubarak's position after his defeat.

The *vali*'s visit was another attempt to try to reconcile Mubarak with Amir Ibn Rashid, and more especially to ask the shaikh to accept a few Turkish officials and a small garrison for his protection.[52] Mubarak refused this suggestion and expressed great dissatisfaction with the Ottoman Government. He told the *vali* that Kuwait had experienced 'only wrongs and troubles' from the Ottomans. Qasim Pasha and Major-General Daghistani, he said, had recently collected troops with a view to attacking Kuwait by sea and land, 'which you had no right to do'. Mubarak told the *vali* that, if he wanted protection, he would call on the British Government for assistance.[53]

Mubarak could support his claim by pointing to the presence of a British warship, HMS *Sphinx* in Kuwait bay. In fact, since the crisis began, there had been at least one British ship in Kuwait bay almost continuously. To emphasise Britain's concern, the commander of HMS *Sphinx*, Captain H. A. Phillips, called on Mubarak while the *vali* was present. When the *vali* expressed surprise at Britain's interest in Kuwait, Mubarak's son, Jabir, repeated that 'we have had nothing but favours and support from them, whereas from the Turkish Government we have experienced only wrongs and troubles.'[54]

Having made this point about the availability of British protection, Mubarak was happy to shower Muhsin Pasha with declarations of friendship for the Ottoman Empire. When the *vali* left Kuwait on 23 May, Mubarak accompanied him to Fao ' ... there to renew by telegraph the protestations of loyalty and devotion of which he is habitually lavish', in the words of the British consul in Basra. On returning to Kuwait, Mubarak wrote to the sultan repeating his professions of loyalty and asking to be granted the rank of pasha as a sign of the sultan's favour, together with a renewal of the Ottoman annual subsidy.[55]

Whilst putting up this show of friendship for the Ottomans, Mubarak was also seeking a much closer defence relationship with the British. During the *vali*'s visit to Kuwait, Britain's news agent wrote to the British resident in Bushire to say that the shaikh would like to see him, as he had something to tell him. Indeed when Mubarak got back from Fao, he at once told Captain Phillips that he wanted Britain to establish a permanent protectorate over Kuwait, and that he was anxious that arrangements should be made to set up this protectorate as soon as possible.[56]

The British resident passed Mubarak's request on to the Government of India, observing that the assumption of the protectorate would be 'only the natural consequence of the Agreement entered into by us with the Chief, and in any case could not have been long deferred.'[57]

Kemball argued that a British protectorate over Kuwait was now necessary to forestall possible intervention in the area by other European powers. In addition, British prestige in the Gulf would suffer if Britain now failed to support the shaikh. Finally, Kemball argued that, in the light of Fahad ibn Sabhan's conversation with British Consul Wratislaw in Basra in April, the declaration of a British Protectorate could lead to the settling of the long conflict between Amir Ibn Rashid and Shaikh Mubarak.

Lord Curzon, as might have been expected, fully endorsed Kemball's arguments in favour of the protectorate, and pressed for an official declaration by London to this effect. Curzon, of course, recognised that Shaikh Mubarak had only requested the protectorate out of a desire for self-preservation. In the viceroy's elegant phrase: 'He is afraid of Najd. He realises that Turkish protection means a Turkish garrison, and he turns to us as the least exacting of his neighbours.'[58] Curzon also supported Kemball's assessment of the likely advantages for Britain from the proposed arrangement, and suggested that a British officer should now be sent via the Red Sea and Aqaba to make contact with Amir Ibn Rashid, so as to negotiate a peace settlement between the amir and Mubarak.

Yet again, Curzon found himself completely out of step with all the departments of state in London. London had by now received from the British consul in Basra, via the Embassy in Constantinople and the Foreign Office, a similar request from Amir Ibn Rashid for the protection of Britain, coupled with a request for British neutrality while Ibn Rashid expelled Mubarak from Kuwait. Any agreement to the request of one of the two sides for protection would therefore certainly stir up the hostility of the other side and would lead to direct British involvement in armed disputes in the area, exactly as Britain had always feared. So the India Office forwarded Curzon's despatch to the Foreign Office with the comment that they were not 'disposed to incur the difficulties and embarrassments which must ensue from the declaration of a Protectorate over either the territories of the Chiefs of Kuwait and Najd.'[59] The Foreign Office of course accepted this view, and Mubarak's request for a formal protectorate was therefore rejected.

Amir Ibn Rashid and Mubarak were once again preparing for battle. Reports came from Bahrain that Mubarak was spending large sums of money to buy camels and saddles. Word reached Kuwait that Amir Ibn Rashid was fortifying his major towns.[60] The Ottoman authorities were also aware of the possibility of further fighting, and moved battalions of infantry northwards from Basra to Nasiriyah, so as to prevent the Muntafiq from gathering under Shaikh Sa'dun. Meanwhile, in a replay of the events of the previous year, Sa'dun and his brother, Sulaiman, were active in the desert cutting off supplies to the amir. Indeed, so effective was their blockade that the amir's envoy, Fahad, found himself trapped in Zubair unable to proceed further. As before, Kuwait's forces were active covering the area between southern Kuwait and al-Hasa and preventing supplies reaching the amir from that quarter. Indeed, Mubarak's blockade had a serious effect on the entire commerce of the region: the Kuwait news agent reported, 'Formerly, Bussorah and Zubeir merchants used to do a lucrative business with Nejd and Hayel. This they cannot do now for fear of Sadun and Sheikh Mubarek. In fact Bussorah and Zubeir have suffered much in this connection.'[61] So successful were his efforts that the people of Zubair were driven to sending a delegate to Mubarak to beg to be allowed to trade with Kuwait again.

The blockade was having even worse effects in Najd. Letters from Najdi merchants reached Kuwait saying that it was now impossible to obtain rice, wheat, sugar or coffee. The merchants also complained of the increasing financial exactions of the amir.[62] It was reported that revolt was being considered as the only solution. Shaikh Mubarak replied he would come to their aid and he had already sent the sons of Abdulrahman al-Sa'ud. By mid-July Abdulrahman's son had departed from Kuwait with a force reported to number 1,000 men to attack Ibn Rashid.[63]

In Basra the *vali* had a long interview with Mubarak's agent. Muhsin Pasha asked if Mubarak would fight, to which the agent replied the shaikh would not fight 'Mohammedan troops', but would seek the protection of the English.[64] The *vali* asked the agent to write to the shaikh and advise him; the agent replied he had on numerous occasions, but without effect, besides what was the hurry? The *vali* replied that there was ' ... no time left: the thing has reached its limit'. Ominously, the agent also reported that Ottoman troops were collecting water skins and were ready to move. He warned the shaikh to send no more letters by land as they were likely to be intercepted. Mubarak had told Captain Phillips that the 'governor' (*mushir*) of Baghdad, Qasim Pasha, had joined the alliance between the amir and Shaikh Yusuf against Kuwait and was assisting them in petitioning the Porte.[65] The 'governor' had now been in Basra for four months considering the Kuwait question, and Mubarak wanted the British to get him sent back to Baghdad.

Meanwhile, the Ottomans had been building what the British consul in Basra described as a 'formidable' force in the Muntafiq district to be under the command of Edhem Pasha. He reported that he believed that a great effort would be made to settle the Kuwait question within the next two or three months, even by force if necessary. He added that, ' … the present crisis is universally understood to be a struggle between the Turks and ourselves for the possession of Kuwait … [the] Sheikh who is much alarmed at the Turkish preparations; he considers that we have got him into trouble and he looks to us to see him through.'[66]

In the face of this danger Mubarak became more conciliatory. He told Kemball at the start of August that he was ready to make a settlement with the amir and presented a list of conditions which Kemball considered 'reasonable'. There were only two main points: the amir would withdraw his support from Shaikh Yusuf and the Sabah nephews, and in return Mubarak would do the same with regard to the al-Sa'ud.[67]

However, mediation would take time and there was the immediate threat of the build-up of Turkish troops. The shaikh had asked Kemball what he was supposed to do if they landed men at Kuwait. He was unwilling to use force against Ottoman troops unless he was assured of British support, and Kemball warned India on 8 August 1901 ' … if he sees that we cannot support him he will have to make the best terms he can with them.' The Government of India directed Kemball to return to Kuwait and assure the shaikh that though they did not wish to have a protectorate over Kuwait he could count on their support as long as he lived up to the Agreement of 1899. If an attack appeared likely O'Conor was to warn the Porte that Britain would resist and naval reinforcements were being despatched to the Gulf.[68]

Meanwhile, Mubarak had received word from Baghdad that the troops build-up at Samawa was continuing under Muhammad Pasha, and Qasim Pasha was expected there with additional troops.

On 22 August 1901, the Turkish gunboat *Zohaf* departed from Basra. When the *Zohaf* entered Kuwait harbour two days later, she found the British warship, HMS *Perseus* waiting.[69] Captain Pears, the commander of the *Perseus*, went on board the *Zohaf* and warned her captain not to attempt to land troops; if he did so he (Pears) would open fire. The Turkish officer said that he had no troops on board and that he had come to speak to the shaikh. He stated that Kuwait was Ottoman territory; the shaikh was an Ottoman subject and foreign nations could not interfere in Kuwait affairs.

The following morning the *Zohaf*'s captain went ashore to see the shaikh. He tried to 'cajole' the shaikh, pointing out that Turkey was a Muslim nation and the British were Christians. The shaikh replied that now he had British support he wanted nothing more to do with the Ottomans. The captain then said he would remain in Kuwait, to which the shaikh replied he could do what he liked as long as he did not attempt to land troops. The Turkish officer then became threatening: he would go to Fao and inform the Ottoman authorities of what had taken place. He would then return with more ships and troops and enforce the sultan's will. Again the shaikh said he could do as he liked, but he wanted nothing more to do with the Turks.

It is difficult to say what the purpose of the *Zohaf*'s mission was. Kemball thought it possible that the Turks would try to land troops; he pointed out that the *mushir* in Baghdad was still in Basra and he was known to be in favour of coercion.[70] He also thought it was possible that the visit had been merely to test the extent of British support for Shaikh Mubarak.

Whatever its origins, the *Zohaf* incident led to intense negotiations at the highest level in London and Constantinople. These discussions also involved the German government, through the German Embassy in London. The German diplomats argued that any British protectorate over Kuwait would be taken in Germany as contrary to the Treaty of Berlin of 1878, and (in view of the German interest in Kuwait as the future terminus of the Anatolian Railway) as an unfriendly act. Meanwhile, the Ottoman Government stressed to the British ambassador in Constantinople on 21 August that their view was that Kuwait was an integral part of the Ottoman Empire. The German government supported the Ottomans in this matter, and on 3 September the German ambassador in London called on the British foreign secretary to confirm that Germany considered 'that Kuwait formed unquestionably part of the territories belonging to the Sultan'.[71]

The result of this brief but intense exchange between the three powers most involved with Kuwait was an argument between Britain and the Ottoman Empire, in the second week of September 1901, which froze the existing situation in Kuwait. The elements of the agreement were:

1. The Ottoman government undertook not to send troops to Kuwait, and stated that it would maintain the status quo in Kuwait.
2. The British government promised that Britain would not occupy Kuwait or establish a British Protectorate over Kuwait, provided that the Ottomans kept their promise not to send troops to Kuwait.

Mubarak certainly never saw the text of this agreement, but if he had been given the chance to read it, he would surely have regarded it as less than completely satisfactory. It did, of course, remove the immediate threat of an

Ottoman military occupation of Kuwait, and so solved his most pressing problem. It also put an end to any hope that Britain would support him in rejecting Ottoman sovereignty over Kuwait. Although he now effectively enjoyed British protection, there was very little chance that he would acquire his ambition of a formal British protectorate.

In any event, the exchanges of telegrams and formal calls between the Chanceries of the Great Powers did not have any direct impact on the confrontation between Arab forces in the desert. Although the Turkish gunboat had now steamed away from Kuwait, the threat from the Ibn Rashid was more intense than ever. In early September, a messenger had arrived in Kuwait from Abdulaziz, the son of Abdulrahman al-Sa'ud, reporting that al-Sa'ud forces had achieved some success against the amir's followers. It soon became clear that the al-Sa'ud raids had stirred Amir Ibn Rashid into action, and late in September the amir was heard to be moving towards the wells at Hafar, only two days from Kuwait. On 23 September, one of Ibn Rashid's raiding parties, 1,000 strong, struck within eight hours of Kuwait town, killing five men and lifting 1,500 sheep. As a result, the tribes loyal to Kuwait began to move closer to the town for protection against the amir. Soon, there was an enormous camp of refugees from the desert, which the shaikh estimated as 89,000 people with their livestock, spreading out for miles around the town.[72]

Two British warships were now on station in the bay of Kuwait: HMS *Marathon* and HMS *Perseus*. The size of the refugee camp made it impossible for the refugees to withdraw to Failaqah Island, where they could easily have been protected by the Royal Navy. Therefore, Captain Field, the senior naval officer in the Persian Gulf and commanding officer of the *Marathon*, began to prepare for the defence of the town. He landed provisions and artillery for the garrison of the fort at Jahra, which he believed was the key to the town's defence, and began training some of the more able Kuwaitis in the elements of gunnery. He created auxiliary gunboats by arming six dhows with threepounder guns. He also requested the shipment of additional artillery from Bombay, both for Jahra Fort and some that could be transported by camel. In the meantime, if any attack did take place he recommended to the shaikh that he adopt the same guerrilla tactics, which had been used so successfully against the British in South Africa.

However, although he raided the immediate Kuwait area, the amir did not press home with an attack on the town itself. He was reported in a number of places, but always stayed a few days' ride from the town. It may be that he was deterred by the presence of the two British warships. In Constantinople, O'Conor reminded Tevfik Pasha that Britain's agreement to respect the status quo ' ... was conditional on the sheikh not being interfered with or attacked. In reply, the Ottoman foreign minister pointed out that the amir had been complaining about Mubarak, and the British ought similarly to restrain the shaikh.[73] Consequently the sultan directed Qasim Pasha to order the amir to withdraw, and to tell Prince Ibn Rashid that he ' ... must keep quite and that His Imperial Majesty did not wish any act of aggression to be committed upon Kuwait'.[74]

On their side, the Indian government ordered Kemball to tell the shaikh that they had used their influence to help him as far as possible, but that he had allowed Kuwait to be used as a base for raids on the amir's territory. They warned the shaikh that he would only be able to benefit from British good offices in future if he allowed himself to be 'guided in this and other matters by their advice'.[75]

Kemball delivered this warning to the shaikh in person. Mubarak promised to comply, and denied 'absolutely' that he had been involved in the raids. Less than a week later, Britain's news agent in Kuwait reported that a message had come to Mubarak from Abdulaziz al-Sa'ud about a successful raid against one of the amir's tribes. The raid had led to the killing of 70 men and the capture of large amounts of property. The agent added that Shaikh Mubarak was very pleased when he heard this news 'because Ibn Rashid's power depended on these tribes'.

However, a new problem now appeared for Mubarak on the Ottoman side. Mubarak's ally and friend Muhsin Pasha had been dismissed as Vali of Basra. His successor, Abdul Latif, was apparently hostile to Mubarak. Indeed, Abdul Latif arrived in Basra on 13 October 1901 in the company of Mubarak's long-standing enemy Shaikh Yusuf ibn Ibrahim. Three days later, Abdul Latif wrote to Mubarak saying that the Porte had ordered Mubarak to obey the orders of the sultan, and to 'expedite' the settlement of the claims of his nephews and of Yusuf ibn Ibrahim against him ' ... so that these matters may not cause troubles and assume another aspect, and thus give cause to various losses to you'.[76] The British consul in Basra rightly concluded that this remark was meant as a veiled threat about the al-Sabah property in Fao and elsewhere in Ottoman territory. Mubarak replied to the Ottoman letter by claiming that it was Yusuf who owed him money, and that he could prove this. As for his nephews, Mubarak said that their cases could be considered if they would behave like their fathers and grandfathers.

The sultan's government, however, was not disposed to let matters rest there. At the end of September, the sultan's secretary had directed the Naqib of Basra to go and see Mubarak, and to explain the advantages of a voluntary submission to Ottoman authority. The secretary asked the Naqib to point out to Mubarak other matters by their advice'.[77]

The Naqib of Basra arrived in Kuwait on 8 November and talked with Shaikh Mubarak on the following day. The *naqib* gave Mubarak a copy of the telegram from the office of the sultan in Constantinople, and presumably tried to persuade Mubarak to follow its recommendations. As an old friend and colleague, we can assume that he warned of the possible consequences of refusal. However, Mubarak now felt he could count on British support, and told Naqib that he wanted nothing more to do with the Turks.[78]

In mid-November 1901, it must have seemed that nothing had changed since the previous August. Ibn Rashid was still in Hafar, just two days away from Kuwait, and was reported to be receiving large quantities of arms provided by Yusuf ibn Ibrahim. The Mushir of Baghdad was still in Basra where the large concentration of Ottoman troops had not been reduced. The Ottoman authorities in Basra were also beginning to drop hints about Shaikh Mubarak's properties at Fao. They were clearly using the nephews' claims to the properties as a means of exerting pressure on the shaikh, just as the British consul had predicted. The British consul in Basra warned the resident that Mubarak was being very stupid. 'He seems to rely on the past disfavour of the claimants in the eyes of the Turkish government and his own former position of protege: ignoring the fact that the position is now reversed.'[79]

At the end of November, the Ottoman government delivered its most serious challenge to Mubarak short of direct military occupation. The Porte ordered the Naqib of Basra to return to Kuwait and to tell Mubarak that the sultan had invited him to come to Constantinople as a member of the Ottoman Parliament. He would live permanently in Constantinople on a large salary. If he refused the invitation, he would be removed from Kuwait by force.

This 'invitation' to Constantinople was a common Ottoman technique for neutralising troublesome rulers. Shaikh Mubarak at once sent his son, Jabir, to the telegraph office at Fao to inform the British resident. At Fao, Jabir met Captain G. L. Quayle, the commander of HMS *Redbreast*, and explained the situation to him. Quayle warned the resident in Bushire that Mubarak did appear to be badly frightened by the telegrams from Constantinople and wanted some very definite support from the British government, failing which he would make terms with the Turks. Kemball immediately dispatched Captain Simmons, the senior naval officer in the Gulf, to Kuwait on board HMS *Pomone*. Meanwhile, Mubarak had passed a message to Kemball, via another British warship, saying that he would have to 'join' the Turkish government unless Britain stopped the Turkish pressure on him.[80]

The decision to intervene so directly in the crisis between Kuwait and the Ottoman Empire was not one which Kemball could make on his own authority. He immediately telegraphed India for instructions, pointing out that if the contents of the telegraph from the sultan's secretary were as reported, this certainly violated the Ottoman promises of September 1901 concerning the maintenance of the status quo in Kuwait. Kemball thought he should be authorised to assure the shaikh of British support in a more definite manner than the assurances of the previous August. In the meantime, Kemball could only advise Captain Simmons to try to get the shaikh to give an evasive reply to the Ottomans and to play for time.

The *Zohaf* arrived in Kuwait bay on the afternoon of 1 December 1901, carrying the Naqib of Basra and Mir Allai Naqib Beg, the brother of the new Vali of Basra.[81] In a replay of the previous confrontation between HMS *Perseus* and the *Zohaf*, less than four months before, Captain Simmons first exchanged courtesies with the *naqib* and then warned him that he had orders to prevent the landing of any troops. The *naqib* replied that he was not landing troops, and that he came simply as the representative of the sultan to see the shaikh.

On the following day, the shaikh sent the British captain a message for transmission to the resident, saying that the Naqib of Basra had given him a letter containing orders from the sultan that he should either go to Constantinople to joint the 'council of state' on a large salary, or else should leave Kuwait for another place and receive a pension. Captain Simmons and the captain of HMS *Redbreast* went ashore to see Mubarak, whom they found to be very upset. The shaikh said he would have to comply with the sultan's orders unless he received a written promise of support from Kemball. Simmons advised the shaikh to ask the *naqib* for time to consider his reply, in the hope that this would give time for an answer to arrive from Kemball in Bushire. The next day, the *naqib* agreed to give the shaikh three days in which to answer, and also told him that he would be allowed to remain in Kuwait if he accepted a small Turkish garrison and promised to abandon his connection with the British. Mubarak wrote another letter to Kemball begging for his support: ' … myself, my children, my subjects, and my country are under British (*sic*) and seek your protection'.[82]

The two British naval officers suspected, correctly, that the *naqib* would not in fact be prepared to wait for three days. They tried to persuade Shaikh Mubarak to gain time by giving an evasive answer to the sultan's request. By now, Mubarak's nerve had gone completely, and he refused to consider this suggestion saying that the sultan would regard an evasive answer as a refusal. So Simmons took the bold decision, at great risk to his own career, of ordering the shaikh not to reply to the Ottoman communication, under threat of a

British bombardment of Kuwait. This idea pleased Shaikh Mubarak, ' … as he considered it cleared him if the English government failed him from the Sultan's vengeance'.[83]

The next day, the *naqib* returned and, as Captain Simmons had feared, said that he could not now wait for three days, but must have Mubarak's answer that afternoon, as he wanted to leave Kuwait that very evening. Mubarak again asked the British officers for a written assurance of support before replying to the *naqib*. Before the *naqib*'s deadline, HMS *Redbreast* arrived in Kuwait with a message from Kemball asking the shaikh to hold out while he consulted India. This was enough to satisfy Mubarak, so Simmons decided that he must now use his threat of bombardment. That afternoon, Mubarak received the *naqib* in the presence of Simmons and his British colleague. When the *naqib* asked Mubarak for his answer, Mubarak simply said that Captain Simmons would not let him reply. Simmons confirmed this, arguing that the Ottoman threat to Kuwait was a violation of the agreement of September with the British government to preserve the status quo. The *naqib* returned to his ship, and Captain Simmons stayed in the shaikh's house throughout the night, in case the *naqib* made a last-minute attempt to persuade the shaikh to change his mind.

The next day, Mubarak and the British officers in Kuwait received the answer from Bushire which they had wanted to hear. HMS *Redbreast* arrived in Kuwait again, this time with a written assurance from Kemball that the Government of India regarded the Turkish attempt to coerce Mubarak as a distinct violation of the sultan's promise of September 1901. Kemball confirmed that His Majesty's Government were prepared to support the shaikh, and would not tolerate an attack on Kuwait by Turkish troops or ships.[84] Understandably, Mubarak expressed his 'great satisfaction' at this message and on 6 December:

> he summoned all the merchants – Persian and Arab and others in a Mijlas and read the letter over to them, and told them that he and his subjects were under the protection of the Brit. Govt. They replied that they were obedient to his orders, and had no wish to act against his wish. They left quite pleased.[85]

Britain had therefore delivered effective support to Mubarak in Kuwait itself, but action was also being taken once more at the highest level on Mubarak's behalf. Vigorous diplomatic pressure by O'Conor in Constantinople gained a disavowal by the sultan of the *naqib*'s action in threatening Mubarak. Kemball in Bushire pointed out that this was scarcely credible: all the *naqib* had done, after all, was to communicate the sultan's telegram to Mubarak.[86]

Although the Porte had denied to the British that there were hostile designs on Kuwait, Ottoman pressure on Mubarak continued during December 1901 and the early weeks of 1902. In mid-December, an Ottoman order was issued prohibiting the export of food from Basra to Kuwait, but this seems to have been a local initiative on the part of the Vali of Basra, and the order was lifted after a protest by the British Embassy in Constantinople. In London, the foreign secretary, Lord Lansdowne, warned the Ottoman ambassador that, if the Porte was '… unable to control its own official, we may find it impossible to acquiesce in continuation of status quo which led to recurrence of incidents such as recent visit to Kuwait of Nakib.'[87]

Meanwhile, Ibn Rashid had only withdrawn his forces as far as Safwan. Here, he was close to Kuwait itself and could also be reinforced quickly from Zubair or Basra, either by Arab levies or by regular Turkish troops. While he waited in the desert near Safwan, he received large quantities of supplies from Basra, and there were reports that the Ottoman authorities had directed that he should receive a gift of $2,000.

At the end of December 1901, there were rumours in Basra that the sultan had ordered the amir to go back to Najd. If these reports were true, the aim seems to have been to use Ottoman troops rather than Ibn Rashid's forces to put pressure on Kuwait. In the last days of December, a battalion of Turkish infantry left Basra for Zubair, and the Ottoman government's contractor, who had already sent a large quantity of provisions to Zubair, was ordered to prepare supplies for more battalions. In fact, the battalion of Ottoman troops, which had been ordered to Zubair, only passed through the town and moved on to Safwan. From Safwan it sent a large detachment to Umm Qasr. This detachment took up a permanent position in 'the mud-walled enclosure called the Fort'.[88] The establishment of a permanent Ottoman presence in Safwan and Umm Qasr was, of course, most unwelcome to Mubarak, who seems to have considered trying to eject the Ottoman troops immediately. In the event, up to the start of the First World War, a reduced force of about 10 Ottoman soldiers was to stay in Umm Qasr and the Ottomans strengthened the fortifications of its old fort, which had crumbled away. In mid-January 1902, the British consul in Basra correctly concluded that the Ottoman aim appeared to be to extend their effective occupation around Kuwait and to hem Mubarak in as much as possible.[89]

Meanwhile, Ibn Rashid continued to linger in the desert and the British consul assumed that any orders which the Ottomans had given to him to withdraw from the area must have been couched in a less-than-categorical form. During January 1902, Ibn Rashid remained in the general area of Basra and Zubair, maintaining communication with the Vali of Basra, with Qasim Pasha and with Constantinople. Shaikh Yusuf ibn Ibrahim was with Ibn Rashid for much of this time, apparently moving between Ibn Rashid and Basra on 'his usual mission of stirring up mischief'. The British consul thought that Amir Ibn Rashid still hoped to obtain permission from Constantinople to attack Kuwait. When this permission was not forthcoming, it seems that Ibn Rashid decided to tighten his own noose around Kuwait, acting either independently or in co-operation with the Turks. In mid-January, the residents of Zubair were warned by Khalid al-Aun, Ibn Rashid's chief supporter in the town, that anyone travelling to Kuwait would certainly be robbed and murdered.[90]

The Turkish advance in Zubair, Safwan and Umm Qasr significantly changed the military balance in the northern Gulf area, by providing Mubarak's enemies with secure bases from which to operate. During the spring of 1902, raids against Kuwait were to be a common event. This was particularly true in the case of Zubair, which had always been a centre for the anti–Mubarak forces. As an example, the British consul in Basra reported in the middle of May 1902 that Khalid al-Aun had led a party of between 100 and 200 men out of Zubair, ostensibly to recover some sheep which had been stolen by Bedouin. The next day, they returned to Zubair with several hundred animals. The consul observed that the general opinion in the town was that these were an addition to their stock, rather than recovered property.[91] In August 1902, reporting on a similar raid from Zubair, which had netted 300 camels, the consul pointed out that ' … there seems at the present time to be a tendency to profit by the presence of the Turkish garrison at Safwan to rob from Mubarak's men without much fear of retaliation.'[92]

Yusuf Ibn Ibrahim Overplays his Hand: the *Lapwing* Incident

As far as Mubarak was concerned, the first months of 1902 were not therefore easy. On the one hand, he could be sure of the support of the British government in the event of a full-scale military threat to Kuwait from the Ottomans. On the other hand, as the Ottomans strengthened their garrisons at strategic points, he had no real counter to the erosion of the military position to the north of Kuwait. Fortunately, one of his most important adversaries, Shaikh Yusuf ibn Ibrahim, was about to make a serious mistake which, by the end of 1902, would remove any serious threat from both Yusuf and from Mubarak's nephews, who had been sponsored by Yusuf in their attempts to unseat their uncle. Before this happy turn of events, Mubarak had to weather some months of indirect pressure from the Ottomans.

In May 1902, the Ottomans opened a new line of attack on Mubarak, by arranging for local Ottoman officials in Basra to raid the house of Abdulaziz ibn Salim Badr Qina'i, Mubarak's agent in Basra, and to arrest the agent on a charge of receiving seditious literature. The arrest took place on 28 May 1902, and when Mubarak demanded an explanation from the *vali* he was told that the arrest had been carried out in response to an imperial trade, which came directly from the office of the sultan.[93]

The reason given for this arrest was that supporters of Ibn Rashid in Basra had denounced Mubarak's agent for receiving a copy of a banned anti-Turkish newspaper published in London. It seems that there had indeed been a copy of the newspaper, *Khilafat*, in the house of the agent when the Ottoman authorities arrived, but that the agent's brother had managed to remove it before it was discovered. Several years later, after his release from prison, Mubarak's agent told the British political agent in Kuwait that the Vali of Basra had admitted that the raid had only been ordered so as to put pressure on Mubarak.[94]

Again, the British ambassador in Constantinople intervened on Mubarak's behalf. He told the Turkish foreign minister that he could only assume that the possession of the newspaper was a frivolous pretext for an action, which was really intended to punish Shaikh Mubarak for his attitude towards Britain. Unfortunately for the agent, sufficient correspondence had been found, when the authorities raided his house, to prove that he had indeed subscribed to the newspaper on Mubarak's behalf. Mubarak made strenuous efforts to obtain the release of his agent. He approached the British consul in Basra and the British resident in Bushire for permission to appeal to the sultan directly. He also complained that the papers seized at the agent's house included five title deeds to his property at Zein in Basra. Representation by the British Embassy in Constantinople to the Porte did eventually result in the return of the title deeds.[95] However, nothing could be done about the agent, who was charged before the Criminal Court of Basra at the end of August 1902 with ordering and receiving a seditious newspaper and with carrying on a treasonable correspondence with the editor. The agent based his defence on orders from Shaikh Mubarak to subscribe to the paper, and was able to produce a letter from the shaikh directing him to order the newspaper as well as a reply from the editor, acknowledging the subscription and encouraging him to persuade his friends to subscribe. This can hardly have endeared the agent to the court! So, although the issue was apparently trivial, the agent was sentenced to ten years' imprisonment in a Turkish fortress.

The imprisonment of Mubarak's agent was in itself a trivial affair, although of course an unpleasant one for the agent. For the historian, the case is interesting because of the light it sheds on Mubarak's method of operation. For, during the trial in Basra, letters were read out from Shaikh Mubarak to the agent, which demonstrate how strongly Mubarak was playing the card of his 'British friends'. In one letter, Mubarak told the agent to go to the British consul if he had any difficulties with the Turkish authorities. In another letter, Mubarak boasted that the British ambassador in Constantinople was kept constantly informed about Kuwait affairs, and that Kuwait was continually guarded by three or four British warships.[96] This was, of course, a considerable misrepresentation of the true state of affairs. What was even more amazing was that the agent had kept these damaging papers in his house. The Vali of Basra, discussing the case with the British consul in the town, said that he had ' ... previously had a high opinion of Mubarak's intellect, but he now considered that a man who could keep such a fool for his agent must not be very bright himself.'[97]

Any embarrassment which the arrest of the agent caused to Mubarak, was soon off-set by a very favourable development indeed. At the start of September 1902, Mubarak's old enemy Shaikh Yusuf ibn Ibrahim decided to try to attack Kuwait with a raiding party, just as he had tried to do in 1898. On the evening of 2 September, a raiding party of between 100 and 200 men left Yusuf's home town of Dora in two dhows. Khalid and Humud al-Sabah were both in the party. They seem to have hoped that they could take Kuwait by surprise and unseat or assassinate Mubarak. In fact, the people of Kuwait were awake and armed. The raiding party withdrew to Failaqah Island, but the raiders were chased away from Kuwait by the boats of HMS *Lapwing*, manned by the British sailors and there was a short gun battle during the pursuit, in the course of which one Royal Navy seaman was killed and two others were wounded.[98]

The fact that a British serviceman had been killed in the action changed the significance of the episode, and ensured that Yusuf ibn Ibrahim would not be allowed to go unpunished, as his involvement in the raid was beyond doubt. The first British approaches to the Vali of Basra were ineffective and the British consul complained to his Embassy in Constantinople that Mustafa Pasha was determined to do his best to prevent guilt being brought home to Yusuf ibn Ibrahim or anyone else for whom the Turkish government was responsible. The consul pressed the ambassador to demand the expulsion of Shaikh Yusuf and the two nephews of Mubarak from the Vilayat of Basra.

The ambassador agreed with the suggestion and spoke accordingly to the Ottoman minister for foreign affairs. The ambassador stressed the enormous amount of evidence, which was available about the *Lapwing* incident, and warned the foreign minister Tevfik Pasha that if no action was taken to remove

Yusuf and the nephews from Basra, the time would come when he would be instructed ' ... to ask for more serious reparation, seeing that the lives of some British sailors had been sacrificed in frustrating and filibustering an expedition organised upon Ottoman territory.'[99]

December passed without any action on the Ottoman side to satisfy the British demands. At the very end of the month, the ambassador returned to the matter, warning the sultan's grand vizier that the time might come when the expulsion of Yusuf and the nephews would not by itself be enough to satisfy the British government. The ambassador added that, if something were not done soon, he would have to make other demands, which might not be so 'agreeable' – a hint that Britain might perhaps demand the removal of the *vali*.

Presumably the Ottoman government took O'Conor seriously, because a week later on 5 January 1903, the minister of foreign affairs told him that the Council of Ministers had agreed to instruct the minister of the interior to expel Shaikh Yusuf and the nephews from the 'neighbourhood' of Basra.

Wratislaw, the British consul in Basra, heard that Mustafa Nuri Pasha had received a 'somewhat severe reprimand' from the Ministry of the Interior and, on 7 January 1993, when the *vali* called on him he displayed a markedly different temper:

The *vali*'s utterances were distinctly propitiatory in tone. He referred only indirectly to the *Lapwing* incident, and made no attempt to champion Yusuf or the nephews, whose guilt he almost admitted by implication. His mention of Sheikh Mubarak was benevolent rather than otherwise, with the exception of one somewhat disparaging sentence, in which he called him 'a liar, a rascal, and an idiot'.[100]

The removal of Shaikh Yusuf from the scene had an unexpected consequence: without his financial support, Shaikh Mubarak's nephews became more amenable to a settlement of their dispute with their uncle.

The property in dispute consisted of five estates within Ottoman territory and a relatively unimportant collection of buildings and property in Kuwait town itself. The Turkish property was made up of date gardens at Ghardilan, Ajirawiyah, Kut al-Zain, and Safiyah. These were of relatively little importance. The real prize was the large date gardens at Fao consisting of about 3,750 acres. All these estates had been acquired by various members of the al-Sabah family by different means, and were registered in a variety of ways, indeed some of them were not registered at all.

It is not known exactly when the *vali* first broached this latest proposal for a settlement to Mubarak, but the shaikh later told Kemball that it was around the end of January 1903 that he had accepted the sultan's *irade* regarding the appointment of 'disinterested' persons and agreeing to accept their decision. The question of who and how many such 'disinterested' persons were to act as arbitrators caused almost as much difficulty as the settlement itself. Throughout the spring of 1903, the two sides wrangled over the composition of the arbitration commission and its terms of reference. Throughout Mubarak displayed an intense suspicion of the entire proceedings, attempting to delay the process at every point, while, at the same time, ensuring the bulk of the property for himself. Even Mubarak's friends became impatient with him. Kemball thought that the shaikh's attitude was 'unreasonable', and the British consul in Basra, informed the ambassador, 'Mubarak's attitude throughout the negotiations has been so tricky and childish, that I can place very little reliance on his promise to submit his differences to arbitration.'[101]

In late July 1903, Mubarak finally gave up the battle and accepted a compromise worked out between the British consul and Haji Mansur, the shaikh's representative. He agreed to allow one-quarter of Fao and of Safiyah to his nephews.[102] However, as he had argued previously, for practical reasons the Fao property was indivisible and, in any case, joint occupation would risk future quarrels and friction with his nephews and possibly with the Ottoman authorities as well, he now offered to give up all his claims to the other property in exchange for the nephews' one-quarter interest in the Fao estates. This was accepted, and, after a number of minor details had been worked out, Crow was able to inform the British Embassy in September that the terms of the agreement had been sealed by both sides and for all practical purposes the dispute was at an end.

The settlement of his domestic disputes appeared to leave the shaikh free to turn his attention once more to affairs in the interior of Arabia. However, the shaikh clearly had undergone a change of heart in regard to his external ambitions. This will be explored in the next chapter.

4

Shaikh Mubarak and Najd: the Final Phase

Following the disaster at Sarif in March 1901, Shaikh Mubarak did not send his forces back into the desert for many years. He seems to have realised after the débâcle of Sarif that his priority must be to secure and maintain his rule over Kuwait, rather than try to extend it. Clearly, he could not neglect the affairs of the Arabian desert altogether, but his approach to tribal politics was now more so than before to use surrogates, supported by Kuwait's money and supplies, to fight his battles. In particular, he used the al-Sa'ud to counter Prince Ibn Rashid, and to neutralise the Ibn Rashid threat to Kuwait.

However, it was not in Mubarak's interests for any one power to dominate Arabia completely. Once the al-Sa'ud had recaptured Riyadh at the start of 1902, and then regained most of Najd and Jabal Shammar from the Ibn Rashid, Mubarak found that he needed to restrain the al-Sa'ud. His policy came to depend on achieving a calculated balance between the al-Sa'ud and the Ibn Rashid, never allowing either side to become so dominant as to be able to dispense with the support of the Shaikh of Kuwait. This policy required great financial resources, which could only be mobilised by straining the Kuwaiti economy to the limit. Mubarak showed great ingenuity in maximising his tax revenues and sources of income. The trouble was that his own people, and particularly the pearl fishers and merchants, who were the main source of income, did not take kindly to this new policy of high and unpredictable taxation. The pearl fishers, in particular, had the ultimate sanction of simply abandoning Kuwait altogether and threatening Mubarak with the loss of a major part of his tax base. Indeed, towards the end of his reign, Mubarak succeeded in impoverishing his people to the point where on one occasion they came close to open revolt. In 1902 these problems lay some time in the future. After a difficult start, 1902 was in many ways an excellent year for Mubarak. In mid-

January, his ally Abdulaziz bin Abdulrahman al-Sa'ud made his epic attack on Riyadh, capturing the town and killing the governor placed there by Amir Ibn Rashid. This event transformed the situation in central Arabia to the immediate advantage of Mubarak. Even more importantly, the Ottomans seem to have been so humiliated by Britain's high-level interventions in support of Mubarak that they abandoned any attempt to subjugate Kuwait by direct military pressure. The visit of the gunboat *Zohaf* in December 1901 was, apparently, the last visit to Kuwait by an Ottoman warship with hostile intent. The Ottomans did try to get Shaikh Mubarak indirectly during 1902, by arresting his agent at Basra. They were further embarrassed by the strong British reaction to Shaikh Yusuf's unsuccessful attempt to take over Kuwait at the start of September 1902 (the '*Lapwing* incident'), for which the British held the Ottoman authorities to bear at least some of the responsibility. We have seen that the Sublime Porte, under strong pressure from the British Embassy in Constantinople, agreed to expel Shaikh Yusuf from the region of Basra. The Ottoman government presumably calculated that Kuwait was now effectively under British protection, whatever the legal niceties of the relationship. Military threats against the shaikhdom would therefore serve no purpose.

This explains why the Ottoman military detachments who had moved into Safwan, Umm Qasr and Bubiyan in the last days of 1901, remained inactive thereafter. Indeed, these unfortunate troops, who had been sent all the way to the coast of the Gulf in order to limit Mubarak's freedom of action, seem to have been virtually forgotten by their own government. In August 1912, Captain Shakespear reported that the Ottoman garrison in Umm Qasr had fallen to somewhere between 8 and 10 men, and that Shaikh Mubarak could certainly have wiped out every Turkish military post on the borders of Kuwait 'with the greatest of ease at any time within the last ten years.'[1]

According to Shakespear, the only reasons why Mubarak had not taken this action was his fear that the Ottomans might retaliate against his date gardens in the Shatt al-Arab, plus a suspicion that a direct military confrontation with the Ottomans might deprive him of Britain's goodwill.

Mubarak's position was further strengthened in his dealings with the Ottomans by the inclusion of Kuwait among the Arab Gulf ports visited by the British viceroy of India, Lord Curzon, on his unique tour of the Gulf in November 1903. The tour was the logical culmination of the splendid viceroy's interest in the region, which dated back to his travels in Persia twelve years before. Although Curzon often stressed the amusing aspects of the visit in his after-dinner stories during the period of political inaction which followed his time as viceroy, there was an intensely serious purpose behind the visit. It was, of course, entertaining to see the viceroy himself being carried through the surf onto the beach three miles from Kuwait, and then being taken in a specially-ordered carriage to Kuwait itself: the carriage was, according to Curzon, kicked to pieces by its horses while the viceroy talked with Mubarak. However, beneath the amusement, Curzon was convinced that the tour affirmed for all to see that Britain now had 'paramountcy' in the Gulf. There would be no question in future of any division of influence with the Ottomans or another power: Britain was the only power which counted from Kuwait down to Muscat. Curzon also acknowledged that Mubarak was 'a striking and powerful type of Arab chieftain'.

So Mubarak could legitimately feel that Ottoman pressure was now off Kuwait. As already mentioned, affairs in Central Arabia were going more favourably for Kuwait after 1902. The main change for the better was the success of Mubarak's protégé Abdulaziz al-Sa'ud in expelling the Ibn Rashid forces from Riyadh in mid-January 1902, the episode which is now commemorated as the birth of the modern Sa'udi state. It is time to consider what role Mubarak played in the recapture of Riyadh.

The story of Abdulaziz's raid on Riyadh, the founding epic of the modern Kingdom of Sa'udi Arabia, is generally presented as a superb and daring initiative by the young Abdulaziz, trusting in God and the courage of his small group of supporters. The available evidence confirms that the raid was indeed planned by Abdulaziz on his own, and that he did not even tell his closest confidants about his intention to attack Riyadh until they were camped in hiding just a few miles away. So the successful attack on Riyadh in January 1902 differed greatly from Abdulaziz's previous unsuccessful attempt to reoccupy Riyadh in the spring of 1931. The earlier raid had been launched by Abdulaziz, in full co-operation with Shaikh Mubarak of Kuwait, as a part of Mubarak's great desert offensive against the Ibn Rashid, which ended with the defeat of Kuwaiti forces at Sarif. In that raid of 1901 Abdulaziz had in fact managed to occupy much of the town of Riyadh and was besieging the Ibn Rashid governor of Riyadh, within the walls of the Masmak Palace, when news came through of the rout of Mubarak's forces at Sarif. Abdulaziz had to abandon the siege and withdraw his forces into the desert.[2] By contrast, Abdulaziz did not plan his successful raid of January 1902 in co-operation with Shaikh Mubarak, but relied on his own skills and the advantage of surprise. When he led his small band through the palm and date gardens towards Ajlan's house and then into the Masmak Palace on that January night in 1902 he had been away from Kuwait for some months, raiding in Sudair and al-Hasa, and keeping his exact movements a secret. Meanwhile, during the winter of 1901–02,

Mubarak was himself facing acute pressure from the Ottomans and from the armies of Ibn Rashid, and cannot have been in a position to give much help to his Sa'udi protege, even if he had known of his plans.

So the most likely supposition is that Abdulaziz did in fact act alone on his epic raid, as tradition has always suggested. If Mubarak had any information about his plans, this would surely have been only very general information of his whereabouts. Indeed, there is a persistent oral tradition that relations between Mubarak and Abdulaziz Ibn Sa'ud had cooled somewhat after the debacle at Sarif. This tends to confirm that Abdulaziz's desert operations in late 1901 and early 1902 were a lone and daring adventure, mounted without direct help from Mubarak.

Once Abdulaziz had recaptured Riyadh, Mubarak appears to have made little secret of his role as a supporter of the al-Sa'ud. At the end of July 1902, the British consul in Basra told his ambassador in Constantinople that Mubarak was 'notoriously aiding and abetting Ibn Sa'ud, who could have done little without his help, and it is to be feared that Kuwait may become actively involved in the hostilities which are locally regarded as inevitable.' When this information reached London, the British government asked Kemball in Bushire to issue yet another warning to Mubarak not to get involved in the affairs of Najd, and to avoid any action which might embroil Kuwait with the Ottomans.[3] Kemball was understandably annoyed at the failure of officials in the India Office and the Foreign Office to comprehend the realities of desert politics. As he minuted his first assistant in the Residency, ' ... the Secretary of State does not seem to be able to grasp that Mubarak has committed himself fully ages ago, as far as Nejd is concerned, and it is absolutely futile to convey any more warnings.'[4] But Kemball was obliged to carry out his orders from London, and sent the usual warning to Shaikh Mubarak. Not surprisingly, he received the usual reply from Mubarak to the effect that he was not interfering in events in Najd, and 'am resting at ease in my country under your shadow and have nothing to do with them.'[5]

Mubarak's reply was sent to Bushire on 13 October 1902. On the margin of the letter, the first assistant noted a report to the effect that Mubarak had recently met one of the sons of Abdulrahman al-Sa'ud at Jahara, and had handed over a considerable body of mounted men to be used against Ibn Rashid. This report was later confirmed by a British naval officer, and shows that Mubarak was definitely not resting at ease in his country.[6] Indeed, he had little choice in the matter. As he had admitted in a letter to Kemball in August 1902, he would face difficulties if Ibn Rashid achieved a success. Mubarak had admitted to the resident in his letter that he intended to offer 'secret assistance' to the al-Sa'ud, which would check any disturbance from Ibn Rashid and keep him engaged.[6]

There were, of course, limits on what Mubarak could do in Najd. He had built his influence on an alliance of tribes such as the Ajman and Mutair, which were not traditionally part of Kuwait. Indeed, not only were they largely Najdi, they were naturally attracted to the al-Sa'ud cause for reasons of tradition, religion and the usual Bedouin enthusiasm for a good fight which promised loot at the end. It is unlikely that Mubarak could have prevented them going to Abdulaziz even if he had wished.

Indeed, there was a limit to his control over his own tribes. Late in 1902 there was a sharp clash between Kuwait and the tribes of Zubair. The Zubairis, who had been raiding Kuwait for months, immediately claimed the Kuwaitis had instigated the attack and reported it to the *vali*. Shaikh Mubarak complained they had raided his tribes and his people had merely resisted. For once Kemball sympathised with the shaikh who, in his eyes, had endured constant provocation, and in any case:

> As an Arab Sheikh, it is of course of vital importance to him to retain his hold on the Bedouin tribes which consider themselves subordinate to him and under the circumstances it is I think impossible for him, even if he had the power to control his tribesmen, to prevent them from carrying out reprisals for the raids to which they have been subjected.[7]

By the beginning of 1904 the al-Sa'ud had driven Ibn Rashid back to the Qasim province, the last bastion between the al-Sa'ud conquests and the heart of Jabal Shammar. Ibn Rashid moved east and early in January he telegraphed the Sultan and again requested permission to attack Kuwait, but was dissuaded from pursuing his grudge by the *vali* on orders from Constantinople.

Prince Ibn Rashid had remained surprisingly inactive following the loss of Riyadh and, in consequence, most of southern and central Najd had come over to the al-Sa'ud banner. By April of 1904, the al-Sa'ud forces had broken through into Qasim and captured most of the province, including Unaizah and Buraidah. By the end of the spring Ibn Sa'ud had recovered all of his ancestral dominions and was in possession of all of Najd.

Ibn Rashid's response was to take the same fatal step which had cost the al-Sa'ud those same lands half a century before and he turned to the Turks for assistance.[8] The first word of this turn of affairs reached Kuwait from a Baghdad correspondent of Mubarak's, who warned him that the Turks were sending troops and artillery to Ibn Rashid's aid and advising him to fill up all the wells on the road from Samawa (where the Ottoman force was concentrating) to

Qasim and to rush men and supplies to Ibn Sa'ud.[9]

It was assumed that the shaikh was behind the al-Sa'ud advance. O'Conor claimed there was 'no doubt' that the shaikh had 'encouraged' Abdulaziz.[10] However, Crow, who was closer to the scene, pointed out that events were perhaps beyond the shaikh's control, and that Mubarak could not afford to stand aside from the struggle in the desert.

> Kuwait is an enclave in Turkish territory with no defined boundaries, and the Turks would readily avail themselves of any opportunity to circumscribe its limits in the hinterland by averting the sympathies of the tribes in that neighbourhood who owe allegiance to Mubarak. If the Sheikh of Kuwait does not help these tribes in the struggle now pending between the Amir, who had gained Turkish support, and the Feysul (*sic*) faction at Riad, it is probable that they will forsake him and join the stronger side, and Kuwait trade and influence, which largely depends on their fidelity, must necessarily suffer. Bearing this in mind, the Sheikh of Kuwait may be involuntarily drawn into the struggle, as his interests are identical with those of the Saoud family.[11]

At least as far as Mubarak's limited ability to control the tribes was concerned, Crow appeared to be correct. There were large numbers of Najdi refugees from Buraida and Unaizah in Kuwait who, upon hearing that Ibn Rashid had called in the Turks, were only too eager to return to fight beside Ibn Sa'ud, 'their Imam'.

The Sa'udi response to the news of the impending Ottoman expedition was also to seek outside support. On 9 May 1904, Shaikh Mubarak forwarded to the Bushire Residency two letters from Abdulrahman al-Sa'ud, one addressed to himself and one to the Residency.[12] In his letter to Mubarak, Abdulrahman reminded the shaikh that, when his son Abdulaziz visited Kuwait in March 1903, he had been approached by both the French and the Russians with offers of assistance. However, on Shaikh Mubarak's advice he had rejected these overtures, and now the al-Sa'ud wanted Mubarak's help in getting British protection. The letter to the Residency pointed out that all the al-Sa'ud had done was to regain the lands which were rightfully theirs by defeating Ibn Rashid. It was Ibn Rashid who had now called in the Turks. He asked for the protection of the British government and British assistance in stopping the Turks. He referred to the Russian offer in March 1903 to assist the al-Sa'ud, but claimed that he would prefer to follow Mubarak's example and have British protection.

The hint was clear enough: the al-Sa'ud held the card that, if Britain did not take their side, there were other European powers who were keen to build up alliances in Arabia. In 1904, a year before the Imperial Russian Navy was comprehensively humiliated by the Japanese, the Russian presence in the Gulf still had the power to frighten British officials.

The Government of India suggested to London that, in view of Ottoman support for Ibn Rashid, the time had come for Britain to appoint an agent in Kuwait 'to watch events'. London agreed and ordered the Indian government to send an agent immediately. Captain S. G. Knox therefore left Bushire for Kuwait on 5 August 1904, where he was welcomed with 'honour' by Mubarak, and was invited to stay in the shaikh's palace while the shaikh sought suitable quarters for the British Agency. Mubarak must have been delighted to have such a tangible sign of his close connection with the British.

Meanwhile, the Ottoman expedition, in support of Ibn Rashid, had turned into a disastrous failure. About 4,000 men and 12 guns had left Samawa at the end of May 1904 to join Amir Ibn Rashid. Following this, no more was heard until early August when conflicting reports reached Basra, suggesting first a victory for Ibn Rashid, and then an al-Sa'ud triumph. In fact, there had been severe fighting over several days in the middle of July in the area of the town of al-Bukairiya. The al-Rashid side had suffered heavy losses, especially amongst the Turkish contingent. Three of the Turkish guns had been taken by Ibn Sa'ud's troops, although they were recaptured a few days later.[13] Details of the battle are unclear, but it is reported that Ibn Rashid himself killed the commander and the second-in-command of the Turkish forces when they refused to march their men in front of the amir's own troops.[14]

The Porte was not deterred by this failure and took steps to prepare for a second expedition in support of Ibn Rashid. This prompted Abdulrahman al-Sa'ud to write again to the British resident in Bushire asking for British protection. However, a change was about to take place in Ottoman strategy, which would help to solve the conflict in Najd. In September 1904, the Ottoman government decided on a change of personnel in Basra, and dismissed Mustafa Nuri Pasha from his post as *vali*. The reason for the dismissal was apparently that Mustafa had failed to keep order in the Basra Vilayat. Mustafa was replaced by Fakhri Pasha, 'a smart and energetic officer', who had previously been chief of staff of the Baghdad Sixth Army Corps. Fakhri was accompanied to his new post by General Daghistani. This suggests that the Porte had decided that its interests would best be served by sending a capable military officer to Basra as *vali*, with full military backing.[15] If the records are correct, it seems that the outgoing *vali*, Mustafa Nuri Pasha, had taken a very important initiative in Najd just before he left Basra for good.[16] In view of the failure of the Ottoman expedition in support of Ibn Rashid, and because the al-Saʻud's star was now in the ascendant, the *vali* told Constantinople that he would take steps to bring Najd under the al-Saʻud into the Ottoman orbit. In August 1904, in pursuance of this strategy, he approached three leading personalities in Basra with an identical request. All three men were asked to write to Shaikh Mubarak urging him to advise Abdulaziz al-Saʻud to send a conciliatory letter to Constantinople blaming all the disturbances in Najd on Ibn Rashid, and asserting the loyalty of the al-Saʻud to the sultan. The three personalities selected by Mustafa for this diplomatic offensive were the Naqib of Basra, Rajab the agent of the Basra–Persian Steam Navigation Company, Agha Jaffir, who was reported to be the *vali*'s 'most trusted and confidential adviser'; and Abdulaziz, Shaikh Mubarak's agent in Basra. The *vali* asked the three to pass on a promise that Abdulaziz al-Saʻud would be recognised as the ruler of Najd under Ottoman protection, and that the Porte would not interfere in the affairs of Najd by sending Ottoman officials or garrisons into the region. The *vali* also authorised the three men to offer rewards and titles for both Abdulaziz and Mubarak.

All three men made excuses to the *vali* for not writing to Mubarak, but all three did in fact write privately. The new Ottoman approach was not entirely welcome to Mubarak, who faced some difficulty in working out what to do. On the other hand, he had an understandable aversion to any involvement with Ottoman officials. He also knew that if he refused to participate in the latest Ottoman initiative, there was nothing to prevent the *vali* from communicating directly with Abdulaziz al-Saʻud. If this was to happen, the consequences for Kuwait could be serious. Shaikh Mubarak seems to have feared that, once the Ottomans established even nominal authority over the al-Saʻud, this would lead to the absorption of Najd into the Ottoman Empire.[17] In this, Mubarak was probably being alarmist, as the Turks had never managed to absorb Najd in the past and Abdulaziz was, in any case, a far stronger character than anyone with whom they had previously dealt in Arabia. However, Mubarak had another worse fear that the establishment of direct political relations between the Porte and the al-Saʻud would compromise his own political position. His position as intermediary between the outside world and central Arabia was a major factor in his status within Kuwait and in the Gulf area as a whole. In addition, his ability to influence the results of any talks between the al-Saʻud and the Ottomans depended on being involved in the talks between the two parties. If he was not asked to attend the talks, he would be virtually bound to accept any agreement which arose from them. Even more importantly, a direct relationship between the al-Saʻud and the Ottomans could undermine Mubarak's relations with the British.

Mubarak therefore decided to launch a diplomatic campaign of his own. At the start of September 1904, he told the British agent in Kuwait that he did not trust Abdulaziz al-Sa'ud, especially in conjunction with the Turks. 'He repeated over and over again that Ibn Saood was a Beduw (*sic*) meaning apparently that he was on his side today, on the other tomorrow.'[18] This was manifestly unfair of Mubarak, as Abdulaziz was known as a man of his word. In a conversation with the British political agent in 1930 Ahmad Jabir, Mubarak's grandson, adopted a similar derogatory attitude describing Najdis and Iraqis as a couple of dogs and Kuwait as the bone![19] However, Mubarak needed to impress on the British that he was the best interlocutor they had in the region, and that Ibn Sa'ud (as we will now call Abdulaziz) was not to be trusted.

As for the *vali*'s request to Mubarak to communicate with the al-Sa'ud and to encourage them to write to Constantinople, we must assume that Mubarak did indeed pass the message on. In late September, Abdulrahman al-Sa'ud finally responded. The timing of the reply is of some importance. The desert campaign, which had begun with the Ottoman expedition of May had continued right through the hot weather of 1904, and had only concluded in late September with the decisive Sa'udi victory at Qasr Ibn Aziz in Qasim. The Sa'udi forces now badly needed a rest. Even before the battle, Ibn Sa'ud's army had been in a state of 'almost open mutiny', and despite his victory Ibn Sa'ud was still not certain of his hold over Qasim. As Shaikh Mubarak's secretary later put it to Knox, ' ... the Nejd people are tired of this everlasting fighting. They don't know how to feed and clothe their children. Nothing but fighting.'[20] So Fakhri Pasha in Basra was able to write to the grand vizier on 8 October forwarding a conciliatory letter from Abdulrahman al-Sa'ud, in which the Sa'udi prince confirmed his loyalty to the sultan and blamed all misunderstandings on the intrigues of officials, stirred up by the tyrant Ibn Rashid. The letter did appear to be the one which Shaikh Mubarak had been instructed to obtain from the al-Sa'ud. Fakhri Pasha noted that it was addressed to him via Kuwait, and indeed had apparently been written in Kuwait for Abdulrahman!

It turned out that Abdulrahman's letter was only just in time to avoid another Ottoman expedition into Najd. In early November, Mr Townley of the British Embassy in Constantinople obtained from a 'secret source' copies of documents including a letter from the grand vizier to the minister of the interior, dated 17 October 1904, which indicated that the sultan had been preparing a second substantial force to assist Ibn Rashid against the al-Sa'ud. Other papers confirmed that the size of the expedition was almost immediately reduced when Fakhri Pasha's letter enclosing the message from Abdulrahman reached Constantinople.[21]

In November 1904, Fakhri Pasha wrote back to Abdulrahman (apparently on instructions from Constantinople) proposing a 'friendly meeting' to find a peaceful settlement to the problem of Qasim. Fakhri sent the letter via Kuwait and, at the same time, asked Mubarak to help to arrange a meeting between Mubarak, Abdulrahman and the Vali of Basra. Mubarak seems to have complied with this request: at the end of November, the new Vali of Basra, Mukhlis Pasha, received a letter which purported to come from Abdulrahman al-Sa'ud, but was actually in the handwriting of Mubarak's secretary. This involvement in the contacts between the Ottomans and the al-Sa'ud brought useful dividends for Mubarak himself in late December, when letters reached him from the *vali*, which contained orders 'in very friendly terms' from the sultan, directing Mubarak and Abdulrahman al-Sa'ud to meet the *vali* at Safwan, and to arrive at an agreement on the future of Najd. The letter to Mubarak promised that the al-Sa'ud would be made rulers of Najd. The letter to Abdulrahman al-Sa'ud said that the Ottomans could do nothing for him unless Mubarak was a party to the agreement. Thus far, Mubarak's position as an intermediary between the Ottomans and the al-Sa'ud seemed secure.

At first, Mubarak felt obliged to pretend to the British agent in Kuwait that he thought nothing would come of the new Ottoman initiative in Najd, and that he would not himself be going to the meeting at Safwan.[22] Mubarak had, after all, been warned by his British friends on many occasions to keep clear of the affairs of Najd. However, it soon became obvious that he would be going to the meeting. He told Knox that he planned to take a 'precautionary guard of 1,000 men', as he did not trust the Turks. He believed that the al-Sa'ud would also bring a large contingent. There were certainly reasons for suspicion: the British Embassy reported at the start of January 1905 that the Porte had changed its mind and, instead of accepting the submission of the al-Sa'ud, now planned a new and more powerful expedition to subdue them. There were also reports that Ottoman troops were being concentrated at Najaf, south of Baghdad, and close to the Ibn Rashid heartland of Jabal Shammar. The new reports presumably reflected disagreements between the factions at the Ottoman court, where both the al-Sa'ud and the al-Rashid had highly-placed supporters. It may be that the Porte simply wanted to keep its options open, so as to be able to intervene if the planned meeting between the *vali* and the al-Sa'ud went badly.[23]

The first meeting between the Ottomans and the al-Sa'ud took place at Safwan, just south of Zubair, on 8 February 1905, Mubarak introduced Abdulrahman to the *vali* and then, as he later claimed to the British agent in Kuwait, withdrew from the discussions.[24] Abdulrahman repeated to the *vali* his oft-stated position that he and his people were loyal to the sultan, that their petitions against Ibn Rashid had been ignored, and they had to fight in self-defence. He said he would not fight the government and he would accept Ottoman officials and even a garrison in Qasim, as long as there was no interference by Ibn Rashid. Immediately after the meeting, the *vali* returned to Basra and communicated the result in a long telegram to the sultan.

The three met again on 13 February. The *vali* brought with him three conditions set by Constantinople: Ibn Rashid would be kept out of Najd affairs, an Ottoman garrison and officials would be placed in Qasim, and Mubarak must be a party to the agreement. Shaikh Mubarak claimed to Knox that he 'flatly refused' this last condition, telling the *vali* that ' … the people of Nejd were a seditious turbulent lot … [and] he refused to have anything to do with Nejd politics'.[25] The *vali* also reproved the shaikh for styling himself in correspondence as ruler and Chief of Kuwait, but the shaikh declined to use the Ottoman title *qaimaqam*. Like his predecessors the *vali* raised the question of a telegraph line and postal service to al-Hasa via Kuwait and, as before, the shaikh rejected the suggestion. On their part both Shaikh Mubarak and Abdulrahman asked for the sultan's pardon for the latter in writing.

It would appear that the two shaikhs did not, at this point, agree to the Ottoman proposals because shortly after the second meeting the *vali* wrote to both Mubarak and Abdulrahman. He told Abdulrahman to make his submission to the mushir commanding the Ottoman expedition, and also directed Mubarak to stop allowing foreign influences at Kuwait and accept the garrison and officials proposed at the second meeting. A few days later he sent a telegram to them 'urgently demanding' a reply to his letters. Abdulrahman asked for a letter of introduction to the *mushir*, but it was over two months before Mubarak replied to the *vali*'s letter with the usual protestations of loyalty to the sultan.

It may be that the shaikh suddenly felt that he had need to improve his relations with the Ottomans: despite British efforts to keep the matter secret, reports had already appeared in local newspapers that Britain was about to withdraw its political agent from Kuwait. This apparently bizarre decision was the result of a fundamental disagreement between the Foreign Office and the Government of India about the role of the political agent. The Foreign Office regarded the post as a temporary one, to cover the period of immediate danger to Kuwait, while the India Office had always envisaged that the agent would stay on in Kuwait *sine die*.

Since the autumn of 1904, the Foreign Office had been pressing for Knox's withdrawal, and the India Office was unable to resist for very long. In May 1905, Knox left Kuwait for what was to be an absence of five months.

There were good reasons for Cox in Bushire and the Government of India to be unhappy about the decision to withdraw the agent. During the meeting at Safwan, Knox had worried that Shaikh Mubarak might decide to switch his loyalty from Britain to the Ottoman Empire, and therefore suggested that a British warship should be stationed at Kuwait during the talks. Cox had also warned in December 1904 that, if Knox was withdrawn, ' ... Mubarak's secession (to the Ottomans) must be regarded as eventually probable'.[26] Throughout the summer and autumn of 1905, there were signs that Cox was right to be worried, in view of the increased cordiality between Mubarak and Basra. Mubarak had subscribed 'liberally' towards new barracks for Ottoman troops in Basra. He regularly forwarded to Basra the deserters from the Ottoman expedition to Qasim, who escaped to Kuwait. The Ottomans returned the favour by releasing Shaikh Mubarak's imprisoned agent in Basra in November, long before the end of his sentence. The shaikh and the *vali* corresponded frequently, and the letters were couched 'in very friendly terms', with Mubarak referring to himself as Qaimaqam of Kuwait, and signing the letters as 'your sincere friend'.[27]

The most significant sign of a rapprochement with the Ottomans was the news that Mubarak had agreed to allow the Ottoman mail for al-Hasa to pass through Kuwait, and for an Ottoman postal official to reside in Kuwait. The news so surprised Cox that he sent Commander Bowman at the start of October 1905 to ask if it was true. Mubarak flatly denied the report that a Turkish postal official had been or would be established in Kuwait, and indeed was said to be very emphatic on the point. However, it turned out that the shaikh had been highly economical with the truth, as the postal service was reported to be in operation by November.

The Government of India was alarmed by these developments. So when it was discovered at the end of September that a party of German engineers would soon arrive in Kuwait to investigate the possibility of building a railway, the India Office warmly endorsed a recommendation by the ambassador in Constantinople that Knox should be sent back to Kuwait. Knox, therefore, arrived in Kuwait to resume his work as agent on 25 October, and received an enthusiastic welcome. He was visited almost immediately by Shaikh Mubarak, his son Jabir and the shaikh's secretary, Mula Abdullah, the first of a long string of visitors 'of all ranks'.

Mubarak gave Knox the latest news from Najd, which was all to the advantage of Kuwait. To start with the Ibn Rashid clan was in marked decline in the autumn of 1905. The factionalism which was to rend the family in 1906 was already starting to appear. Humud Ibn Rashid, the uncle of the Amir Abdulaziz, ruled in Hail itself, and his nephews wandered the desert. Hail itself was largely populated by soldiers, as the rest of the population had fled. Meanwhile, the remnants of the Turkish garrison in Qasim were in a sorry state, as barely 700 of the original expedition and its subsequent reinforcements remained alive.[28]

Indeed, Mubarak told Knox that the situation in the interior of Arabia was ' ... entirely satisfactory from the point of view of himself and his friends of the Bin Saood faction'; the al-Sa'ud were well-established and firmly in control, and caravans passed freely and unmolested between Kuwait and Najd, while Qasim itself was prosperous. At the same time, there was an interesting hint of strains in the relationship between Kuwait and the al-Sa'ud. Knox was told by someone who 'was not usually favourable' to Mubarak that Ibn Sa'ud's men had recently raided followers of Ibn Rashid, and that Mubarak had remonstrated with Ibn Sa'ud about this, pointing out that unprovoked aggression in the desert was not wise. According to this informant, Mubarak had threatened to withdraw his favour for the al-Sa'ud if such lawlessness continued.

There were other signs that the friendship between Mubarak and Ibn Sa'ud was under strain. In the summer of 1905, Ibn Sa'ud had arrived in the region near Qatar, ostensibly to settle some tribal disagreements, but before the summer heat caused him to leave, he wrote to the Shaikh of Dubai to say that he would be back in the spring 'to look into certain affairs'.[29] Both the Shaikh of Abu Dhabi and the Sultan of Muscat were worried about the effect such a visit would have on their tribes. The British were also unhappy about the disruption which Ibn Sa'ud's visit might cause on the Gulf coast. The Government of India therefore recommended that Mubarak should be asked to dissuade Ibn Sa'ud from his planned visit. The government pointed out that Mubarak's control over most of the supply of weapons going into Najd gave him considerable leverage over Ibn Sa'ud. So Knox was asked to sound Mubarak out casually on the subject, and to indicate that the British government would not approve of Sa'udi interference with the Trucial shaikhs or the Sultan of Muscat.[30]

Mubarak was happy to co-operate with the British request. He had already heard of Ibn Sa'ud's plans to visit the Lower Gulf, and told Knox that he thought the visit was just an attempt to extort money from the shaikhs of the region, so as to meet Ibn Sa'ud's constant need for extra funds. Mubarak said that he had already written to Ibn Sa'ud to point out that it was unwise of him to admit, as a ruler, that he needed money. Mubarak claimed that he had also reminded Ibn Sa'ud that the power of Amir Ibn Rashid was 'scotched, not killed', and that Ibn Sa'ud's power in Najd was anything but firmly established. Mubarak's own assessment in his conversation with Knox in mid-January 1906 was that Ibn Sa'ud would not in fact make the visit, but he had to admit that he could not ' ... answer for the opinions and policy of an ignorant savage'.[31]

A few weeks later, at the start of February, Mubarak again raised the subject of the visit, and told Knox that he did not think Ibn Sa'ud would go ahead with it. Knox suspected, probably rightly, that Mubarak's keen interest in the visit concealed his own worry that Ibn Sa'ud might negotiate access from Najd to the Gulf via one of the ports of the Lower Gulf, so as to bypass Kuwait. The British agent therefore argued that, on the grounds of self-interest, 'we may reckon on Sheikh Mubarak's support in this matter'.[32]

In fact the major changes of 1906 were destined to take place in Najd rather than on the Gulf coast. In February 1906, Shaikh Mubarak received a friendly letter from Amir Ibn Rashid, who suggested that Mubarak should be on the same terms of friendship with Ibn Rashid as the rulers of Kuwait had been with Ibn Rashid's uncle and grandfather. Mubarak replied in guarded but friendly terms. There may have been further correspondence between Mubarak and Ibn Rashid, but we do not know what the contents would have been. In any event, before the peace negotiations between Mubarak and the amir could bear fruit, Amir Ibn Rashid was himself dead. In the early spring of 1906, he had set out with a small group of companions to raid a Sa'udi caravan on its way from Baghdad to Najd. He was unaware that Ibn Sa'ud was waiting nearby with a large force, and was caught unprepared in camp at Rawdhat Muhanna on the night of 11 April. In a short, sharp fight, Ibn Rashid who ' ... in regular Arab style declared his presence and recited *rajaz* (war songs) ... ' was killed.[33] Abdulaziz Ibn Sa'ud sent the amir's signet ring to Shaikh Mubarak in Kuwait, perhaps as a sign of his debt to the shaikh in the difficult years of his exile. When the news of Ibn Rashid's death reached Kuwait, Knox tells us that Mubarak's eldest son, Jabir, appeared to be moved to regret, and said to the British officer, 'in a sentimental kind of way' that Ibn Rashid had been a 'fine brave man'.

Ibn Rashid was succeeded as amir by his son Mitab. The young amir's family fortunes were at a low ebb, with little of their old domain and power remaining to them. Despite his youth, Mitab showed that he had inherited a significant amount of the political skill of his grandfather, the powerful Amir Muhammad Ibn Rashid. He was careful to consult the elders of the al-Rashid tribe, so as to secure their goodwill and support for his decisions. He also remitted all tribal taxes for the year in which he took power. Perhaps as a result of his decision, he was eager to achieve a breathing space in the conflict between his family and the al-Sa'ud.

On his side, Ibn Sa'ud was ready for a truce. Although he claimed to be the ruler of the whole of eastern Arabia, he had to take account of the fact that the

Ottoman sultan had recognised Mitab Ibn Rashid as amir in succession to his father, and that there was still an Ottoman garrison in Qasim. Ibn Sa'ud ruled a collection of turbulent and fickle tribes, and needed time to consolidate his position. He was notoriously short of the money needed to maintain support among the Bedouin and not everyone was loyal. In addition, he may already have been planning his move against the Ottoman Garrison in al-Hasa, which in fact took place in 1913. His trip to the environs of Qatar in 1905 may have been intended as a first reconnaissance for this move, and his decision to send a supporter, Mus'ad Ibn Suwailim, to Bahrain in February 1906 was certainly taken as part of the preparations for a move into al-Hasa. For such a move to succeed, he needed peace on his north-western flank.

Shaikh Mubarak also saw advantages in ending the incessant struggle between the al-Sa'ud and the al-Rashid. As a trading community, Kuwait needed peace in the desert to secure its own prosperity. From the shaikh's point of view the political situation in Najd had changed dramatically. Not only was Amir Ibn Rashid dead, but Mubarak's arch-enemy, Shaikh Yusuf Ibn Ibrahim, had died in Hail the previous December and Mubarak had begun to reconcile himself with his nephews. He had secured British backing for Kuwait against Ottoman military and diplomatic pressure, and had used this British support to develop an easier and more equal relationship with the Ottomans. He was now widely regarded as a ruler of considerable influence, who commanded respect and whose views should be sought on a wide range of regional affairs. As a sign of his high status, the Ottomans had made their original approach to Ibn Sa'ud, which led to the Safwan meeting of February 1905, through Mubarak. In 1905–6, the British government had seen him as their best hope of persuading Ibn Sa'ud not to visit the Lower Gulf region. Indeed, the Sultan of Muscat had sought Mubarak's advice and so had the Shaikh of Bahrain during a period of difficulty between Bahrain, and the British in 1905. On the tribal front, Mubarak had in mid-1906 recently settled a serious tribal quarrel between the Ajman and the al-Murra, and was soon to be involved in settling tribal differences in al-Hasa. With his increased prestige, he had every interest in avoiding conflict and upset in the desert.

At the same time, Mubarak's relations with Ibn Sa'ud were less happy in 1906 than during earlier years. Even before the death of Amir Ibn Rashid, Mubarak had been sensing that his protégé was less willing than before to accept the guidance and support of the older ruler. At the time of Ibn Sa'ud's proposed visit to the Trucial coast, Cox had remarked that the shaikh's '... disapproval of Bin Saood is due to the fact that while his own relations with the Turks are getting more friendly, Bin Saood's are becoming decidedly strained, and this means no doubt that the latter is less inclined than before to be guided by the Sheikh of Kuwait's advice in his relations with the Porte.'[34]

These signs of growing independence on the part of Ibn Sa'ud must have worried Mubarak, as much of his influence in the region depended on his role as the main channel of communication and control between the al-Sa'ud and the outside world.

Now Ibn Sa'ud had made peace with the Turks, destroyed the amir and was courting the British. With Abdulaziz dominating central Arabia, what then of the shaikh and Kuwait? Mubarak was no fool and he was undoubtedly concerned about his own future. Knox reported in May 1906 that since the death of the amir, Ibn Sa'ud had ' … adopted in public durbars and other places, a very different tone in speaking of the Chief of Kuwait.'[35] Furthermore, a Najdi remarked to Knox that Ibn Sa'ud '… considered Kuwait as his and that the conquest of Kuwait would be quite a simple matter.'[36] Finally, one cannot ignore the likelihood that there was a natural personal resentment, even jealousy, on Mubarak's part for this young man who had as a boy sat in his own majlis and now, in a few short years, was on the verge of dominating all central Arabia.

The suspicion seemed to be mutual. In February 1906 a representative of Ibn Sa'ud, Mus'ad Ibn Suwailim, called on Prideaux, the British political agent in Bahrain, seeking British support should Ibn Sa'ud eject the Turks from Al Hasa and Qatif.[37] He then travelled on to Bushire from where he sent a long telegram to the sultan, ostensibly from Shaikh Jasim Ibn Thani of Qatar, but probably from Ibn Sa'ud, boasting of Ibn Sa'ud's loyalty and complaining about Ibn Rashid.[38] Shaikh Mubarak later confessed that he knew nothing of the telegram except what Mus'ad Ibn Suwailim (apparently after the event) had told him, and that he had had no correspondence with Ibn Sa'ud about it. It was a marked change from the previous year when Ibn Sa'ud's correspondence with the Ottomans was written in Kuwait by the sheikh's own secretary.

Finally, there was the vexed question of the *zakat* take over of the desert tribes. The *zakat* question may have been the original cause of the conflict between Mubarak and Ibn Rashid, and it now appeared that Shaikh Mubarak and Ibn Sa'ud were on a similar collision course. When in the spring of 1906 the *zakat* collectors from Kuwait visited the Ajman who had previously paid *zakat* to Shaikh Mubarak, they were told that the Ajman had already paid Ibn Sa'ud and could not be expected to pay twice. Mubarak complained to Ibn Sa'ud, but did not get a satisfactory reply and there were soon rumours of an imminent break between the al-Sa'ud and the al-Sabah, and a rapprochement between the latter and Ibn Rashid.[39]

What form such a settlement might take was revealed in a series of meetings between Shaikh Mubarak and Cox in March 1906. The shaikh told Cox that he envisioned a peace settlement based on a tripartite partition of Arabia under which Ibn Rashid would receive Hail, Kahafa and the rule of the Shammar; Mubarak would take Kuwait, Unaizah, Buraidah, Sudair and Wushm and their tribes; and Ibn Sa'ud would have Najd and the Wadi Dawasir.[40] Cox thought that such a settlement between Ibn Rashid, Ibn Sa'ud and Mubarak '... would probably be found to amount to a defensive alliance for resistance to Turkish expansion in Nejd and Hassa, and is an interesting, if somewhat utopian, prospect to contemplate.'[41] But it is difficult to believe that Mubarak was really serious about his territorial ambitions to take over the Qasim region. Even Cox thought they '... were likely to form the chief obstacle to such a development'.[42]

Within a month of the amir's death, Shammar messengers were seen in Kuwait. Mubarak's son, Jabir, told Knox that they had been sent by Mitab seeking the protection of Shaikh Mubarak. A short time later the shaikh himself told Knox that he had received a submissive letter from the young amir and other members of his family asking for his friendship and protection. Then in early June Khalid al-Aun, who had been Ibn Rashid's chief lieutenant in the area, arrived as the representative of the new amir, with 40 followers including the son of the Naqib of Basra. The subsequent course of the negotiations is unclear, but there is no doubt that Mubarak acted as the mediator between the al-Rashid and the al-Sa'ud. The al-Rashid wanted to retain Hail, Shammar, the Harb and the control of the *hajj* route from Majid Ali to Medina, but Ibn Sa'ud was only prepared to leave them with Hail and Shammar. The essence of the final settlement, concluded in Qasim early in August 1906, was that the two sides would stay in their own territories, while arrangements would be made to settle inter-tribal disputes. Mubarak agreed to guarantee the settlement. A few weeks later, an envoy from the al-Sa'ud and the al-Rashid visited Kuwait to report to Mubarak that the peace was being maintained, and to ask him ' ... to inform either party if he noticed that they were infringing the conditions or committing acts likely to endanger the peace'.[43]

Unfortunately, this truce between the al-Rashid and the al-Sa'ud was only a result of exhaustion on both sides. In the future, the fighting would resume whenever one side felt sufficiently strong or saw an advantageous opening. However, Shaikh Mubarak's interests now depended on maintaining an equilibrium between the two powerful desert families, so that he was basically opposed to any resumption of the fighting. Captain W. H. Shakespear (who took over as British political agent in Kuwait in 1910) summarised the situation at the start of 1910 as follows:

I have been told more than once that all Shaikh Mubarak's dealings with the Bedouin tribes have for their ultimate object this balance (between the al-Sa'ud and the al-Rashid) together with his own aggrandizement, whereby his support becomes and remains the most desired end of each of the rival chiefs.[44]

In the months immediately following the 1906 truce, it was the al-Rashid who needed Mubarak's support. In January 1907, less than six months after the truce was concluded, Amir Mitab Ibn Rashid, his two brothers and a cousin were murdered by their uncle, Shaikh Sultan ibn Humud Ibn Rashid. Shaikh Sultan immediately sent a close relative to Mubarak in Kuwait, bringing letters which professed friendship and promises to consult Mubarak on all matters. In April 1907, Shaikh Sultan again approached Mubarak to ask his assistance in consolidating his position. Sultan proposed to follow a twin-track strategy: either he would seek to come under British protection or he would try to get the Porte to acknowledge him as the head of the al-Rashid house.

Mubarak was, in principle, keen to maintain the al-Rashid as a political force and did not, therefore, want to see Shaikh Sultan weakened too much. He was aware of rumours that the Ottoman authorities now wanted to meet with Abdulrahman al-Sa'ud (who was technically still the head of the al-Sa'ud, despite the great prestige of his son Ibn Sa'ud) at Safwan. There seemed to be a chance that the Ottomans were considering switching their support from the Ibn Rashid to the al-Sa'ud. The danger to Mubarak, if this happened, was that the Ottoman-backed al-Sa'ud would become the major regional power in Arabia, and that Kuwait would lose its special role as the arbiter of desert politics. An Ottoman-backed Sa'udi state would also be a threat to the independence of Kuwait itself. So he edged a little closer to the al-Rashid, As Knox reported in May 1907,

... there is little doubt that the pendulum has swung in the other direction and that Sheikh Mobarek is now more inclined to the Bin Rashid faction than to that of Bin Sa'ud. Nobody, whether Turks, Sheikh Mobarek, or Nejd towns like Boraida or Anaiza wish to see either of the rival factions betray and be betrayed incessantly.[45]

Shaikh Mubarak could not afford to become an unconditional supporter of the al-Rashid, because of the risk that the al-Rashid, in their present weakened state, would make dangerous concessions to the Ottomans, in order to gain additional support. These concessions might allow the Ottomans to build up a position in Arabia to Mubarak's disadvantage. This fear of Ottoman encroachments into Najd seems to have been the reason why Mubarak carried out a particularly skilful manoeuvre in the autumn of 1907 to break the alliance between the Ibn Rashid and the Mutair tribe. It was the alliance between Sultan Ibn Rashid and the powerful Mutair tribe which had enabled Sultan, in August 1907, to recapture Buraidah from the al-Sa'ud. Mubarak believed that the overwhelming desire of the people of Buraidah and of the Qasim region as a whole was simply for peace, irrespective of who ruled them. Mubarak's fear was that the people of Qasim would despair of seeing no end to incessant warfare, and simply call in the Turks, ' … not perceiving that (the Turks) in the end would be a harder master than Bin Sa'ud'.[46]

Mubarak decided to send Abdulaziz al-Hasan, one of his most trusted followers and a native of Qasim, into Qasim to detach the Mutair from Ibn Rashid. Mubarak told Knox that he planned to achieve this difficult aim by offering the people of Qasim a guarantee of peace against both Ibn Rashid and Ibn Sa'ud. Knox was impressed by the ambitious scale of the plan, which he described as worthy of Mubarak's genius, but felt that only a 'deus ex machina' could possibly bring it off. Somehow, Mubarak's envoy did achieve the apparently impossible. The Mutair withdrew their support from Ibn Rashid, and Ibn Sa'ud was able to reassert his position in Qasim.

Looking back at the events of 1907, Knox believed that:

> The despatch of Abdul Aziz Al Hassan and the general trend of events have given rise to the assumption – by no means unwarranted – that the disturbances of this year were skilfully engineered by Sheikh Mubarak. He wished to show the ruler of Riadh that he could not afford to stand independent of Kuwait support and yet, at the critical moment, when Bin Sa'ud was seriously threatened, Sheikh Mubarak threw his weight into the opposite scale and has, for the time being completely destroyed the power of the bin Rashid family, who, he probably realises, are irreconcilable enemies.[47]

Knox exaggerated both the extent and power of the shaikh's influence and, moreover, in describing his manoeuvrings as 'treachery' failed to appreciate the shaikh's position. Indeed, the al-Sa'ud and the al-Rashid were 'irreconcileable enemies', but the continuation of their struggles was of no advantage to either the shaikh or Kuwait. As Shaikh Mubarak explained to Cox, ' … the inhabitants of Nejd are people who are dependent on our side and cannot do without keeping up intercourse because their requirements are purchased from our side'.[48] The converse was also true; Kuwait depended on trade with the interior and war in the desert meant poverty in Kuwait. Shaikh Mubarak was not Ibn Sa'ud trying to regain his patrimony, nor Ibn Rashid trying to defend his; he had only Kuwait, which he was becoming increasingly concerned with preserving. Mubarak wanted peace and quiet and, as he lacked the power to impose peace on Najd, he had to use guile to achieve that end.

Another problem was that Kuwait and Shaikh Mubarak were suffering economically from the conflict in Najd. Mubarak was known to be the chief source of financial and material support for the al-Sa'ud forces. What has conveniently been forgotten by all, especially the Sabah, was that the real and actual financiers were the Kuwaiti people. The years of warfare had strained his finances and the finances of his small state. Back in September 1904, his chief clerk, Mula Abdullah, had complained to Knox that ' ... the Sheikh had poured out money in the interior like water and God alone knew what would be the end of it all'.[49] Knox commented that, apart from British support, Mubarak's power and prestige depended almost entirely on the Bedouin, so that he had to supply them with money and arms while they provided the men to promote his schemes and to keep danger away from Kuwait.

Mubarak's need for a more stable situation in Najd may have been the reason why, from time to time, he expressed support for Ibn Sa'ud's attempts to acquire British protection. On the face of it, a direct relationship between Ibn Sa'ud and the British would not be in Kuwait's interests as it would deprive Kuwait of her special position as an intermediary between Najd and Britain. However, the British must have seemed to Mubarak as the only real source of peace and stability. On one occasion in May 1907, when he had again asked Knox why the British did not extend their protection to Ibn Sa'ud, Mubarak added: 'It would be so good for trade and general quiet'.[50] But Britain was unlikely to risk incurring serious Ottoman hostility by declaring a protectorate in Najd, and Mubarak was therefore left to his own devices. The cost of his attempts to maintain a favourable balance in Najd were to have a serious impact on Kuwait itself.

The Financial Strains of Desert Diplomacy

The earliest indication which has come down to us of Mubarak's growing need for money is in the British record of Mubarak's private meeting with Lord Curzon during the viceroy's Gulf tour of November 1903. During the meeting, the shaikh assured the viceroy that he had broken all connections with the Turks and had also turned down approaches from both the French and the Russians. He asked Lord Curzon for some form of title or decoration and a financial allowance from the British government as a reward. Curzon thought that Mubarak made this request simply as a way of consolidating and acknowledging the present relationship with Britain, rather than as an attempt to change the relationship, but Curzon was wrong. When more detailed enquiries were made by British officials at the start of 1904, Mubarak made it clear that he wanted a very substantial subsidy indeed, and that ' ... a merely nominal allowance would not be of any use'.[51] However, it was to be more than three years before the British granted a subsidy to Mubarak, disguised as a rent for the lease on Bandar Shuwaikh. In the absence of British help, Mubarak had to step up the pressure on his own people to provide him with revenues. At the time when Britain began to collect detailed reports on Kuwait from 1905 onwards via the British agency in Kuwait, Shaikh Mubarak was starting to squeeze the economy of his small state rather hard.

The best picture we are ever likely to get of Mubarak's sources of income during the early years of his reign comes in Lorimer's *Gazetteer of the Persian Gulf*, in which the entry for Kuwait is largely based on information gathered during a visit in December 1904. Lorimer pointed out that Shaikh Mubarak did not make any distinction between his state income and his private income, and did not reveal any information about the volume of trade coming into Kuwait. A Persian merchant in Kuwait gave Lorimer an estimate of Mubarak's total income, apparently referring to 1904 itself or to an earlier year. The merchant put the total annual receipts of the shaikh at $399,000, which divided into the following main headings:

	Dollars
Mubarak's private income from his date plantations	108,000
Customs duties on imports and exports	170,000
Tax on pearl divers	60,000
Zakat tax on Bedouin flocks	25,000

Other items:—
  (rent on shops in the bazaar,
  taxes on butchers and sheep-imports,
  fines and interest on loans to merchants)   36,000

The figures do unfortunately present some difficulties. As we might expect, they confirm the great importance of the date gardens at Fao for Mubarak's finances. Indeed, he would hardly have been able to balance his books without these gardens. The figures also show the extent to which Kuwait depended on trade and the consequent revenues from customs. The small figure for revenue from *zakat* tax on the Bedouin is not surprising, in view of the difficulties involved in collecting the tax and the rather limited extent of Mubarak's base in the desert. The very low figure of $60,000 for income from the tax on pearl divers is really surprising, in view of Lorimer's estimate that the Kuwait fleet numbered 461 boats by this time, carrying a total of 9,200 men. In principle, Mubarak levied a tax equivalent to one diver's share of each boat's profits during the season, which must surely have produced a larger figure. To make matters worse, Lorimer mentions that another source had told him that the figure of $60,000 was a considerable over-estimate, and that Mubarak really only collected $29,000 a year from the tax on the pearl boats.

Lorimer's estimates cannot therefore be regarded as absolutely reliable, but they throw some light on the resources which were available to Mubarak. Lorimer also confirms that the Kuwait economy had been expanding rather fast in the years between 1896 and 1904, even despite the serious fighting in Najd and around Kuwait in 1901–2, which must have damaged the import–export trade, and even despite the ups and downs in the pearling sector. In trade, Kuwait seems to have benefited from its inclusion in June 1901 on the route of the mail steamers of the British India Company, which sailed once a week from Bombay to Basra. The introduction of a steam-ship service to Kuwait must have helped the trade with India, and especially the export of horses from Najd and Jabal Shammar to India.[52]

The pearl-fishing industry was also passing through one of its best periods in the early years of Mubarak's reign. Despite the chronic instability of the industry, the money which it generated during the first years of the century had a great effect on the small and rather rudimentary economy of Kuwait. In general, the good years seem to have outweighed the bad ones. Briefly, storms devastated the pearling fleet in 1896 and 1897, but there was a strong speculative boom in prices in 1899 in expectation of high European demand for pearls during the Paris Universal Exhibition of 1900. The boom collapsed in 1900 and prices fell. In 1901 pearls of good quantity and quality were gathered, but prices were low in 1902. The next year, 1903, was again a good year for the merchants, but in 1904 the market suffered from an overhang of unsold stocks. Thereafter 1905 and 1906 were excellent seasons but were followed by a near-catastrophic downturn in the catch in 1907 and 1908, which provoked a general economic slump in Kuwait.

We can conclude that Kuwait was expanding strongly in 1900–5, despite the fluctuations in trade and pearl fishing. During his 1904 visit, Lorimer found that house-building activity was intense, as people took up the free sites which Mubarak granted on all sides of the town and constructed houses on these sites as a commercial speculation. Lorimer ascribed this activity to the 'increasing prosperity of the place'. The administrative report which Britain's agent in Kuwait, Major Knox, submitted for the year 1906–7 confirms this picture, talking of the high level of building activity in Kuwait and claiming that the town had grown to 'four or five times' its original size. Knox may have exaggerated the rate of growth but there certainly were a lot of houses for Shaikh Mubarak to tax when in 1907 he tried to impose a levy on all buildings constructed in years. In addition, the rise in Kuwait's population seems to have overwhelmed the always limited capacity of Kuwait's fresh-water wells during periods of low rainfall. In 1908 some enterprising Kuwaitis had the idea of shipping water into Kuwait from the Shatt al-Arab, and selling it in competition with the brackish water from the depleted walls around town. Kuwaitis were apparently happy to pay for the superior quality of the imported water.

The rise in prosperity during the early years of Mubarak's reign was, of course, starting from a very low base indeed and the standard of living for most Kuwaitis remained fairly precarious. In the slump of 1907–8, caused by the failure of the pearling industry, many Kuwaitis seem to have fallen back very quickly to real poverty. The trade report of the British agent for 1909–10 shows a sharp increase in imports of tallow, when prosperity was also affected by the lack of rainfall in Najd and the decline of the export trade. The agent commented that the poorer classes in Kuwait were now being compelled to use tallow instead of ghee for cooking.

Despite these fluctuations, there were plenty of opportunities for Shaikh Mubarak to 'enhance' his revenues in order to finance his diplomacy in Najd and his growing taste for luxury. Indications of a concerted attempt to maximise the shaikh's revenues came almost as soon as the British agent started to compile regular reports in 1905. In that year, the shaikh ordered the construction of a stone customs warehouse, to store goods which had previously been left in the open. He also increased customs duties ' … in some cases to a very great extent'.[53] In 1906, the shaikh added grain-storage areas, and again increased customs duties to the point where Captain Knox believed that total customs income might have doubled. There was a further increase in import duties in 1907 and the rate of assessment was changed from a fixed duty per package or bag to a rate based on the value of the contents: this step caused real discontent amongst the merchants. In the same way, import and export duties on livestock were increased in 1907 and changed from a flat rate per animal to a percentage of the sale price. In 1908, Mubarak took personal charge of all customs receipts, ordering that payments should be made to him personally rather than passing through the customs house in the first instance. By

1913 all Kuwait's trade passed through the shaikh's warehouses in the town and any merchant who broke this rule had his goods confiscated.[54]

Quite apart from his increased levies on the external trade of Kuwait, Shaikh Mubarak took every opportunity to tax other aspects of commercial activity. In 1907, he imposed heavy taxes on the *hajj* (pilgrimage) caravans from Kuwait: T£5 on each woman's litter and T£1 on each camel rider, as well as Rs. 16 on each slave accompanying the caravan. The taxes on pilgrims were so heavy that there were virtually no Kuwaitis in the 1908 caravan.[55] As well as the pilgrimage, the shaikh struck out at the necessities of life. In 1909, there were large increases in duties charged on staples of the Kuwaiti diet such as dates and tea. In 1910, the shaikh placed a tax on between $20 and $50 per boat on the ships, which brought drinking water to Kuwait from the Shatt al-Arab.

Harder to trace is the taxation which the shaikh certainly imposed on rifles brought into Kuwait from Europe for re-export to Najd and smuggling into Persia. In 1904, Mubarak had signed a number of agreements with Britain to ban all trade in rifles, but despite his denials to British officials the trade certainly continued. By 1907 he had raised the import tax from the 1904 level of $1 to $6.

Mubarak's exactions on his people were imaginatively oppressive. In 1907, he began a census of all new houses built in Kuwait since his accession in 1896. He then ordered the owners to pay 75 per cent of the estimated value of their houses to the shaikh. If they were unable to pay, the shaikh would take over the title to the property, paying just 25 per cent of the estimated value to the owner in compensation.[56] Although the valuations were apparently set low, Captain Knox estimated that this single action had transferred at least Rs150,000 (£STG16,666) from the pockets of the townspeople to the coffers of the shaikh. This was perhaps the clearest single example of Mubarak's favourite dictum that everything in Kuwait belongs to him as his personal *mulk* (property). With some understatement, Knox commented that 'the order is generally condemned by public opinion'.[57] However, Shaikh Mubarak did not stop with the tax on houses. In May 1908 he introduced a special 'contribution' from merchants and shopkeepers for two of his own family's weddings. The first of these was the marriage of his youngest son Humud to the daughter of one of his nephews, Shaikh Sabah Ibn Muhammad, while Shaikh Sabah, at the same time, married one of Shaikh Mubarak's daughters. The second wedding, also in May 1908, was between Mubarak's grandson Abdullah Ibn Salim, and the daughter of his son, Jabir. This spate of family celebrations weighed heavily on the people of Kuwait. Although the richer merchants had already presented substantial presents to the shaikh to mark the occasion, the smaller shopkeepers and merchants also found that they were directed to contribute as well, and there were rumours of taxes being extracted from the workers on the shaikh's personal estates in Fao. The British Administration Report for April–December 1908 concluded that about T£30,000 had been collected through these levies from the people least able to afford it.[58] The pearl industry was of course an obvious target for extra taxation. Beginning in 1907 the direct levies on each pearling boat based in Kuwait were substantially increased. In 1907, Shaikh Mubarak also ordered Kuwaiti divers not to go to work in the Ceylon pearl fisheries during Kuwait's off season. Kuwaiti divers had apparently started to go to Ceylon in 1904 and the shaikh was finding that they came back to Kuwait too exhausted to work effectively during the Gulf season, with a loss of income to himself. The exactions on the pearl fleet, both in financial terms and in terms of conscription of divers and boatmen to fight in desert wars, led to the drastic decision of three leading *towashis* in August 1910 to leave Kuwait and go to Bahrain, where they approached the British to ask for protection for themselves, their *nakhodas* and sailors, so as to avoid the shaikh's constant demands for money and the conscription of men for desert service. British reports suggest that the people of Kuwait were generally sympathetic to the move, as they understood and no doubt sympathised with the problems, which the shaikh's demands for money caused to the *towashis*. The potential impact of this defection was very great, as the three *towashis* between them controlled about 250–300 pearling boats, which they were prepared to transfer to Bahrain, Dammam or any place prepared to welcome them. Partly as a result of British pressure, Shaikh Mubarak took a conciliatory line, and by October 1910 the *towashis* had returned to Kuwait. This episode gives an idea of the damage which Mubarak's aggressive and shameless financial policy was beginning to cause to the economy of Kuwait and to its major industry.

To make matters worse, Mubarak began to spend substantial sums on what can only be called personal whims. He bought new property in Ottoman territory and then in 1908 purchased a yacht. His earthly houris, unlike the heavenly variety, were costly. Soon afterwards, he bought an automobile, probably the first to be owned by a Gulf ruler. He made extensive improvements to his place and Captain Knox commented in July 1908 that the increase in his revenue had 'revealed in him a hitherto unsuspected taste for luxury and ostentatious display'.[59] In this report, Knox gave a frank and accurate estimate of the way Mubarak's financial policies were likely to develop. In his words:

> the taxes are still low, but have increased rapidly of the past years and new extortionate demands have been levied on the people. Everything points to lean years to come and it's problematical whether the Sheikh will have the strength of

mind to economise. It is far more probable that he will increase his demands on the people and drive trade out of the town. At present the people, who complain continually, look to us as their deliverers. It will be an unpleasant moment for us when they arrive at a juster view of the situation and realise that it is our support chiefly that has enabled and will enable Sheikh Mubarak's despotisms to flourish and taught him that he need no longer rely on the affections of his people and their confidence in his strength, wealth and justice.[60]

Knox was wrong in only one respect. There does not seem to have been any anti-British element in the undoubted souring of the political atmosphere in Kuwait in the later years of Mubarak's reign. Indeed, apart from complaining, most people of Kuwait were in no position to do much. Only the very wealthiest such as the *towashis* could afford to take the drastic step of deserting Kuwait altogether. Even the three *towashis* who made such a move in 1910 were worried about possible retaliation against members of their families by the shaikh. The fact was that Shaikh Mubarak continued the old tradition of tight control over the population and an authoritarian approach to problems of law and order. We have already seen that nineteenth-century travellers agreed that Kuwait was the best-ordered and least crime-prone town in the region. From the first day of his rule in 1896, when he announced his accession to the leading men of Kuwait with a drawn sword across his knee, Mubarak made little secret of the fact that he would back his rule by force if necessary. This brought the benefit of a general absence of crime and swift punishment of any crimes that did occur. As Knox commented in December 1908, 'Whatever may be said of his methods, Sheikh Mubarak has the town well in hand.' In 1911, Knox's successor Captain W. H. Shakespear wrote that 'the town continues under the strong hand of Shaikh Mubarak to be the most peaceful and best governed in the Gulf.'[61]

In the early years of his rule, Shaikh Mubarak seems to have been able to make his authoritarian rule acceptable to his people by regular consultations with the leaders of the community, in the traditional manner of the Gulf. In later years, we get the impression that he felt secure enough to dispense with consultation, and to become increasingly arbitrary and self-indulgent. This tendency was to create problems for Shaikh Mubarak and for Kuwait during the conflict which broke out at the start of 1910 against Mubarak's old ally, Shaikh Sa'dun of the Muntafiq.

The Breach with the Muntafiq

Mubarak's alliance with Shaikh Sa'dun of the important Muntafiq tribe, back in 1899, had been for many years an important element in Mubarak's desert strategy. With the help of the Muntafiq, he was able to confront the Ibn Rashid and even to weather the difficult period which followed Mubarak's defeat at al-Sarif in 1901, when the al-Sa'ud were unable to provide much help. The alliance with Sa'dun was to prove no more durable than other desert alignments. In late 1909, the split became final, when Shaikh Sa'dun granted sanctuary to Shaikh Ibn Hallaf of the al-Saif, an important sub-section of the Thaffir tribe. Shaikh Ibn Hallaf had attacked a Kuwaiti merchant in the region of al-Hafar as the merchant was returning from a trading trip to Najd. To make matters worse Shaikh Ibn Hallaf raided some Kuwaiti camels in the al-Batin depression shortly after receiving sanctuary with the Muntafiq. Mubarak then asked Sa'dun, as the protector of Ibn Hallaf, to return the looted property to its Kuwaiti owners. Sa'dun refused the request, and rubbed the humiliation in by himself raiding one group of Kuwaiti tribesmen and trying to raid another. By March 1910, the total accumulated loot was 300 sheep and some camels.[62]

The enmity between Mubarak and Sa'dun seems to have started before 1909. The British consul in Basra blamed it on 'some disagreement in commercial matters', which might refer to an incident in the summer of 1907. At that time, Mubarak had tried to buy some property near Fao from Shaikh Sa'dun. Mubarak had paid a deposit of T£500 to Sa'dun, but when the Ottoman government refused to sanction the sale Sa'dun did not return the deposit to Mubarak. Whatever the cause of the split, it had become serious by the start of 1910, and early in February 1910 Mubarak held a *majlis* with the leading men of Kuwait, where it was decided to mount an expedition against 'desert offenders'. Mubarak did not at this stage announce the identity of these offenders, and rumours pointed to the Muntafiq, the Ajman and the Thaffir, or even the people of Shammar. Whatever the target, Mubarak conceived the expedition on a large scale. Britain's agent, Captain Shakespear, said that nothing on this scale had been planned since the expedition, which ended with the disaster at Sarif in March 1901. Everyone had to contribute. The town of Kuwait itself had to provide 2,000 men, and further levies were made from the Bedouin tribes. The leading merchants were required to provide between 160 and 200 *khabras* (tents), each housing seven men and five camels. Even the prostitutes of the town had to supply coffee pots for the expeditionary army.[63]

As the preparations went ahead, it became clear that Mubarak's extortionary tactics of demanding as much money as possible from his people had acted against him. Shakespear commented that the expedition was unpopular in the town, mainly because of the heavy expenses it entailed on all, and also because of an understandable fear that the shaikh would use it as a pretext for further tax increases. At this stage, Shakespear believed that the Ajman were the most likely target. His reasoning was that Ibn Sa'ud had agreed to join Mubarak's expedition and, while Ibn Sa'ud certainly had a score to settle with the Ajman, he had no known grudge against Sa'dun and the Muntafiq. Captain Shakespear had already heard that the shaikh had been attempting to use the Najdi leader against the Ajman, ' ... so that if anybody's fingers should be burnt in the process they will not be Kuwait (Mubarak's) fingers'.[64] The Ajman also thought that they were the target of the expedition and, according to Shakespear, were 'simply terrified' by the prospect. They came to Kuwait to seek Mubarak's forgiveness for all the offences they had committed against Kuwaitis, and offered to make good any property which they had looted. When Ibn Sa'ud arrived in Kuwait at the end of February with his contingent of 3,000 men, he was able to restore peace between Mubarak and the Ajman, and even persuaded them to join him and the Kuwaiti forces on the expedition.

In mid-March, the force assembled at Jahra and marched out in search of Shaikh Sa'dun and his followers. Within a few days, the entire force was streaming back to Kuwait in defeat. The expedition had met Sa'dun on 16 March 1910 between al-Rakhaimia, Waguba and Zaraibat. Sa'dun had the advantage in numbers and quality of fighting men. He struck at the right wing of the Kuwait force, which was mainly composed of townsmen who quickly broke under the attack of the experienced desert raiders. The rout was only saved from becoming a tragedy by the speed with which the Kuwaiti contingent raced from the battlefield, and by the fact that Ibn Sa'ud was able to hold his contingent together and to organise a valiant covering retreat.

Despite this serious humiliation, Mubarak ordered the preparation of a second expedition, even larger than the first. He placed an embargo on the sale of firearms to foreigners, and seized the stocks of arms dealers in Kuwait. Those merchants who had been ordered to provide a *khabra* for seven men and five camels were now ordered to provide one for ten men and seven camels. This time, instead of sacrificing their coffee pots, the prostitutes had to contribute their bedding. Ibn Sa'ud apparently gave Mubarak permission to conscript into his force the men in any caravans which arrived in Kuwait from Najd. Captain Shakespear believed that Mubarak was planning a force of about 15,000 men.[65]

The preparations had an effect on Shaikh Sa'dun, who decided in mid-April to open negotiations for a compromise with Mubarak. At the same time, Humud Ibn Swait, the shaikh of the Thaffir, came into Kuwait to seek Mubarak's friendship. Mubarak rejected the approaches from Sa'dun, and told Humud to return to his camp. Even so, despite the size of the force which he was assembling, Mubarak hesitated to act. His explanation to Shakespear was that he was waiting for the hot weather, which would weaken Sa'dun's largely horse-mounted army, a force which was more dependent on water than the camel mounted Kuwaitis and Bedouin. Mubarak would also have been aware of reports that Sa'dun's forces were superior to the Kuwaiti expedition in terms of numbers and fighting ability. To make matters worse for Mubarak, his most effective military ally, Ibn Sa'ud, had to return to Riyadh in the middle of May in order to deal with a military threat from the Ibn Rashid whose forces had successfully raided the Western borders of Ibn Sa'ud's territory. Ibn Rashid had left letters announcing to the people of Qasim that Ibn Sa'ud had now deserted them for Shaikh Mubarak, so that they would have to submit to Ibn Rashid's control. Without the participation of Ibn Sa'ud, Mubarak must have appreciated that he risked another defeat in the desert on the scale of the disaster at Sarif in 1901, which was something he certainly could not afford. Indeed, a defeat on that scale would probably mean the end of his rule in Kuwait, as practically all sections of the population were already unhappy about the strain on the economy from the maintenance of large military forces.

During May 1910, there were rumours that Shaikh Mubarak now only intended to keep his force in being for the sake of appearances, and that he would disband it as soon as he found a plausible excuse. Disbanding the force would also present a risk to Mubarak, who needed to maintain his reputation as an effective ruler. As he explained to Shakespear at the end of May, if he gave the impression that Kuwait could be raided with impunity, the country would be ' ... open to the raids of any large force of Bedouins, and so all security would be destroyed'.[66] Understandably enough, Mubarak was crippled with indecision throughout the summer of 1910, and his forces remained idle in Kuwait, but some tribes and sections of tribes in the Kuwait confederation became frustrated at the idleness and lack of opportunity to plunder. These Bedouin slipped away from Kuwait to mount raids on their own account. These raids were extremely embarrassing for Mubarak, as the targets were often tribes faithful to him. For example, rumours spread during the summer that the Jiblan section of the Mutair, who had gone raiding despite Mubarak's protests, planned to raid pro-Kuwaiti tribes. Some of the Ajman actually did attack 'Awazim of Kuwait near the wells at Wafra. By early August, the men from the Najd caravans who had been impressed into the Kuwaiti army were demanding that the great expedition should start soon, or that they be allowed to go home.

There can be no doubt that the presence of this large force in Kuwait during the summer of 1910 seriously strained the economy. Shakespear put the size of the force at about 12,000 men from the town, plus the tribesmen.[67] He believed that it was costing Mubarak $60,000 a month to keep the force in being. A ten-day raid could cost the shaikh himself about $330,000 and a further $351,000 to the town as a whole. Shakespear added that these figures related purely to the Kuwait-based contingent, and did not include contingents provided by Ibn Sa'ud but paid for by Shaikh Mubarak.

The direct costs listed by Shakespear did not reflect the full extent of the burden the expeditionary force placed on the Kuwaiti economy. Many of the townsmen who had been forced to join the expedition were pearl fishers, who would normally have left Kuwait in May to spend the summer fishing. To keep his army up to strength, Mubarak simply announced in May that the pearl fleet would not be allowed to leave Kuwait: a drastic step, which threatened the main source of income for most of the population. Mubarak later softened his position and allowed the fishermen to leave as long as they found and paid for substitutes to take their place in the expeditionary force. The measure had little effect, as most pearl fishers were in their usual pre-season state of poverty and so had to continue to wait around in the expeditionary army. Shakespear sadly observed that the town was now quiet and almost empty. If Mubarak maintained Kuwait on a war footing, he feared that 'there won't be much capital left in the place for trade'.[68] The fears which Knox had expressed in 1908 on an anti-British reaction on the part of the population were unfounded. Far from blaming the British for supporting their extortionate shaikh, a number of Kuwaitis approached the British Agency to ask about obtaining protection from the British government. As Shakespear put it, there was little chance of a rising 'for the simple reason that there is no leader and the whole population lives in such mortal terror of the Sheikh.'[69]

So Mubarak did not face a full-scale political revolt during the summer of 1910. However, he did provoke something almost as dangerous: the three leading *towashis*, who controlled a very large part of the pearling fleet and who decided to abandon Kuwait altogether and to seek permission to settle in another part of the Gulf, where they would be free from Shaikh Mubarak's *zulum* (tyranny). This potential body-blow to the Kuwait economy was the event which forced Mubarak to see reason, and to abandon his desert expedition. In a sense, it was the second major crisis of his post-1899 reign, comparable with the defeat at Sarif in 1901.

Even though Mubarak had relaxed his ban on the departure of the pearl fleet in May 1910, his requirement that all pearl fishers from the expeditionary force should pay for substitute soldiers meant that only about half the normal number of boats had managed to sail by the end of May. The three leading *towashis,* Hillal Mutairi, Shamlan ibn Said and Ibrahim ibn Mudaf, together with many of their *nakhodas* and fishermen, left Kuwait with most of their valuables secretly stashed on board their ships, in preparation for abandoning Kuwait. In late August, at the end of the season, the three *towashis* kept their boats on the pearl banks instead of returning to Kuwait. For some days about 200 boats stayed at anchor at Ras Abu Ali, debating what to do next. About 17 of the Kuwaiti boats went to Bahrain to discuss the chances of settling there. Others stayed on the banks, arguing that it would be better to approach the Ottoman *qaimaqam* at Qatif for permission to settle in Dammam. Their reasoning was that the Ottomans were less likely than Shaikh Isa of Bahrain to yield to pressure from Shaikh Mubarak and to order them back to Kuwait.

By acting in this way, the *towashis* were taking a desperate risk. Their families remained in Kuwait, and they told the British in Bahrain that it was fear of reprisals by Shaikh Mubarak against their families, which prevented them from writing directly to the shaikh to try to settle the dispute. In their words, 'it was inadvisable to expose particular persons to the shaikh's vengeance'. The British political agent in Bahrain recorded in his diary for the week to 9 September 1910 that two of the *towashis,* Hillal Mutairi and Ibrahim ibn Mudaf, were convinced that Mubarak would incite some Bedouin to murder them in the desert or even in Kuwait itself if they returned, even if they had previously offered safe-conduct. The general view in Bahrain was that 'a man who would kill his brother would not hesitate to do anything.' When he heard of their fears, Mubarak told Shakespear that they were being foolish, as he (Mubarak) 'had never killed anyone in Kuwait'. It soon became clear that the protest of the *towashis* against the conscription of their men and against the shaikh's financial exactions struck a chord with most of the people of Kuwait. British reports show that the news of the defection was received 'with great joy and satisfaction in all quarters' in Kuwait. There were many who said that, if the defection was successful, they would follow the example of the *towashis* and leave Kuwait. Even Shaikh Mubarak's blind son Nasir apparently 'much regretted his father's action and tyrannical treatment of the people.'[70]

The defection of the *towashis,* against a background of real popular discontent in Kuwait is best seen as a Kuwaiti version of the traditional tendency of desert tribes in the Gulf region to desert one ruler if he made unreasonable demands and transfer their men and loyalty to another. Tribal defections of this kind were a feature of life in Trucial Oman (now the United Arab Emirates) even after 1945. In late 1968, a group of the al-Za'b tribe left Jazirat al-Hamra in the Emirate of Ras al-Khaimah and migrated to Abu Dhabi because of a deadlock in their dispute with their ruler, Shaikh Saqr of Ras al-Khaimah.[71] However, migrations of this kind were serious steps and often other rulers would hesitate to grant protection and accommodation to a defecting tribe or sub-tribe because of the risk of serious political consequences. Shaikh Mubarak certainly wrote strong letters to Shaikh Isa of Bahrain in the summer of 1910 warning him against allowing the pearl fishers and *towashis* to settle in Bahrain. The defection of a tribal grouping was generally a blow to the prestige and power of the ruler who was deserted: the defection of the three *towashis*, who between them were thought to control between 250 and 300 boats, was certainly a major threat to Mubarak's economic base. We have already pointed to the way in which the pearl fishing culture of Kuwait adapted many Bedouin ideals of behaviour and heroism to the conditions of the fisheries. In this light, we can perhaps see the *towashis* as imitating a Bedouin style of conduct.

Fortunately for Kuwait and for his own position as ruler, Shaikh Mubarak quickly saw that he had gone too far by provoking the defection of the *towashis*. He was, therefore, unusually receptive to the advice he received from Shakespear about the need to conciliate the *towashis*. More importantly, he appreciated at once that he could no longer afford to strangle Kuwait's economy by maintaining the expeditionary force in being. On 30 August 1910, the day after he received the first detailed report of the defection, he ordered the disbandment of the main forces waiting at Jahra. The order to disband the expedition was given 'quietly', as Mubarak apparently did not want the news to spread too fast into the desert. In mid-September, Mubarak sent his son, Salim, to Bahrain to negotiate with the leading *towashis*. The *towashis* asked for full safe-conduct and guarantees that there would be no reprisals. Salim answered that he had no powers to negotiate any safe-conduct, but he was able to persuade Ibrahim ibn Mudaf and Shamlan ibn Said to return with him to Kuwait on 13 September. Hillal Mutairi stayed in Bahrain, holding out for a full promise of safety. Only when Shaikh Mubarak journeyed to Bahrain, many months later in July 1911 to see Hillal, did the last rebel *towash* agree to return.[72] Even then, he refused to travel back to Kuwait in the company of Shaikh Mubarak. When he did finally return, Mubarak paid him the unusual honour of calling on him to welcome him back: the honours were certainly with Hillal at the end of this episode.

The action of the *towashis* was indeed a turning point for Mubarak, forcing him to abandon his plans for a large expedition into the desert against Sa'dun. The prospect of losing a large part of his pearl-fishing population also seems to have made him, for a time at least, more careful about the feelings of his subjects. On 12 September, Shakespear wrote that he had heard that Mubarak 'is now most gracious in returning salutes of passers-by', but the old high-handedness and greed soon resurfaced in his inept handling of the dispersal of his expeditionary force. When the members of the expedition returned to Kuwait from Jahra, Mubarak only allowed the larger merchants to take away their camels and rifles, and held on to the animals and weapons of the less important members of the force. Only when a man called Jasim Budai, who enjoyed Mubarak's confidence, explained the ill-feeling which this step had created did Mubarak allow everyone to recover their property.

Now that he had abandoned his plans for an expedition against the Muntafiq, Mubarak faced the prospect of an attack on Kuwait by Sa'dun, with possible support from the Ottomans. The Ottoman involvement on Sa'dun's side may have been provoked by members of Mubarak's own tribes. In July 1910, some Kuwaitis of the Rashayidah and Tuala tribes had raided a few camels, donkeys and sheep belonging to the people of Zubair. The Ottoman Vali of Basra protested to Shaikh Mubarak, and demanded that the raiders should be punished and the property returned. Mubarak gave a rather unsatisfactory reply, saying that ' ... though he had influence with the Bedouin, he was not the Sheikh of all the tribes round Basra and Koweit'.[73] However, by way of contracting this statement, he did return some of the livestock and then, in August, Mubarak learned that Shaikh Sa'dun had moved his main force to Bargasaiah, only an hour from Zubair. This was an area into which he would not normally have ventured without the permission of the authorities in Basra. Shakespear learned that Sa'dun was indeed contemplating an attack on Kuwait, and at once suspected Ottoman involvement. Indeed, Mubarak told him that he had learned from an old and trusted friend, who was a member of the Council of the Vali of Baghdad, that the Ottoman authorities in Basra were using the conflict with the Muntafiq to induce Shaikh Mubarak to seek Turkish protection and to break his links with Britain. Mubarak told Shakespear that he was confident that he could deal with Sa'dun on his own, but that he was worried about the Turks. By the middle of January 1911, about four-and-a-half months after the disbandment of the Kuwaiti expeditionary force, the threat from Sa'dun had not abated, and Mubarak asked the British if a warship could be stationed off Kuwait until the crisis had passed.[74]

Shakespear strongly endorsed the request for a warship, arguing that Mubarak was in fact being subjected to continual Ottoman harassment and intrigue. At the same time, Shakespear pointed out, the Ottomans were offering Mubarak an easy way out of his difficulties. All he had to do, in order for the harassment to cease, was to acknowledge Turkish sovereignty, either by agreeing that he or his sons should take Turkish nationality, or by accepting an Ottoman subsidy. The only way to stop this Ottoman pressure on Kuwait was for the British government to make plain to the Turkish government that it was aware of Ottoman aims, and would not allow the Ottomans to disturb British relations with Shaikh Mubarak. In response to Shakespear's arguments, HMS *Philomel* arrived in Kuwait at the end of January 1991, but before the British warship arrived a peace settlement had been signed. Shaikh Mubarak seems to have realised that the continuation of the conflict with Sa'dun was not worth the cost to himself or to Kuwait. In fact, the conflict with Sa'dun, which ended in January 1911, was Mubarak's last initiative of any importance beyond the borders of Kuwait. This chapter of his reign was to be dominated by the question of the definition of these borders, and this was a matter which turned out to be totally beyond the shaikh's control.

5

Kuwait and the Baghdad Railway Project

The history of the project to build a railway from Constantinople to Baghdad and the Gulf is a complicated story. Five great powers were involved in a struggle for commercial and political influence: Britain, Germany, France, Russia and the Ottoman Empire. The Ottoman Empire was constrained by its economic weakness, and by the fact that its public debt was under international management. This weakness meant that the other Great Powers had ample scope for pressure on the Ottomans, and for rivalry between themselves. The discussions about kilometric guarantees and percentages of participation in fact conceal a hard-fought battle for strategic advantage. In this battle, Kuwait was generally a fairly minor consideration: by the time that the 1914 War halted the project, the line was still a long way from the Gulf, but the negotiations on the project did lead, as a by-product, to the establishment of Kuwait's practical independence from the Ottoman Empire and the first official definition of Kuwait's territory.

The negotiations also revealed the fundamental weakness of Shaikh Mubarak in his dealings with his Great Power associates. In the years after 1899, he had used his new-found friendship with Britain to manoeuvre Britain into acting as the protector of Kuwait against the Ottomans and against Ibn Rashid. The result had been a great gain for Kuwait in terms of political and diplomatic freedom of action, but there was always the risk that his new British friends would seek a comprehensive settlement of their differences with the Ottomans over the head of Mubarak, in a sense which was not to his liking. The railway project led to just such a settlement, involving serious potential dangers for Kuwait's independence. Only the outbreak of war in 1914 saved Mubarak from these dangers.

The Anatolian Railway Company

The Russian Count Kapnist's railway concession, which had caused such a stir in Whitehall and in the Gulf during 1897–99, had come to nothing. Very soon after the agreement between Mubarak and the British in January 1899 (which Kapnist had unwittingly done so much to provoke), it became clear that the concession had no serious support in Russia or anywhere else. As we have suggested, the entire project may have been no more than an attempt by the much more serious German-backed project, the Anatolian Railway Company, to distract British attention from its own designs.

The company had been established in 1889, and by December 1899 it had received a preliminary concession. The concession granted the right in principle to extend the company's railway (which had already reached Konya) to Baghdad, and beyond Baghdad to Basra and the Gulf.[1] However, the German-backed company suffered from a serious shortage of finance. The British government was, therefore, confident that the German promoters of the railway would have to call on Britain for assistance. Even before the company signed its preliminary concession, the British ambassador in Constantinople anticipated that there would be long and difficult negotiations, which would quite possibly lead to a demand for British financial co-operation. The company faced two problems. Firstly, the project could only succeed on the basis of 'kilometric guarantees' in the form of a subsidy from the Ottoman government to assist in the construction and subsequent operation of the railway. However, the Ottoman government could not possibly generate the money for these subsidies from its internal resources, and would have to increase tariff revenues. Under the terms of its agreements with the European powers, this could only be done with the consent of the main powers. The second problem was that the German company could not raise sufficient capital on its own. It would therefore need to turn to foreign sources of finance, which would necessarily involve British and French lenders. British and French funds could only be obtained for the project if the governments of Britain and France approved of the project.

The British attitude to the project in the years immediately after 1899 was conditioned by the belief that Britain could control the project by its ability to control the Ottoman customs increases. Kuwait was also an integral part of the project from the beginning. Even before the Anatolian Railway Company signed its preliminary concession in December 1899, the company sent a commission to examine the possible routes for the railway. The head of the commission, Herr von Kapp, believed that the success of the project depended on access to a port on the Arabian Gulf, and the commission's engineers had concluded that Kuwait was an essential part of the scheme. They specified Kathama Bay, at the western end of Kuwait Bay, as the preferred site for the terminus.

As early as 7 January 1900, Britain's ambassador in Constantinople, Sir N. O'Conor, was able to report to London that Kathama Bay was the likely terminus. He also warned that Germany would probably try to gain access to Kathama Bay by direct negotiations with the Ottoman authorities, going over the head of Shaikh Mubarak of Kuwait. Later in January, O'Conor suggested that the promoters of the Anatolian Railway project should be given a 'friendly warning' of Britain's interest in Kuwait. He argued against any formal notification of the details of Britain's relationship with Kuwait (i.e. the agreement of January 1899), as he feared that publication of the agreement could provoke an international scramble for influence in the northern Gulf. In his view, Britain would be badly placed in such a scramble, because of the loss of prestige caused by the disastrous performance of the British Army in the opening campaigns of the South African war.[2]

We should remember that, although Britain had not made the 1899 agreement with Shaikh Mubarak public by January 1900, the special relationship between Britain and Kuwait must already have been known in European and Ottoman chanceries. The strong warnings which the British Embassy had given to the Ottoman Foreign Ministry during September 1899 about Ottoman plans to establish a customs house in Kuwait demonstrated that Britain was keenly interested in Kuwait and was alert to any plans which might compromise Kuwaiti independence. If more proof were needed, the Ottomans and presumably the Germans would have received reports from Basra and from the desert around Kuwait of Mubarak's boasting in the summer of 1899 about his new friendship with Britain. Perhaps because the 1899 agreement was no longer a real secret, the British government seems to have ignored O'Conor's warning, and to have decided that the time had come to disclose the 1899 agreement to the Ottomans and Germans. In April 1900, O'Conor revealed to the German ambassador in Constantinople, Baron von Marschall, the full sense of the 1899 agreement. The German ambassador's reply casts light on the German government's attitude towards the railway project. On the other hand, the ambassador mentioned that Kuwait was in Germany's view part of the Ottoman Empire. On the other hand, he conceded that the Anatolian Railway Company could not afford to provoke ill-feeling in Britain, as this might prevent the participation of badly-needed British capital in the project. Equally tactfully, O'Conor concluded the conversation by saying that Britain did not want to disturb the status quo in the region, but that Shaikh Mubarak was no longer a free agent when it came to making grants of territory.

Also in April 1900, O'Conor explained to the Ottoman foreign minister that Britain did not want to interfere with the status quo in the Gulf region or with the sultan's authority, but that Britain could not 'view with indifference' any agreements which gave another power special rights or privileges over territory belonging to the Shaikh of Kuwait, 'with whom Her Majesty's Government had certain Agreements'. Without spelling out the details, O'Conor had therefore revealed the main point of the January 1899 agreement to the Ottomans.

For more than a year, the British initiatives of April 1900 were enough to stabilise the diplomatic position in respect of Kuwait, although there was some alarm in London during the summer of 1900 over reports that the Anatolian Railway Company was already preparing to construct a pier on Kuwaiti territory. In July 1901, Kuwait again became an issue in relations between Britain and Germany, when Dr Rosen of the German Foreign Office at a meeting with a senior British Foreign Office official objected to a remark describing Shaikh Mubarak as 'technically a subject of the Sultan but enjoying a considerable measure of independence'. Dr Rosen said that in Germany's view Mubarak was 'merely a subject of the Sultan'. To make matters worse, the Ottoman government began to suspect during the summer of 1901 that Britain would soon declare a protectorate over Kuwait. This was, after all, the time of the stand-off between the Ottoman warship *Zohaf* and the British ship HMS *Perseus* in Kuwait harbour. So, on the 29 August 1901, the British government received two rather unwelcome communications about Kuwait: the Ottoman Foreign Ministry pointedly asked if Britain was intending to establish a protectorate, and the German government stated through its Embassy in London that a British protectorate over Kuwait would be contrary to the Treaty of Berlin of 1878, and that Germany would be compelled to regard any protectorate as an 'unfriendly act' in view of German interest in Kuwait as the future terminus of the Anatolian Railway.

We have already described how Britain managed to defuse the potential conflict with the Ottoman Empire over Kuwait by means of the exchange of telegrams between London and Constantinople of 9 and 11 September 1901. Briefly, the Ottoman government promised in this exchange that it would not send troops to Kuwait and would maintain the status quo in Kuwait, as long as the British did not occupy Kuwait or establish a British protectorate. As far as the railway project was concerned, this informal agreement to preserve the status quo greatly strengthened Britain's diplomatic hand in its dealings with

Germany. The foreign secretary, Lord Lansdowne, told the German ambassador in London during September that 'where minor Eastern states were
concerned, it was not unusual to find that they owed a divided allegiance to
more than one Power.' This effectively rebuffed Dr Rosen's claim during July
that Shaikh Mubarak was 'merely a subject of the Sultan'. In fact, the German
Foreign Ministry had during September already submitted a memorandum
on the railway question to the British Foreign Office. The memorandum can
only be described as very conciliatory towards Britain, since it included the
following points:

1. Kuwait's only importance to Germany was as the proposed terminus for the
   Baghdad Railway.
2. When the time came for the Railway Company to purchase land in Kuwait
   for a railway terminus and landing-place, the Manager of the Company would
   be instructed to 'come to an understanding' with the British government.

A few weeks later, in mid-October, the German ambassador spoke to the
British foreign secretary, confirming these important assurances and saying
that, whenever the railway was constructed, it was important for Germany to
find 'peaceful condition of things' in the northern Gulf.

The exchanges of 1900–1 between Britain and Germany had therefore gone
in Britain's favour. Without giving widespread publicity to the January 1899
agreement, and without provoking an international scramble for influence of
the type which O'Conor had feared, Britain had secured Ottoman agreement
to a status quo which recognised Britain's special interest in Kuwait, and had
also secured a German undertaking that the Anatolian Railway Company would
not try to obtain land in Kuwait without a prior understanding with Britain.
Britain's success was largely due to the fact that the German government and
the German banks and companies involved in the railway project could not
afford a direct quarrel with Britain. As we have seen, it was generally felt that
only Britain could provide the capital resources to build the railway. In addition, German companies were aware that the railway itself could not succeed
commercially if it was seen as a purely German project. In February 1900, the
directors of Germany's mighty Deutsche Bank told Mr W. A. Buchanan (a
partner in the leading British trading house Gray, Mackenzie and Company)
that ' they were keenly desirous to interest the principal European Powers in
the undertaking, with a view to making the railway a neutral highway, and so
(to) avoid the international jealousies which are certain to arise if it were to
remain a purely German enterprise.'[3]

On the British side, we should not assume that sensitivity about Kuwait meant that Britain was opposed to the railway project in principle. Far from it, the general inclination in British government circles was to regard the construction of the railway as beneficial to British interests, provided that no other European power had absolute control over the project. In December 1899, Lord Salisbury and Sir N. O'Conor had agreed that the construction of the railway would tend to strengthen the Ottoman Empire both politically and economically.[4] In their view, Britain would benefit from a strong and well-disposed Ottoman Empire, which could support British interests on the flank of any Russian moves to threaten Persia or India. Indeed, as Russia was still the main worry for Britain in the Near East, O'Conor argued that internationalisation of the railway project to include participation by Germany or France was the best way to forestall any Russian objections to the project or Russian retaliation against British interests in Persia and the Gulf.

In January 1902, the Sublime Porte awarded a 99-year concession to the Anatolian Railway Company. This provided for a kilometric guarantee of 16,500 francs per kilometre, to be paid out of the tithes on the various *sanjaks*. The agreement gave the company rights with regard to the use of public lands, minerals, navigation and other tax and customs concessions. The route of the railway was to be down the Tigris Valley to Baghdad, and then down to Basra, with a branch line to Zubair and another line from Basra down to the Gulf. Probably, in view of the earlier British protests, the concession left the exact location of the Gulf terminus to be decided in the future. As for the financing of the project, negotiations between British, German and French financial groups during 1902 and early 1903 reached a broad agreement that the financiers of the three countries would each receive 25 per cent of the equity capital of the new railway company, which would be created to build and operate the railway. The remaining 25 per cent would go to the original Anatolian Railway Company and to other countries interested in the project. It must be noted that the British financial consortium was only prepared to participate in the project if the British government gave very substantial support to the project. At a meeting with the British foreign secretary in February 1903, the British consortium, led by Sir Clinton Dawkins and Sir Ernest Cassel, obtained an agreement that the British government would pay the railway company a subsidy for carrying the Indian mails on the line, and would agree to changes in the Ottoman customs tariff so as to increase the revenues available for loan guarantees. The British foreign secretary also agreed to give assistance in obtaining a terminus on the Gulf, 'at or near Kuwait'.[5] The record of this meeting shows that the British government was indeed keen for the project to go ahead with British participation.

However, the government soon found that it was badly out of step with British public opinion on the matter. When news of the talks on financing the railway leaked out in April 1903, there was a furious outcry from the anti-German elements of the British press. The British government immediately broke off the contacts with the financial consortium and, after a brief attempt to defend its involvement in the project, abandoned all support for the railway on 23 April 1903.

The Second Phase of the Railway Project: Britain Obtains a Lease on Bandar Shuwaikh

The British government apparently thought that its decision to withdraw support for the Anatolian Railway Company project in early 1903 would signal the end of the project for a long time to come. There was an assumption in London that the project could only go ahead on the basis of an adjustment of Ottoman customs revenues to provide the funds for loan guarantees and, such an adjustment would require British consent under the 1881 agreement on the Ottoman Public Debt. To the surprise of the British, the Germans managed to finance the first stages of railway construction by loans, which were guaranteed simply by the existing Ottoman tariffs. The German task was made easier by the fact that the first stages of the line involved relatively easy country between Konya and Eregli. By the start of 1905, the line's builders faced the far more difficult and expensive task of cutting a route through the Taurus mountains. For this, the London capital markets would clearly play a vital role.

In May 1905, O'Conor in Constantinople learned that the Germans would shortly approach Britain again to ask for financial backing for the railway. The German strategy this time would not be to involve Britain in an internationalised line, but instead to offer the British exclusive control of the southern section of the line, running from Baghdad to the Gulf. O'Conor saw at once that there were strong arguments for accepting an offer of this kind, as it now seemed likely that the railway would be constructed sooner or later, whether or not Britain was involved. The old argument that Britain would be able to influence the project through its control of the Ottoman customs tariffs or through the provision of capital could no longer be taken for granted.[6]

The international situation in 1905 looked very different from that which had prevailed when the Anatolian Railway Company first submitted its request for a concession. Britain's relations with Germany were now more tense, and her relations with France and Russia were correspondingly better, as Europe moved towards the pattern of alliances of 1914. In addition, the Ottoman Empire was starting to show signs of the more aggressive policy in the Gulf region, which would develop after the removal of Sultan Abdülhamid in 1909 and the triumph of the military wing of the 'Young Turks'. In the earlier years, Britain had wanted to gain access to the project primarily so as to render it neutral in terms of international politics. The emphasis after 1905 was, above all, on safeguarding Britain's strategic and commercial influence in the Gulf and, in due course, preserving the existence and effective independence of Kuwait itself from Ottoman and German designs.

However, before the Germans could make an offer to Britain on the lines which O'Conor anticipated, the British political agent in Kuwait came up with an idea which was to change the rules of the game as far as Kuwait was concerned. In November 1905, shortly after returning to Kuwait from his six-month absence, Captain Knox learned of a report by Captain Hemming of the Indian survey ship 'investigator'. During his work in the northern Gulf, Captain Hemming had found a sheltered deep-water anchorage at Bandar Shuwaikh, a few miles along the shore of Kuwait Bay and to the south-west of Kuwait town. Hemming saw Bandar Shuwaikh as the natural harbour for Kuwait, and also as the best location for a railway station if the railway ever came to Kuwait. Knox passed the news on to the British resident in Bushire, Percy Cox, and stressed that with fairly minor improvements the water near the site could accommodate fully-laden ocean-going steamers. In Knox's view, the best course would be to purchase 'a considerable plot of land' from Shaikh Mubarak. An excuse for the purchase could be the need for a berth for the steam-powered launch which the agency planned to acquire, but the importance of the site would, of course, be far greater than a simple berth for a launch.[7]

Knox's report to Bushire fell on receptive ears. Sir Percy Cox knew that in the spring of 1905 Britain's Committee of Imperial Defence had sent a British officer, Captain E. W. S. Mahon of the Royal Engineers, to the northern Gulf to report on the possible locations for a terminus for the Baghdad–Gulf railway. Mahon's report of July 1905 had recommended Bandar Shuwaikh as the best location in Kuwait.[8] So Cox immediately sent Knox's suggestion to London, adding his approval for the idea as long as right over Bandar Shuwaikh could be acquired without 'attracting attention'. Cox's communication to the Government of India was sent in November 1905; this did not authorise an approach to Shaikh Mubarak until September of the following year. The main reason for the delay seems to have been a warning from O'Conor in February 1906 that the step might arouse Turkish suspicions and lead to a violation of the status quo. O'Conor's objections seem to have been overruled only after pressure from the Admiralty who, on the basis of Mahon's report, expressed great enthusiasm for the idea of acquiring Bandar Shuwaikh.

On the morning of 6 September 1906, Knox raised the question of Bandar Shuwaikh with Shaikh Mubarak, who was about to leave for a week's visit to Fao. Knox told Mubarak that the Government of India was about to provide the agency with a steam launch. As the beaches near the town were not suitable for the boat, the government would like to buy a strip of the shore at Bandar Shuwaikh for a pier and coal shed and quarters for the crew. The shaikh expressed little interest in the property and seemed more concerned that the political agent's new steam launch would outshine his own new steam yacht, which was about to arrive from India. Knox reassured him on this point and he agreed that, when he returned from Fao, he would visit the site with Knox and settle the arrangements.

Knox raised the subject of Bandar Shuwaikh again on 29 September, when Shaikh Mubarak visited the agency. This time, Mubarak was evasive on the question of the price he would require for the land. He also emphasised the number of approaches he had received and refused in the past, including one from the Germans, which was backed up by a letter from the sultan. Knox soon saw that Mubarak had a good idea of the real reason for the British enquiries, as the shaikh suddenly pointed out that Bandar Shuwaikh was an ideal place for warships and large cargo steamers to come close to the shore. Knox, of course, denied that Britain had any such intentions, and repeated that he only wanted a small plot for a pier and a coal shed. He guessed that Mubarak was seeking 'a large sum of money for the concession during his life time, and with the ulterior object of enlisting (British) sympathies and influence on behalf of his port as a terminus for the railway.'[9]

Negotiations between Knox and Mubarak continued into 1907. In November 1906, Mubarak told Knox that he believed the railway would never be a success, unless the British controlled the Baghdad–Gulf section, an observation which prompted Cox in Bushire to note the 'astute concern which he takes in the political situation'. On 21 January 1907, under cover of a visit to his new yacht, Shaikh Mubarak took an apparently casual stroll along the shore with Knox to visit the site. He still refused to name a price, but Knox was sure that he was in fact anxious to sell, either because he expected to make a large amount of money or else because he hoped to involve the British more closely in Kuwait.

A few days later, Knox asked the shaikh if he would grant the concession, and how much money he wanted. Mubarak was obviously expecting the question, and gave a long and careful reply.[10] He claimed that he was not wealthy and depended on his customs revenues for his income. At the same time his expenses were increasing as a result of his growing prestige and the need to provide more lavish hospitality. He again mentioned that he had received offers from both the Germans and the Russians, and had only turned them down because of his agreement of 1899 with Britain. He also reminded Knox that Lord Curzon had promised during his visit to Kuwait in November 1903 to try to obtain an allowance for him. Although he was prepared to leave the price for Bandar Shuwaikh up to the 'liberality' of the British government, he asked for something 'substantial' to help with expenses. He would prefer to lease the site in return for an annual rent, but would not object to selling the site if this was what Britain wanted. Knox said that Mubarak's wish for something 'substantial' was far more than Britain had been proposing, and that the British government would therefore expect to receive a much larger piece of land. Mubarak seemed happy with this, and Knox concluded that Mubarak really wanted something more like an annual subsidy, and not a lease of ground.

Cox in Bushire had long been in favour of a subsidy, and thought that a subsidy disguised as a rent for Bandar Shuwaikh would be a good solution, as it would give the Turks as little ground as possible for objection or suspicion. Despite Cox's support, Knox's summary of his conversations of January 1907 was not sent to London for six months, and then only in response to a request from the India Office for news about the state of negotiations. During this time, the Foreign Office had been reassessing its policy on the Baghdad railway. On 12 June 1907, a Foreign Office under-secretary wrote to the India Office (apparently unaware that Knox had already opened discussions with Mubarak) to say that, under the changed circumstances of the railway project, it might now be expedient to come to a decision about buying a plot of land at Bandar Shuwaikh.

The Foreign Office enquiry at last stirred the Government of India into sending the details of the conversations between Knox and Mubarak the previous January. These suggested Britain could obtain a site 600 yards long by 100 yards deep, but that the cost would probably be high, as the shaikh was fully aware of the potential value of the site. The price might be as much as Rs200,000 for an outright sale, or an annual rent of anything up to Rs15,000 (although part of the rent could be treated as a subsidy). The Secretary of State for India, John Morley, agreed that the price was high (he used the word 'exorbitant'), but felt that it would be a mistake to hesitate, particularly as part of the rental payments could be considered as a subsidy. Indeed, Morley was in favour of obtaining the largest possible site, and the India Office therefore suggested that an option should be obtained on other parts of the foreshore which might be possible sites for a rail terminus.[11]

The Foreign Office considered that purchase would be better than rent, and the Government of India was therefore instructed to get the largest possible site, in the form of an outright purchase if possible. The government was also asked to try to get a pre-emptive right over other possible sites. The instructions from London arrived in India at a particularly good time, at the end of July 1907, because reports from Knox in Kuwait were suggesting that Shaikh Mubarak as he got older was becoming reluctant to part with any land at all. In June, Shaikh Mubarak had decided to erect a building right in the middle of the site in which Knox had expressed an interest, a move which Knox saw as a worrying sign that he would not be bound by any promises he might have made earlier in respect of the site. Then, Mubarak had refused to donate the land required for the construction of a lighthouse in Kuwait, even though construction would be at British expense. Knox pointed to his 'increasing disinclination to gift or sell land on any consideration whatever'.[12]

However, Knox immediately acted on the new instructions from London and by the middle of August he was able to report that the negotiations were going ahead better than he had expected. Shaikh Mubarak was now offering a lease on a plot twelve times the size of the plot originally sought. The rent of Rs60,000 (£4,000) per year was proportionally well within the limit laid down by the British government. The lease also included the right to pre-empt any offer on the island of Shuwaikh (Qurain) in the bay of Kuwait, and a similar pre-emptive right over Ras Kathama and its foreshore for two nautical miles in any direction. Knox pointed out that Mubarak had in a sense removed the 'pearl from the oyster' by reserving a piece of land for himself in the middle of the concession. Even so, Knox urged immediate acceptance of the terms, adding that the offer would be good for two months.

Mubarak's sudden willingness to co-operate over the concession could be due to the fact that he had recently been frustrated by the Ottoman authorities in Basra over plans to purchase more estates in Ottoman territory. At the start of his negotiations with the British over Bandar Shuwaikh, he had expressed some concern to Knox over the possible reaction of the Ottoman authorities if they discovered that he had been leasing territory to the British. In mid-1907, the Vali of Basra took an obstructive attitude over the shaikh's attempt to purchase the estates, and Mubarak was apparently so annoyed that he forgot about his fears over the British lease. Knox had to listen to his complaints about the 'deceitful rotten Turkish Government', and the British Residency in Bushire told the Government of India that Mubarak's fury against the *vali* had almost certainly influenced his attitude on the subject of Bandar Shuwaikh to a degree far greater than the *vali*'s attitude could justify. The Residency argued that Mubarak's anger with the *vali* might only be temporary, which was an argument for concluding the argument over Bandar Shuwaikh as soon as possible.[13]

On 21 August, Knox was able to send Bushire a draft agreement with a letter from Mubarak promising to accept its terms. The agreement covered the larger area offered by Mubarak earlier in August. It also included a clause by which Britain guaranteed the internal independence of the shaikh. The one problem was that Mubarak had insisted on including a clause to reserve all the customs revenues collected in the concession area to himself. Mubarak was clearly worried that, at a later date, the British might try to divert the customs revenues from the area to themselves. In fact, there was no such intention on the British side, but Knox found the inclusion of the customs-clause objectionable. However, he agreed to leave the clause in the draft agreement as he thought that the course of the negotiations could be imperilled if he had tried to insist in removing it.

Bushire was pleased with the draft, and Percy Cox and his first assistant both sent congratulations to Kuwait. In India, the government not only endorsed Knox's draft, but wanted to extend the proposals by taking out options over a much wider area. As well as the foreshore and Shuwaikh and Ras Kathama, the government wanted the area of the options to cover Warbah Island (to the north of Bubiyan) with its northern and southern anchorages, as well as the adjacent foreshores for a distance of three nautical miles. The Government of India argued that, if these areas were not included in the pre-emptive rights, it would still be possible for a railway terminus to be placed at Umm Qasr and reached via Khaur Abdullah. [14] This ambitious suggestion by the government raised the problem that Britain had no detailed information about the boundaries of the shaikh's territories and therefore the land which he was entitled to lease.

The Eastern Limits of Kuwait: Bubiyan, Warbah and Umm Qasr

When the Government of India suggested in August 1907 that Britain should acquire pre-emptive rights over a wider area around Kuwait, departments in London had to look urgently at the status of the two islands of Warbah and Bubiyan, as well as the question of Umm Qasr on the West bank of the Khaur Zubair. Between them these three sites controlled all access to the Khaur Zubair via the Khaur Sabiyah and the Khaur Abdullah. Shaikh Mubarak was quite

convinced that Warbah, Bubiyan and Umm Qasr belonged to Kuwait, but he
had difficulty in proving his claims, partly for lack of any convincing documents, and partly because the Ottomans had sent military detachments to
occupy Umm Qasr and a place called Ras al-Gai in Bubiyan Island during the
last days of 1901 and the first days of 1902 when Shaikh Mubarak himself was
in a weak position. On 24 March 1902, the British ambassador protested to the
Ottoman government about the occupation of Umm Qasr and Bubiyan, on
the grounds that it disturbed the status quo agreement between Britain and
the Ottomans of September 1901. The Ottoman garrisons stayed at Umm Qasr
and Bubiyan until they were expelled in November 1914 as British forces moved
up the Shatt al-Arab to occupy Basra. British sources suggest that the garrisons were rather depleted by 1907, but the major departments of state, and
especially the Foreign Office, had no wish to provoke a clash between Britain
and the Ottomans in 1907 on the issue of the islands and Umm Qasr. A further problem was that there was little information available in London in 1907
about the history of the three places. Detailed enquiries by British officers to
try to determine the loyalties of fishermen and Bedouin in the area only started
in 1908.

To simplify this complex story, we will discuss the three places in turn, pointing out that some of the information below would not have been known to
British officials in the summer of 1907:

Bubiyan Island

Britain had repeatedly given diplomatic support to Mubarak's claim to Bubiyan
ever since the Ottoman troops arrived at Ras al-Gait in 1902, but this support
had produced no results. O'Conor's first protest about Bubiyan, delivered in
March 1902, was fobbed off by the Ottoman minister of foreign affairs on the
grounds that he was 'unaware' that any Ottoman troops had gone to Bubiyan.
In 1904, Curzon in India recommended that the Porte should be asked to withdraw the garrison, and that Britain should either set up a military post on
Bubiyan on Mubarak's behalf or assist him to do this himself. O'Conor in
Constantinople did request the Ottomans to withdraw from the island once in
May 1904 and again in September 1905, but to no avail. On the first occasion,
the Ottoman foreign minister Tevfik Pasha did seem prepared to discuss the
arguments about Bubiyan in a reasoned manner. He conceded that Shaikh
Mubarak by now enjoyed a 'sort of semi-independence' from the Ottoman
Empire, and had a 'special understanding' with the British government, but he

also reminded the British ambassador that the limits of Kuwait were very vague. It was therefore desirable that proofs should be produced that Bubiyan Island belonged to him. As Tevfik Pasha put it, 'the mere fact that Kuwait fishermen repaired there annually was in itself no proof of possession or ownership, and if an incident like this justified a claim to possession, there was no saying where (Mubarak's) demands would end.' O'Conor replied that he considered Mubarak's claim to Bubiyan to be fully justified, as the Ottomans had shown no interest at all in the island before 1902.

Despite their strong support for Mubarak's claim, the British government did not proceed with plans to set up a military outpost in partnership with Mubarak. The reason for this was that Mubarak made rather extravagant requests for help, including a demand that British warships should regularly visit Kuwait and Khaur Abdullah, and a demand for financial help.[15]

Warbah Island

The British generally felt that Mubarak's claim to Warbah was less solid than his claim to Bubiyan. Warbah Island had never been inhabited, and was described by one British official as 'of no use to anyone' (apart from its location, of course). The British investigations during 1907–8 mainly focused on the difficult question of whether the island should be regarded as a northern extension of Bubiyan Island, or as a southern appendage of the mainland coast between Khaur Zubair and Fao. If Warbah was an extension of Bubiyan, then ownership would logically belong to Kuwait, but if it was seen as attached to the coastline of the mainland, then the matter was more difficult. Mubarak claimed that he was in any case the owner of the 'mainland swamp between Fao and Khaur Zubair', but Knox established in his researches during 1908 that this was in Mubarak's capacity as some form of private tenant of the Ottoman authorities, rather than as the ruler of Kuwait.[16]

Umm Qasr

In June 1904, Captain Smyth visited the Umm Qasr area as part of an investigation into the likely route of the railway. He reported that it was generally believed by the inhabitants that the old fort at Umm Qasr had been built by Mubarak's grandfather Jabir al-Sabah, and that the fort had been 'occasionally occupied' by Arabs from Kuwait during the spring seasons up to 1902. The

Ottoman garrison had occupied the old fort in 1902, and then built themselves a new fort when the old one crumbled away. In 1912, Shakespear, who was of course inclined to favour Mubarak's side of the story, said that Mubarak had frequently come close to evicting the Ottomans from Umm Qasr altogether between 1902 and 1912, but had only restrained himself because he feared that the Ottomans could retaliate against his estates in the Shatt al-Arab, and because he did not want to lose British support by stirring up a military confrontation with the Turks. [17] Shakespear also pointed out that, even after the Ottomans occupied Umm Qasr in 1902, disputes between Bedouins about the use of the wells at Umm Qasr were always referred to Kuwait for arbitration. There were some arguments in support of Mubarak's claim to Umm Qasr, although the claim was not always popular in British government circles. Back in 1902, the British consul in Basra, Mr Wratislaw, had described Mubarak's claim to Umm Qasr as 'very shadowy'.

One general point has to be remembered. Although Mubarak was certainly vociferous and plausible in his claims to Bubiyan, Warbah and Umm Qasr, some British government departments had interests of their own in the area which must have coloured their judgement. Quite apart from the risk that Umm Qasr could provide an alternative outlet to the Gulf for the railway project, there was the possibility that Bubiyan, Warbah and Umm Qasr could be developed so as to provide the basis for an 'impregnable harbour' to rival Kuwait itself. During his Gulf tour of November 1903, the Viceroy of India made a point of inspecting the Khaur Zubair, and was impressed by the potential of the location for a harbour. The Government of India was thereafter strongly inclined to back Mubarak's claim to all three places, so as to prevent the nightmare of another great power gaining direct access to the Gulf.

Knox Exceeds Instructions: The Lease Agreement on Bandar Shuwaikh

Britain's foreign secretary, Edward Grey, decided in mid-September to ask his ambassador in Constantinople for a view on Mubarak's claim to Bubiyan, Warbah and Umm Qasr. Although O'Conor had been prepared to protest about the Ottoman move into Bubiyan and Umm Qasr in the past, he now replied in a more negative sense. [18] His reasoning was that the major priority for Britain was now to obtain British participation in the construction and operation of the railway. Kuwait was only important as a bargaining counter to achieve this end. He therefore concluded that, of the three places under discussion, Mubarak only had a claim to Bubiyan Island, and even that claim was 'meagre'. He argued against any British attempt to extend Shaikh Mubarak's jurisdiction which might be resented by the Porte or, worse still, might lead the Ottomans to seek the assistance of another foreign power. Instead, he though that the 'wily shaikh' should be left to seize any opportunities to extend his territorial jurisdiction without British involvement. In the light of O'Conor's views, the India Office ordered that the agreement to lease Bandar Shuwaikh should be concluded quickly, but that the lease must exclude any mention of Warbah Island or any other doubtful site, but the lease which Knox and Mubarak did finally sign on 15 October 1907 included a specific reference to Warbah Island.

Once again, as in 1899, the British officer on the spot had apparently ignored a specific directive from London. Knox explained the inclusion of Warbah as an oversight on his part, and this time the authorities in India and London were happy to accept the explanation. In Bushire, Cox's deputy in the British Residency, Mr Bill, said that the inclusion of Warbah should be welcomed as it would obviate the need for 'two bites at the cherry'.[19] The Government of India was also happy to approve Knox's action, on the basis that the extension of the lease to include pre-emptive rights over Warbah could not be a cause of embarrassment in the future, since even if Mubarak's title to Warbah was doubtful, the clause only transferred to Britain Mubarak's rights 'for what they are worth', and did not represent a formal statement of position on the claim. London also saw no need to protest over the clause relating to Warbah.

In the months which followed, the British administrative machine began to look in detail at the question of the borders of Kuwait. This question became increasingly urgent after 1909 as the new government in Turkey flexed its muscles and developed a more aggressive policy towards the Gulf. This new and unwelcome policy forced Britain to abandon its previous vagueness about boundary matters. The agreement signed by Meade and Shaikh Mubarak in January 1899 had not specified the area to which it applied: the shaikh promised not to give or sell or lease 'any portion of his territory', but did not state what this meant in terms of area. When it became clear that (despite all hopes to the contrary) Britain was effectively committed to defending Shaikh Mubarak's territory against the Ottomans, this vagueness became a source of annoyance to British officials. As the foreign secretary, Lord Lansdowne, noted in a memorable note during the crisis of early 1902: 'We have saddled ourselves with an impossible client in the person of the shaikh. He is apparently an untrustworthy savage, no one knows where his possessions begin and end, and our obligations towards him are as ill-defined as the boundaries of his Principality.'[20] Lansdowne decided that the obligations of the British government towards Kuwait under the 1899 agreement should be taken as limited to the 'district adjoining or close to the bay of that name'. Later in 1902, Lansdowne's very narrow definition of Mubarak's territory became official policy, when Britain had to respond to a request from Shaikh Mubarak for the loan of two pieces of artillery to help Kuwait against Ibn Rashid. After consulting the Foreign Office, the India Office instructed the Government of India to refuse the request, while assuring Mubarak that Britain would defend the Kuwait 'district' on the basis that this area was 'clearly defined as that adjoining or close to Kuwait Bay', and there the matter rested until the summer of 1907.

There were of course great difficulties about the definition of frontiers in any part of Arabia. British officials thought of frontiers as clear lines on a map, but apart from a few settled habitations, Arabia belonged to nomadic tribes who wandered over vast areas in search of water and forage for their herds and flocks. Changes in the climate could force tribes to change their areas of ranging, or to encroach on the areas normally regarded as belonging to other tribes, and the tribes themselves might change their allegiance from one ruler to another in the light of the shifts of desert politics. To make sense of this confusing picture, the British approach in all parts of the Gulf region was generally based on trying to establish the allegiance of the more settled areas (by asking the leading figures in the community to whom they felt they owed allegiance) and trying to establish the traditional rights over the major wells and grazing areas. A secondary indication of sovereignty over a district might be the fact that the Bedouin of the area admitted to paying *zakat* to a particular ruler (but *zakat* was not a very reliable indicator of allegiance, as it was sometimes paid to more than one ruler and in any case most tribes only paid up if a team of tax-collectors arrived in their area). To add to the confusion, the areas covered by the tribes in their wanderings – their 'ranges', or *diras* – were roughly set by custom, but were often modified in detail and were sometimes shared with other tribes on a seasonal basis. So any attempt to draw a border-line on the map was bound to be a hazardous business, since the line could only give a temporary indication of a highly fluid and dynamic situation. In 1902 a merchant who knew Kuwait well gave a judicious account of the problems Britain would face in defining its frontiers during a conversation with Mr William Davis, the first assistant to the British resident in Bushire:

Shaikh Mubarak's boundary may be considered to comprise the tract of desert occupied by Bedouin tribes which owe him allegiance, or with whom he is on friendly terms, and as these tribes are constantly moving about and often have misunderstandings with him there can be no such thing as a defined boundary of his country. [21]

It is probably true that, when Shaikh Mubarak seized power in Kuwait in May 1896, his effective authority was limited to a small area around the town of Kuwait itself. The only areas which certainly acknowledged his authority outside Kuwait were the wells and village at Jahra at the head of Kuwait Bay, the little hamlet of Zaur on Failaqah Island, and a few small villages on the mainland coast to the south of Kuwait. As we have seen in our examination of the claim to Bubiyan Island, previous rulers of Kuwait had certainly been able to exercise some form of control over a very much wider area. Using his powerful network of tribal alliances, especially the links with the Ajman and Mutair tribes, Mubarak soon extended his authority over a wide area of inland desert and coastline. By the time that J. G. Lorimer visited Kuwait in December 1904 to gather information for his long geographical and historical survey *The Gazetteer of the Persian Gulf*, Mubarak could plausibly claim that his rule extended over an area of about 30,000 square miles.

The geographical section of Lorimer's *Gazetteer* was published in Calcutta in 1908. Like most works of this kind, its circulation was restricted to military and political officers of the British Government of India. The *Gazetteer*'s views on questions of sovereignty and boundaries came to enjoy great authority in British thinking, but very soon after the publication of the *Gazetteer* some British officials were expressing criticism of the conclusions relating to Kuwait. In particular, Sir Percy Cox and Captain Shakespear were unhappy with Lorimer's rather cursory treatment of Umm Qasr and Safwan. So, important though his book is, Lorimer should not be seen as giving a final view on Mubarak's territory.

Lorimer stated that Shaikh Mubarak's authority covered an area some 190 miles long and 160 miles deep. Starting with the north-eastern frontier, he was happy to accept that Mubarak had a strong claim to Bubiyan Island despite the presence of the Ottoman garrison on the island. He recorded the fact that the Ottomans occupied Umm Qasr, and said that the Kuwait frontier should therefore run to the south of the Ottoman fort. He used the same argument in Safwan, where he thought that the fact of Ottoman occupation of Safwan since 1902 meant that Kuwaiti authority only extended 'up to the walls' of Safwan. Some years later, in August 1912, Cox expressed unhappiness with this abrupt dismissal of Mubarak's claim to Safwan. Cox thought the claim was a 'good deal stronger' than had generally been thought, and pointed to a report by J. C. Gaskin of the Bushire Residency in September 1897 which had given Safwan as the northern limit of Kuwait. Cox also referred to a statement by Mubarak in February 1902 to the British senior naval officer in the Persian Gulf, to the effect that there were families in Safwan which supplied him with grass and onions in recognition of his authority.[22]

In Lorimer's view, the northern boundary of Kuwait's territory ran from a point south of Umm Qasr along a line passing south of Safwan and on for another 20 miles or so to the west, until it reached the northern end of the great Batin depression. The Batin depression ran to the south-west until it reached the great Wadi al-Rummah in Najd. As far south as Hafar, Lorimer thought that the Batin depression should be taken as the western limit of Mubarak's territory, although he admitted that Mubarak claimed that his influence extended to the north and west of the Batin. Lorimer pointed out that the Riqai wells, about 105 miles from Kuwait Town and situated in the Batin depression, were a major halting-place on the route from Kuwait to Qasim and were generally recognised as marking the Kuwait frontier. Sixty miles further along the Batin came the wells of Hafar, which Lorimer saw as marking the frontier between Kuwait and Jabal Shammar. In his letter of August 1912, Cox strongly endorsed Mubarak's claim to control over the important wells at Hafar on the grounds that possession of the wells by Mubarak and the tribes under his control had never been seriously questioned, and that the wells had been used as a rallying-point for troops in 1901.

South of Hafar, the frontier was harder to fix. Lorimer thought that it ran more or less southwards, along a line dividing Summan from Dahanah region, until this line intersected the route from Wafrah to Riyadh. Here, the frontier turned east and passed by the Wadi al-Miyah, until it reached the coast. It was hard to determine exactly where the frontier reached the coast. Lorimer thought that Kuwaiti control over the coastline to the south of Kuwait extended as far as Jabal Manifah, which marked the border between the Shaikhdom and the Sanjak of Hasa in his view. He was inclined to ignore Mubarak's claim to authority extending south of Jabal Manifah to the bay of Musallamiyah. His argument was that the Ottomans maintained a garrison at Musallamiyah. In 1912 Cox was able to provide some powerful arguments in support of the Kuwaiti claim to Musallamiyah: the Ottoman occupation was of comparatively recent date, and Musallamiyah had long been the main base and provisioning-centre for the Kuwait pearl-fleet. Again, Cox could point to Gaskin's useful report of September 1897, which designated Jazirat al-Amayir in the bay of Musallamiyah (which Gaskin called Bulbul Bay) as the southern limit of Kuwaiti territory. Cox also had to admit that both the Foreign Office and the India Office had in the past refused to support Mubarak's claim to the area of the bay of Musallamiyah, even though he did not know 'on what evidence or absence of evidence that decision is based'.

So Lorimer's account, while confirming that Mubarak had by late 1904 managed to extend his authority over a fairly wide area, was not the final word on the frontier problems. In particular, Lorimer had shied away from any areas which were actually under Ottoman military occupation, even if this occupation was a recent matter. But the Ottoman threat to Kuwait was now about to intensify in a way which would enmesh Britain even more deeply in the frontier issue.

The Ottoman Revolution of 1908 and the Gulf

The 'Young Turk' movement scored its first success in the summer of 1908, just a few months after Mubarak had leased Bandar Shuwaikh to Britain. This success was the transformation of the government of Sultan Abdülhamid into a constitutional monarchy. At the start the new government was rather pro-British, but the failure of Sultan Abdülhamid's conservative counter-revolution in April 1909 and the replacement of Abdülhamid by his brother led to a change of tone. The original 'Young Turks' had been exiles of a rather liberal persuasion, mainly based in Paris and other Western capitals. In late 1907, these exiles had linked up with Ottoman Army officers such as Niazi Bey, who began the revolt in Macedonia which forced Abdülhamid to re-introduce the constitution. The crisis of late 1908 and early 1909 led to a strengthening of the position of the army group within the movement at the expense of the more liberal-minded exiles, and the tone of Ottoman policy after 1909 was to be more 'Turkish' and nationalistic than had been the case under Abdülhamid.

The new regime in Constantinople soon took action to strengthen the Ottoman presence in key areas of the Gulf in a way which was calculated to alarm Great Britain. In March 1909, Ottoman troops placed a garrison on Zakhnuniyah Island, ten miles south of Uqair, and raised the Ottoman flag. Zakhnuniyah had traditionally been claimed by the ruler of Bahrain, and in any case it lay well to the south of the section of the Gulf coast which the British regarded as falling under Ottoman jurisdiction. A British protest led to the withdrawal of the Ottoman garrison at the start of June 1909, but by April 1910 the Ottomans were back on the island and the Ottoman flag was flying again. To make matters worse, the Ottomans appointed a *mudir* at Udaid, on the Qatar peninsula, which was an area in which the British had always denied Ottoman jurisdiction. In Basra, the Ottoman authorities imprisoned subjects of the ruler of Bahrain who did not possess Ottoman nationality certificates, thereby challenging Britain's position as the protecting power in Bahrain. They also made difficulties over the properties of Shaikh Mubarak of Kuwait and

Shaikh Kha'zal of Muhammarah in Ottoman territory. British merchants and British Indian businessmen were harassed, especially in Baghdad where the Ottomans destroyed the premises of the Lynch Brothers trading firm on the grounds that they were a threat to public safety. The Vali of Baghdad even threatened to drive an unnecessary road through the Residency of the British consul-general. All the signs were that the new Ottoman regime was seeking a full-scale confrontation with Britain in Mesopotamia and in the Gulf.

The British Ambassador to Constantinople, Sir Gerald Lowther, stressed in his reports to London that the new Ottoman regime had a strong national programme of 'Asiatic or Turkish revival'. He saw Mesopotamia and the Gulf as the most likely zones of conflict with Britain, and said that Kuwait could be expected to be one of the major flash-points. He pointed out that Constantinople regarded Kuwait as an integral part of Ottoman territory, and that the Ottomans believed that the Kuwait question could be settled in a manner favourable to the Ottoman claim when final arrangements were made for the construction of the railway terminal.[23]

The importance which the ambassador attached to Kuwait was borne out by an interview in December 1910 between Hakki Pasha, who was now the Ottoman grand vizier and Sir Henry Babington Smith, the head of the Banque Nationale de Turquie. During the conversation, the grand vizier frequently raised the question of Kuwait, which he described as a 'thorn stuck in the side of Turkey' and the major cause of Ottoman suspicion of Britain's aims in Mesopotamia.[24] When Babington Smith complained about a recent violently anti-British article in the Turkish press, Hakki Pasha pointed out that the writer of the article had just made a visit to Baghdad and Basra, and 'what had produced more impression on him than anything else was the question of Kuwait'. Clear notice was being given, as Babington Smith noted in his report of the meeting to the British Foreign Office, that friction over Kuwait would become more acute unless a settlement could be reached. Hakki Pasha had also established a link between progress on the Kuwait issue and a satisfactory solution of Britain's needs for involvement in the railway project. The British chargé d'affaires in Constantinople, Charles Marling, saw the note of the conversation with Hakki Pasha, and argued that the Kuwait question and the railway question should now be discussed together. As he put it, 'the prospect of gaining something at Kuwait would be a powerful inducement for (the Ottomans) to obtain from the Germans the latitude requisite for them to satisfy our requirements in the railway question.'[25] In Marling's view, the entire British rationale for being in Kuwait was to secure British interests in the railway project, and this might now be the time to use the Kuwait issue as 'leverage' for

Britain's participation in the Baghdad–Basra section of the railway.

Marling followed up this despatch with an even stronger communication to the Foreign Office on 17 January 1911, in which he argued once more that the time had come to trade concessions over Kuwait for a role in the railway project. 'The Turks expect that in return for their making the arrangements we desire concerning the Baghdad–Persian Gulf section of the railway, we shall restore them to complete sovereignty over Kuwait. They attach immense importance to the latter point.'

Marling's two despatches reflect a common view among Foreign Office decision-makers during 1911–14. These officials argued that the independence of Kuwait was not sufficiently important to justify a confrontation with the Ottoman Empire, especially when Britain had so much to gain from an understanding with the Ottomans over the railway issue and, indeed, from good relations with the Ottoman Empire in general. Predictably, the India Office and the Government of India took a much less conciliatory line. Cox in Bushire argued during December 1910 that the time had come to assert clearly and publicly Britain's traditional position in the Gulf, so as to limit any Ottoman action. He thought that this could best be done by publishing the texts of Britain's treaties with Kuwait, by removing Ottoman military posts from areas such as Bubiyan which Britain did not recognise as falling within Ottoman jurisdiction, and by negotiating a treaty with the Shaikh of Qatar to block further Ottoman advances in the Udaid region. The Government of India forwarded his views to London with full approval, and the India Office also was inclined to go along with Cox's suggestion of a strong public assertion of the traditional British position in the Gulf. Ritchie of the India Office minuted to the under-secretary at the Foreign Office on 30 December 1910 that, if the public assertion of Britain's position in the Gulf did not achieve the desired result, it would probably be necessary to strengthen the British naval squadron in the Gulf and to remove 'summarily' all signs of Turkish authority from places where Britain did not admit that the Ottomans had right. Finally, Ritchie advocated giving material support to Shaikh Mubarak of Kuwait and Shaikh Kha'zal of Muhammarah in their disputes with the Turkish government, so as to convince the Turks that Britain was serious in its intentions.[26]

Anglo–Ottoman Talks Begin: the Exchanges of 1911

Ritchie's ambitious memorandum of 30 December 1910 did not at first meet with a favourable response from the British Foreign Secretary, Edward Grey.

Grey felt that this was a bad moment to open negotiations as he could not see anything which Britain could offer in return for the concessions which Cox and the Government of India wanted the Ottomans to make. But a few days later, Marling's despatches from Constantinople arrived in London and caused Grey to change his mind. Following Marling's suggestion, he wondered whether Her Majesty's Government could now exploit their 'acquired position' in Kuwait to secure British participation in the Baghdad Railway. He accepted the view of the India Office and the Foreign Office that no foreign power should be allowed to secure a foothold in the Gulf. So, while he proposed that Britain should now acknowledge Turkish suzerainty over Kuwait, he stressed that any agreement with the Ottomans must include a provision for joint Anglo–Kuwaiti control over Kuwait Port itself. He also said that the agreement must include a 'full measure of home rule' over Kuwait's internal affairs, especially in the matter of customs revenues, where he rightly pointed out that the shaikh was particularly jealous of foreign interference. He argued that Shaikh Mubarak should in future pay tribute to the Ottoman government on condition that the Ottomans gave equitable treatment to the shaikh in respect of his properties on Ottoman territory. Grey thought, rather naively, that it would be fairly easy to persuade Mubarak to agree to such a proposal. He admitted that the planned solution was not an easy one because of the long-standing relations between the British government and Kuwait and the close nature of these relations in recent years. This would make it impossible to abandon the shaikh to the Turkish government 'without incurring a disastrous loss of prestige'. [27]

At the start of February 1911, Cox in Bushire gave his reactions to Grey's proposals. Except for the suggestion that Mubarak should pay tribute to the Ottomans, Cox thought that the proposals were not unreasonable. Cox had recently discussed with Mubarak the idea that Mubarak's sons should take out Ottoman nationality papers in exchange for an Ottoman *firman* which would guarantee freedom from interference for Mubarak's properties in Ottoman territory. Mubarak had seemed to accept this as a possibility, as long as he retained British support. Cox of course agreed that it was essential for the shaikh and Britain to keep control of the port. The one point of difficulty, in Cox's opinion, was the idea that Mubarak should pay tribute to the Ottomans. He considered that the shaikh would greatly resent any such suggestion. Although Cox had not been asked for any comments on the boundaries of Kuwait, he said that Shaikh Mubarak's rights to Bubiyan, Warbah and Umm Qasr should now be recognised, and the Turkish military posts on Bubiyan and Warbah must be removed. Cox did not deal at any length with the way that Mubarak might react to a formal admission of Turkish sovereignty over Kuwait. He only warned that any such admission would have to be linked to a definite agreement that the terminus of the railway would be at Kuwait.

The Government of India endorsed Cox's comments, and added a few of their own. These together made up the list of conditions which the Government of India saw as essential in any settlement. The main conditions were:

1. British control of the Baghdad–Gulf section of the railway, through a British stake of at least 60 per cent in the new company.
2. A binding commitment that Kuwait would be the terminus of the railway.
3. Absolute control of Kuwait Port by Britain and the shaikh.
4. An agreement on the division of customs revenues between the Ottoman government and the shaikh.
5. Settlement of all the shaikh's disputes over property.
6. Recognition of all outstanding agreements between Shaikh Mubarak and Britain.
7. Recognition of Umm Qasr, Bubiyan and Warbah as part of Kuwait territory and the withdrawal of Turkish military posts.

In return for these very substantial concessions on the Ottoman side, the Government of India suggested that Britain would recognise Turkish suzerainty over Kuwait, provided that the shaikh retained internal autonomy. The Government of India and the India office did not apparently realise that the Ottoman government would see this as a very unequal bargain.[28]

By this time, however, hints were reaching the Foreign Office that the Ottomans were anxious to achieve a settlement with Britain on issues relating to the Gulf. In mid-February 1911, the Ottoman foreign minister Rifat Pasha told the British ambassador in Constantinople of the lines along which his government was working. The Ottoman plan was to persuade the German company to abandon its concession for the construction of the Baghdad–Basra section of the line. Instead, the Ottomans proposed to create an international company, of which the Ottoman side would hold 40 per cent and Britain, Germany and France would each hold 20 per cent. Rifat Pasha indicated that the Ottomans would prefer Kuwait as a terminus on the Gulf, but that this would need an 'arrangement' with Britain on the political position of Kuwait. The Ottomans could not accept that the terminus of the railway was not in Ottoman territory. On 1 March, the Ottoman Foreign Ministry delivered a memorandum to the ambassador, confirming the points made by the minister. The memorandum also drew attention to 'the utility of arriving at an understanding as to the respective rights of the two Powers in the Persian Gulf.'[29]

The immediate problem which the Ottoman memorandum presented for the British government was the stipulation that no country other than the Ottoman Empire could have a stake larger than 20 per cent in the new railway company. The Government of India, which had insisted on a British stake of at least 60 per cent, thought that the Ottoman proposal of 20 per cent for Britain was 'hardly possible to take seriously'. Also, the Ottoman requirements in respect of Kuwait would, in the viceroy's view, represent a surrender of Britain's position in Kuwait, and the complete destruction of the British position in the Gulf. Rather than accepting the Ottoman conditions, the viceroy thought it would be better to let the railway go to Basra after all.[30] The Foreign Office, however, took a more moderate line. The Foreign Office view was that the protection of British commerce from unfair discrimination did not necessarily require a controlling stake in the railway company.

Was the percentage of British participation really so important, as long as the Baghdad–Gulf section of the railway was internationalised? In any event, the Foreign Office thought it likely that the railway would be built with or without British participation. If Britain stood aside from the railway project, this would only increase the scope for Turkish pressure on Kuwait, and in terms of prestige, it might be better to participate at 20 per cent than not to participate at all.[31] The Foreign Office also indicated that it was prepared to make substantial concessions on the territory of Kuwait in order to secure settlement with the Ottomans. Foreign Secretary Grey appeared to accept Lord Lansdowne's definition of Kuwait of 1902 as being limited to Kuwait town and the immediate environs. He did not accept Mubarak's claims to Umm Qasr in the north-east or Musallamiyah to the south. He also argued that the importance to Britain of Bubiyan, Warbah and Umm Qasr would largely disappear if the Ottomans gave a firm commitment to put the rail terminus at Bandar Shuwaikh: the main reason for British interest in Umm Qasr and the islands had been to prevent the railway from reaching the Gulf by an alternative route which would by-pass the British concession at Bandar Shuwaikh. In effect, the Foreign Office was ready to give a large part of Kuwait to Constantinople as long as Britain could achieve some participation in the railway.

The Government of India was certainly not happy with Grey's very restrictive view of Kuwaiti territory. India agreed that Umm Qasr was probably unobtainable, but otherwise considered that there was an obligation to defend all the shaikh's territory as defined in Lorimer's *Gazetteer*, including the islands of Bubiyan and Warbah. Before the Government of India's views arrived in London, however, Britain's ambassador in Constantinople had reported on a new development which made previous arguments about levels of participation in the railway project irrelevant. On 22 March 1911, Lowther signalled to the Foreign Office that the Ottomans and the Germans had signed a new convention which made all previous discussions about the level of British participation in the railway project completely irrelevant. The Ottoman–German convention specified that Germany would give up all rights in the section of the railway from Baghdad to the Gulf. In return for this concession, Germany was given an assurance that the German share in the new Turkish-sponsored company to operate the railway would not be less than the share of any other power. As the Ottomans had already reserved 40 per cent of the capital of the new company for Ottoman interests, it was now impossible for Britain to have a controlling interest in the new company.

When news of the Ottoman–German convention reached India, the Government of India expressed its alarm in the strongest terms. The viceroy commented on 23 March that it was now even more important than before to secure absolutely Britain's position in Kuwait. Indeed, the viceroy's paper raised the possibility of withdrawing from the negotiations altogether, and then checking the first sign of any forward moves by Turkey in the Gulf region by military means, 'with the aid of our naval forces'.[32] By coincidence, the India Office became aware, just a few weeks after the signature of the Ottoman–German convention, of a new opportunity to put military pressure on the Ottoman Empire in the Gulf region. This opportunity arose out of a discussion between Britain's agent in Kuwait, Captain Shakespear, and Ibn Sa'ud during April 1911, while Shakespear was touring in the desert. During this conversation, the al-Sa'ud leader stressed the general Arab hatred of the Turks, and the desire to drive them out of Arabia. Ibn Sa'ud again pressed for British recognition, and offered to accept British agents in his territory. Shakespear's account of the meeting greatly interested the political secretary of the India Office, Arthur Hirtzel, who wrote a short un-dated and un-signed comment on the cover of the file:

This is a very interesting report ... the information may in certain contingencies prove valuable. It wd. evidently take very little encouragement to make the Wahabis turn the weak Turkish garrison out of Hasa, and if our ships held up Turkish reinforcements in the Gulf, Turkish authority must disappear from the Arabian coast of the Gulf. It is worth thinking of, in case they drive us to extremities.[33]

So the attitude of the Indian government and the India Office towards the Gulf region had changed very fundamentally in a few short weeks. The long-standing policy of non-involvement in the affairs of inland Arabia was no longer sacrosanct. If the new Ottoman policy towards Germany, the railway and Kuwait became unbearable, the India Office would apparently be prepared to back a Sa'udi push against the weak Turkish garrison in al-Hasa by giving naval support, so as to remove all Turkish power on the Arab coast. This drastic change of stance is not hard to understand. No matter how the secretary of state for India looked at the case, either commercially or politically, there no longer seemed to be any good reason why Britain should continue to negotiate with the Ottoman Empire. As a result of the Ottoman–German convention, Britain was being asked to consent to an increased customs tariff in order to finance a railway in which her participation would be so low that British capital would probably not want to contribute. To make matters worse, the impact of the increase in tariffs would fall mainly on British companies as the main traders in the region. The secretary of state ended his comments with a reference to Kuwait, where he felt that the requirements of the British and Ottoman governments were now so contradictory that a settlement would be impossible. Taking everything into account, he concluded that the balance inclined markedly towards non-participation.[34]

Although the India Office had now shifted away from continuing the negotiations with the Ottomans, officials of the India Office agreed to a meeting with the Foreign Office to try to reach a compromise on the reply to be given to the Ottoman note of 1 March. The meeting took place on 30 March. Much to general surprise, Foreign Secretary Grey suggested that Britain should still ask for a 50 per cent British share in the new railway company, and said that there was a good chance of getting this. The Board of Trade, which was represented at the meeting, stressed that only a 50 per cent British stake would be adequate to protect British interests. If this could not be obtained, it would be better to withdraw from participation altogether.

The meeting also agreed that the negotiations with the Ottomans should include an attempt to settle all outstanding points of dispute in the Gulf region, including Kuwait, Bahrain, Qatar and the limits of Ottoman jurisdiction in Arabia. The importance of Kuwait is shown by the fact that 11 of the 26 points settled at the meeting concerned Kuwait. For example, the agreed British aims included the siting of the railway terminus at Kuwait, joint Anglo–Kuwait control over the port, retention of internal affairs in the hand of the shaikh, a guarantee by both parties of the territorial status quo, recognition of the 'suzerainty' of the Porte and the definition of the territory of Kuwait.

The new British negotiating position was welcomed by the Government of India, which commented that it gave 'better hope of a satisfactory settlement'. India still regarded the preservation of Kuwait's independence as essential, together with the maintenance of the special British position in Kuwait. The Government of India also insisted that no opening should be created in Kuwait for Turkey or any other power.[35] Back in London, the India Office expressed concern about the tension between Britain and the Ottoman Empire in Mesopotamia and the Gulf. Turkish authorities in the region continued to make difficulties over Britain's position in Bahrain, and over the setting of buoys in the Shatt al-Arab. There were also protests from the authorities in Baghdad about the use of sepoys from the Indian Army to guard the British consulate-general in Baghdad. All these developments made the senior officials of the India Office extremely cautious about the prospects for successful negotiations with the Ottoman Empire.

Then, at the start of April, the Foreign Office suddenly cut the ground from under the feet of the India Office by changing the terms of the reply to be sent to the Porte. The new draft reply, which was composed without any attempt to consult the India Office, called for five countries to participate in the new railway company instead of the original four: Russia was added to the proposed consortium, alongside the Ottoman Empire, Britain, France and Germany. The Foreign Office draft suggested a 20 per cent stake for each participant. It also dropped Kuwait as the terminus, and specified Basra instead. As might have been expected, Hirtzel at the India Office was dismayed to hear of the new draft. He described it as the 'bankruptcy of British diplomacy in the Middle East'. He particularly criticised the idea that the inclusion of Russia, now considered as an ally of Britain, would strengthen the British position in the company. In his view, the only security for British interests in Kuwait and the Gulf would be a 50 per cent British stake. Interestingly, he suggested strong action to defend the British position in the Gulf:

We are claiming nothing new, and it is for others to put themselves in the wrong by acts of aggression on us. If they put down buoys, I would take them up again; if they agree on Kuwait or Bahrain, seize their date-dhows; and in an extreme case – as Sir E. Grey himself suggested – hold up their reinforcement for the Yemen, or for Hasa.[36]

Hirtzel discovered 'privately' that Sir Arthur Nicolson, the permanent under-secretary at the Foreign Office, was responsible for the new draft. Nicolson told Hirtzel that the new terms were necessary because Britain was too weak to do anything against Germany. Hirtzel was unimpressed by the argument, and pointed out that it was illogical for Britain now to seek refuge with the Russian Empire, one of the weakest powers in Europe. There was little he could do, as the Government of India expressed satisfaction with the new proposals, calling them 'satisfactory on the whole, and a great advance on those made hitherto'.[37] The one comment of importance from the Government of India was about Kuwait. The government stressed that the situation to be desired for Kuwait was a situation of complete autonomy under the suzerainty of the sultan. Great care should therefore be taken to avoid any ambiguity in the formula to be adopted for Kuwait which might provide an opening for Turkish interference or aggression in the future.

On 29 July 1911, the British government gave the Ottoman ambassador in London its reply to the Ottoman proposals of 1 March. The reply specified Basra as the preferred terminus for the railway, but said that if the railway was ever to be extended beyond Basra, then the terminus should be at Kuwait. On the subject of Kuwait, the reply stated that Britain was prepared to recognise Turkish 'suzerainty' over the Shaikhdom, with the shaikh holding the title of *qaimaqam*, as long as 'in other respects the status quo is guaranteed, and the validity of certain agreements which the shaikh has concluded with the British Government is recognised.' In effect, the British reply proposed that the elements of the Anglo–Ottoman exchange of September 1901 on the status quo in Kuwait should now form part of an international agreement. The British reply included a summary of the position which Kuwait would occupy under the new agreement: 'Kuwait would thus form a sort of enclave within and forming part of the Ottoman Empire, but enjoying complete self-government under Turkish suzerainty'.[38]

The reply did not specify the boundaries of Kuwait, but did say that Bubiyan and Warbah islands would be recognised as lying within Kuwait, and that the Ottoman garrison on Bubiyan should be removed. The Porte seems to have interpreted these conditions as representing support for a 'Greater Kuwait', to judge from a conversation three weeks later between Britain's ambassador in Constantinople, Sir Gerald Lowther, and the grand vizier. In this conversation, Hakki Pasha gave an informal reply to the British memorandum in which he commented that the British proposals 'seemed to provide for an enlargement of the dominions of the Sheikh of Kuwait', which could not be accepted by the Ottoman government. The grand vizier confirmed during this conversation that Kuwait had especial importance for the Ottoman Empire. He said that the Ottoman government did not anticipate any great problem in resolving differences with Britain about Bahrain, Qatar and other places in the Gulf, but that Kuwait was a different matter. The other places were 'as it were, detached from the main possessions of the Empire, while Kuwait ate right into it.'[39]

Hakki Pasha during this conversation pointed out to Lowther that the British memorandum referred to various arrangements between Britain and Kuwait which were not known to the Ottoman government. He asked to be provided with copies of these arrangements. This caused some problems for London. In particular, no-one was in favour of releasing the text of the 1907 lease of Bandar Shuwaikh. Shaikh Mubarak argued that, quite apart from the fact that he had refused requests from other countries for similar leases in the past, disclosure of the Bandar Shuwaikh lease would possibly bring difficulties with the Ottomans and might cause 'inconvenient gossip' at home. Cox in Bushire argued that disclosure of the lease could put Britain at a disadvantage if the negotiations proved abortive. The Government of India was worried about revealing the details of the rent for Bandar Shuwaikh, which was in all but name a subsidy to the shaikh. Faced with this strong set of arguments, Foreign Secretary Edward Grey decided only to tell the Ottoman foreign minister, in his message of 24 October 1911, that His Majesty's Government held 'a lease of land' from the Shaikh of Kuwait. Grey also had to skirt round the question of Britain's obligations to defend Kuwait. Here, the problem lay in Meade's agreement of January 1899 with Shaikh Mubarak, or rather in the letter accompanying the agreement, in which Meade had promised Mubarak the 'good offices' of the British government. What was Britain obliged to do as a result of this letter, and what was the area of ground to which it applied? Cox in Bushire and the Government of India took the position that the terms of Meade's letter of 1899 had been expanded by the assurances which Britain had given Mubarak in 1901 and 1902 to protect 'Kuwait and district' from Turkish attack. When the India Office was asked to comment on this interpretation of the 'good offices' promise, it at first accepted the Government of India's view. Hirtzel, who had been absent from the Office when the request arrived, objected strongly to the interpretation when he returned. Hirtzel argued, in the first place, that this unconditional obligation to defend Kuwait with military force went far beyond the terms of Meade's original letter. Secondly, he pointed out that, whatever the nature of the obligation which Britain had taken on, it now applied to a far larger territory than had originally been envisioned. In practice, any British commitments during 1901 and 1902 had been limited to Kuwait town and its immediate environs, but now Britain had defined Kuwait as the area specified in Lorimer's *Gazetteer*.

The Foreign Office accepted the force of Hirtzel's arguments. As a result, Sir Edward Grey's message to the Ottoman foreign minister on 24 October simply said that, in addition to the agreement of January 1899, the British government had promised the shaikh and his heirs and successors 'to support them and accord them their good offices', but that the British government reserved the right to interpret that term at its discretion. [40] Grey also gave the Ottoman ambassador the texts of Britain's agreement of 1900 with Mubarak prohibiting the arms trade, and the 1904 agreement on post offices.

Grey's message of 24 October concluded the diplomatic exchanges of 1911 between Britain and the Ottoman Empire. The main result of the exchanges had been to identify Kuwait as the single largest obstacle to any agreement between London and Constantinople about problems in the Gulf region. The exchanges also highlighted the dangers inherent in the British approach to the northern Gulf. Important obligations had been taken on, generally in secret and often without any clear timetable or agenda. In one major respect, the 1899 promise to provide good offices, the obligation had been incurred by the British official on the spot, Lt. Col. Meade, without any mandate from the British government and to the considerable alarm of officials in London when the existence of the obligation was discovered. Despite this rather casual and unplanned approach, it could be argued that Britain had succeeded up to 1911 in its major aim: Britain had managed to consolidate its political position as the dominant foreign power in Kuwait (and virtual protector of Kuwait) at minimal cost in terms of military resources, and without provoking a major clash with the Ottoman Empire. This success had been based on a studied vagueness in its dealings with the Ottoman Empire, and above all on a careful avoidance of exact definitions of the status of Kuwait and the limits of British responsibilities. The wording of the British exchange of messages with the Ottoman Empire on 9–11 September 1901, when both powers agreed to maintain the status quo in Kuwait, is a masterpiece of vagueness in this respect. Questions of the status of Kuwait or the area which it covered were simply ignored in these messages. This lack of precision, which had been so useful up to 1911, became something of a handicap to Britain once it decided, for reasons of wider diplomatic advantage, to tidy up its relationship with the Ottoman Empire in the Gulf region.

Departmental Strife in London: the Negotiations of 1912

Grey's message of 24 October 1911 was followed by a silence of nearly five months, mainly because the Ottoman Empire was involved during this time in a war with Italy over Italian claims to Libyan North Africa. Eventually, the

Ottomans replied to Grey's message in the form of an aide memorie, presented by the Ottoman ambassador in London on 15 April 1912, but in the weeks before 15 April, informal discussions took place in London between senior British and Ottoman officials. On the British side, the Foreign Office was represented by its expert on railways, Alwyn Parker, and the India Office fielded its political secretary, Arthur Hirtzel. The Ottoman Empire was represented by Tevfik Pasha (now Turkish ambassador to London) and by Ahmed Rashid, a legal expert sent from Constantinople. The details of the discussions have not survived, but subsequent events indicate that the talks gave the British side reason to hope that a compromise could be achieved. In particular, the Ottoman side apparently raised no objections when Hirtzel put forward the British definition of the territory of Kuwait, based on the entry in Lorimer's *Gazetteer* and including the islands of Warbah and Bubiyan. The only real difficulty during the talks seems to have concerned the British demand that Russia should be a participant in the railway. The Ottoman side did not reject the demand outright, but did stress their strong political objection to the inclusion of Russia. Hirtzel recorded that they said that the Turks would demand the inclusion of Switzerland in the consortium if Britain insisted on Russia.[41]

Given the rather pleasant atmosphere during the talks in March, it was a considerable surprise to the British government when Tevfik Pasha called on the Foreign Office on 15 April to present his government's formal aide memoire in reply to Grey's message of 24 October. The aide memoire stated simply that there was no doubt in the Ottoman government's view that the Shaikh of Kuwait and his people were subjects of the Ottoman Empire, and that the shaikhs of Kuwait had borne the title of *qaimaqam* since 1871. The aide memoire rejected the definition of the territory of Kuwait put forward by Hirtzel during the talks in March. The Ottoman government now said that the shaikh's influence did not extend beyond Jahra, Kathama and Sira, indeed no more than 20 kilometres beyond the town. It also refused to abandon the post on Bubiyan Island, and, while offering to come to a definitive arrangement to secure Britain's commercial interests in Kuwait, insisted that this purely commercial agreement must replace all Britain's previous treaties with Shaikh Mubarak [42]

Alwyn Parker was dismayed at the strong line taken in the *aide memoire*. He wrote a private letter to Cevad Bey of the Ottoman Embassy in London to express his disappointment, and to point out what at enormous gap had now opened up between the Ottoman statement on Kuwait and the British government's determination not to allow any interference with 'the succession or with the internal administration or any infringement of the complete autonomy of the sheikh'.[43] Arthur Hirtzel, while unhappy about many elements of the Ottoman reply, took a more positive line about the sections relating to Kuwait. He persuaded Parker to co-operate in submitting a joint minute, which suggested that it might be better to drop any reference to the boundaries of Kuwait for the time being. Hirtzel argued that the British request for the withdrawal of the Ottoman garrison from Bubiyan Island was bound to appear to the Turkish public as a cession of the territory of the Empire, to which they would naturally be opposed. Since Britain's real aim was to prevent any further Ottoman occupation of territory around Kuwait, and to 'save Mubarak's face', there was no benefit to be gained from an immediate confrontation on the subject of the islands, although he conceded that the limits of Kuwait would eventually have to be defined in order to avoid misunderstandings.

The Foreign Office decided that the immediate priority was to put the exchanges between London and Constantinople on a more formal basis, by obtaining an official statement from the Ottoman government that the British reply of 29 July 1911 was acceptable as a basis for a settlement of the Kuwait question. On 10 May 1912, the Foreign Office therefore presented an interim note to Tevfik Pasha, asking if the Porte was willing to accept an arrangement based on British acknowledgement of Turkish 'suzerainty' over Kuwait, with the shaikh holding the title of Turkish *qaimaqam*, and with a guarantee of respect for the status quo, plus recognition of existing Anglo–Kuwaiti agreements and a commitment that Shaikh Mubarak's property in Ottoman jurisdiction would not be disturbed. The Foreign Office accepted the arguments of Parker and Hirtzel, and omitted any reference to the claim to Bubiyan and Warbah on Shaikh Mubarak's behalf, or to the withdrawal of the Ottoman garrison on Bubiyan.

The Foreign Office and India Office now agreed that there should be an inter-departmental meeting to work out an agreed British position on the difficult questions of participation in the railway, the status of Qatar and the frontiers of Muhammarah. Before the meeting took place relations between the Foreign Office and the India Office started to deteriorate. In particular, the India Office considered that the inter-departmental meeting should only be held after the Ottomans had replied to the British note of 10 May accepting the principles set out in that note as the basis of any agreement. Sir Arthur Nicolson, the permanent under secretary at the Foreign Office, had told the Ottoman ambassador that there was no need for the Ottoman government to reply to the note in writing. Worse was to come. On 11 June, Nicolson met with Hirtzel of the India Office and a representative of the Board of Trade to discuss participation in the railway. Nicolson favoured a 20 per cent British stake, but the other two departments insisted on 50 per cent. Nicolson agreed to see what the Russians and French thought about a 50 per cent British stake. When the group of officials met again at the end of June, Nicolson reported that the Russian and French governments were both opposed to allowing Britain and Germany to participate alone in the new company. The attitude of the Russians and French meant that Britain could no longer secure a 50 per cent stake, and so the only alternative was for Britain not to participate in the railway at all. Hirtzel suspected that Nicolson had not in fact made the enquiries which he claimed to have made. In Hirtzel's words, 'Nicolson was far from explicit as to what had passed with Russia and France, and we really know no more than we did at the last meeting – we have simply his bare assurance that the 50 per cent proposal is impracticable.' Hirtzel's suggestion that Nicolson should be asked to provide copies of his communications with the French and Russians 'for purposes of record' was over-ruled by his superiors as unduly offensive.[44]

In addition to the difficult question of participation, the meeting at the end of June did settle some important aspects of the British negotiating position. In particular, the meeting decided that Britain would agree to an increase in Ottoman customs revenues in exchange for some technical concessions about the railway and an undertaking from the Ottoman government that the railway would only be extended beyond Basra if Britain consented to the extension. The meeting also agreed that the Porte should be asked to recognise all Britain's territorial claims in the Gulf, and a major change was proposed to the British position on the subject of the boundaries of Kuwait.

In this account of the meeting, Hirtzel set out the new formula which the India Office suggested should be offered to the Ottomans in regard to Kuwait. The formula can best be described as a 'two-zone' approach to the question of the territorial limits of Kuwait and the related question of the extent of Ottoman jurisdiction. The diplomatic exchanges up to 10 May 1912 had given grounds for thinking that the Ottoman government would accept a 'little Kuwait' definition of the borders of the Shaikhdom, limiting the Shaikhdom to the town, the bay and the immediately surrounding area, but rejecting the other areas included by Lorimer in his account of Kuwait in the *Gazetteer*. So the India office suggested that Britain should negotiate on the basis that Shaikh Mubarak's authority would be recognised in the area of 'little Kuwait'. Beyond this area and up to the frontiers which Lorimer had set out, the British should insist that the 1901 status quo continued in effect. In other words, the shaikh would enjoy practical autonomy in this outer zone, and would be entitled to British 'good offices'. The intention behind this formula was clearly to offer the Ottomans a face-saving way out of the problem, by recognising Ottoman jurisdiction in the outer area while imposing so many limitations on it as to render it symbolic.[45] When communicating the formula to the Government of India for its comments, the India Office assured the government that the proposed concession was indeed one of appearance only, and was only made in order to avoid an Ottoman loss of face.

The Government of India and the resident in Bushire were not at all sure that the concession to be offered was simply a matter of appearance. Cox in Bushire was convinced that Kuwait had been a target for Ottoman intrigues for more than a decade. As recently as June 1912, the German shipping firm Wonckhaus and Company had tried to persuade Shaikh Mubarak to allow them to establish an office in Kuwait, and just a few days before he received news of the new compromise-formula, Cox heard that another representative of Wonckhaus had tried to obtain a lease for a terminus at Kuwait on behalf of the German railway company.[46] Cox was especially unhappy that the latest British formula did not settle the question of Warbah and Bubiyan. He pointed out that, if the Ottoman garrison was left on Bubiyan, Kuwait would be subject to constant intrigues on the part of the local Ottoman authorities, with British good offices representing no real protection. The result of this would be constant anxiety to the British and to Shaikh Mubarak, who would certainly feel badly treated.

The Government of India also felt concerned about the new formula, which appeared to them to involve the loss of a large part of the shaikh's territory. They proposed that the final agreement should be carefully drafted so as to exclude the Ottomans, and to place on record that Shaikh Mubarak had acquired administrative influence throughout the wider area attributed to Kuwait in Lorimer's *Gazetteer*. If Warbah and Bubiyan were also returned to the shaikh, the Government of India was prepared to accept that the formula would be practicable.

The India Office, which was now intensely suspicious of the attitude of the Foreign Office, welcomed the criticisms and reservations from India and from Bushire. In the view of the India Office, these comments strengthened the case for holding the 'two-zone' formula in reserve, rather than pushing it forward at the start of negotiations.

Partly as a result of these comments, the Foreign Office presented a new memorandum to the Ottoman ambassador on 18 July 1912, which made no mention of any division of Kuwaiti territory. The memorandum confirmed that Britain now withdrew entirely from participation in the railway company, but it included as a condition of any Anglo–Ottoman agreement the recognition of Warbah and Bubiyan as part of the territory of Kuwait. It was accompanied by a paper defining the British view of the territory of Kuwait, corresponding to the definition in Lorimer's *Gazetteer*.

Disappointment for Shaikh Mubarak: the Anglo–Ottoman Convention

The delivery of the Foreign Office memorandum of 18 July 1912 was followed by another period of inactivity, caused by Turkish involvement in yet another war. This time, the war was the disastrous First Balkan War of October 1912, when Ottoman forces suffered heavy defeats at the hands of a coalition of Greece, Serbia, Bulgaria and Montenegro. It was not until the spring of 1913 that an Ottoman delegation arrived in London to resume negotiations. The 1913 talks involved Hakki Pasha himself, Louis Mallet (assistant under-secretary at the British Foreign Office) and Arthur Hirtzel of the India Office.

As far as Kuwait was concerned, the discussions centred on two major questions: the exact status of Kuwait itself and the limits of Kuwaiti territory. On the matter of the status of Kuwait, the two sides were unable to agree to the two terms proposed by the British ('sovereignty' and 'suzerainty'), so both terms were dropped and it was agreed that Kuwait should be described as an 'autonomous Caza of the Ottoman Empire'. Kuwaiti ships would fly the Ottoman flag, but this would include a special device indicating Kuwait. On the vital question of Ottoman authority in Kuwait there were hard discussions. Hakki Pasha proposed a formula under which the Ottoman government would agree not to become involved in the internal affairs of Kuwait. The obvious implication of this formula was that the Ottomans would be entitled to be involved in external affairs, so the British side put forward a counterproposal to prevent any Ottoman interference in either internal or external affairs. Hakki Pasha could not accept this, so all references to internal and external affairs were omitted.

On the question of the frontiers of Kuwait, the progress of the talks is hard to determine in detail. From the start, Hakki Pasha objected to the wider definition of Kuwaiti territory set out in the British note of 18 July 1912 (i.e. the frontiers specified by Lorimer). To the great surprise of the British negotiators, Hakki Pasha suggested a 'two-zone' solution to the problem, very similar to the solution which the India Office had proposed in June 1912. At the request of the Foreign Office, the India Office produced an official statement of its own proposals for a two-zone solution. Hakki Pasha seems to have received the India Office proposals with favour, as the British negotiators reported that they had managed to obtain a rectification of the southern frontier in favour of Kuwait so as to include Ant'a town, about 100 miles to the south, in the outer ring of Kuwaiti territory. Hakki Pasha also agreed, although with great reluctance, that Bubiyan and Warbah Islands should be included in Kuwait's territory.[47]

However, the British side became aware that the Turks would only agree to this solution of the frontier-problem on one important condition: Britain must accept the Ottoman demand for the right to appoint an Ottoman agent in Kuwait. The India Office decided to ask the Government of India to instruct British officials in the Gulf to talk to Shaikh Mubarak, and to prepare him for the bad news which he would probably have to accept as the price of the settlement between Britain and the Ottoman Empire: the appointment of an Ottoman agent in Kuwait, and the formal abandonment of Kuwaiti claims to Umm Qasr and Safwan in the north-east and to Musallamiyah in the south. The Government of India sent instructions to Cox on 1 and 15 April 1913 to approach the shaikh accordingly.

Cox delegated this task to Shakespear, who had to report on 21 April that Shaikh Mubarak was dangerously ill with arteriosclerosis. The illness was so serious that his life was thought to be in danger, and Shakespear did not want to take the risk of giving him such unpleasant news at this time. In the event, Shakespear was only able to call on the shaikh to discuss the Anglo–Ottoman negotiations at some time on or after 21 May (the exact date cannot be determined from Shakespear's report of the visit, which he sent on 28 May). Before Shakespear could make this visit, Shaikh Mubarak had learned of reports in the Arabic press in Basra, which suggested that the British and the Ottomans had settled all outstanding points, and had agreed on the autonomy of Kuwait … Mubarak apparently interpreted these reports as a sign that all his claims were to be recognised, and Shakespear told Bushire at the end of April that both the shaikh and the general public of Kuwait were extremely pleased with the news. Mubarak must have been all the more disappointed when he finally heard from his old friend, Captain Shakespear, just what had been agreed in London.

Indeed, Shakespear's account of his meeting with Mubarak at the end of May 1913 makes a sad final chapter to Mubarak's relationship with Britain.[48] The old man listened carefully and, for the most part, calmly to Shakespear's presentation of the likely terms of the Anglo–Ottoman convention. Shakespear did his best to stress the positive aspects of the settlement for Kuwait: namely, that the agreement stressed the autonomy of Kuwait within the Ottoman Empire, recognised most of his boundary claims and confirmed his right to undisturbed enjoyment of his properties on the Shatt al-Arab. Shakespear had to point out that Mubarak would pay a price for these advantages: the Ottoman military occupation of Safwan and Umm Qasr would probably continue and there would probably be a demand by the Ottoman government to install a permanent representative or agent in Kuwait.

At this point, when Shakespear mentioned the possibility of a Turkish agent in Kuwait, the tone of the meeting changed sharply. Mubarak was at first so surprised that he asked Shakespear over and over again to explain what he meant by this. Then, the old shaikh became 'most vehement in his opposition to the idea' and begged Shakespear to send an immediate telegram to stress that he would refuse to accept any kind of Turkish official in Kuwait. Mubarak apparently said that any Ottoman agent would intrigue against the ruler of Kuwait and would weaken his authority in Kuwait itself and in the desert. Indeed, Mubarak argued the intrigues would be likely to involve the British government in fresh difficulties before too long.

It is hard not to sympathise with Mubarak's feelings. Whatever concessions he may have made to the Ottomans in the past, he had always maintained the effective independence of his small state by refusing to allow a permanent Ottoman presence in Kuwait. When the Ottomans threatened to install such a presence, he reacted strongly and quickly to prevent this. In 1897, he had turned to the British for protection, and a few years later he had simply frog-marched an Ottoman official out of Kuwait. The one fixed point in his thinking was that, by making an agreement with the British in 1899 (an agreement which prevented him from dealing with any foreign power without British consent) he had acquired a guarantee against any Ottoman attempt to force him to accept their agent.

The day after his meeting with Shakespear in his palace, Mubarak came to the British Agency for another meeting. Shakespear was surprised to see him, as he knew that Mubarak was still in poor health, but it soon became clear that Mubarak wanted to make one final effort to persuade his British friend of the strength of his case against the Ottoman agent, before accepting the inevitable. The arguments which he put forward were, in effect, the principles of his foreign policy:

1. The agreement he had signed with Meade in January 1899 had been framed with the sole purpose of preventing the advent of foreign officials in Kuwait.
2. In the 1907 lease agreement on Bandar Shuwaikh, the British side had expressly named the Turkish government as one which it was desirable to exclude from Kuwait.

3. Mubarak had repeatedly since 1899 refused German overtures to establish a German firm in Kuwait, even though such a firm would have increased his customs revenues.
4. In all respects, Mubarak had faithfully observed his side of the bargain made with Lt. Col. Meade 14 years before.
5. There was no need for Britain to make any concession to the Sublime Porte at the moment, as the Turks were 'a beaten and weak nation', who were not able to dispute his authority in the desert or in Kuwait. He argued that he had never been subject to the Ottomans. If they chose to address him as *qaimaqam*, this meant nothing to him, as he never used the title himself.

This second meeting ended with Mubarak again pleading to Shakespear to telegraph his objections to a Turkish agent as quickly as possible to the Residency in Bushire. He offered Shakespear the use of a boat to take the text of the message from Kuwait to the nearest telegraph office at Fao.

In the event, Shakespear put his comments to Bushire in the form of a long letter describing the meeting. Shakespear had got to know Mubarak well over the past four years, and was clearly fond of him. The comments he made show his affection for Mubarak and also his deep understanding of the mood of Kuwait as a whole. As he pointed out, Kuwait had become more influenced in the past ten years by the Arabic language press of Mesopotamian towns such as Basra, and by newspapers published in Egypt and in India. The shaikh and his people now spent almost all their leisure on 'the discussion of high politics on the mischievous lines supplied by the vernacular press'. These newspapers encouraged a general feeling that the Christian powers of Europe were determined to reduce the Islamic world to impotence. There was, therefore, likely to be a suspicion in Kuwait that the Anglo–Ottoman convention was sacrificing Kuwait to the Ottomans in exchange for gains for Britain elsewhere in the Middle East. In Shakespear's words, the convention would appear to be 'a formal delivery of Kuwait into the hands of Turkey by the Power which has hitherto safeguarded them from the menace of that very Power', and the most disappointed of all would be Shaikh Mubarak, who 'more than anyone else has combated anti-British notions ... and has always held up the British government as the only one which could be trusted to keep its word, deal even-handed justice, not to discriminate between the religious beliefs of its subjects and not to oppress the weak'. Shakespear concluded that there was every chance that the convention would destroy 'with a stroke of the pen' the position which Britain had built up in Kuwait over the past ten years, at considerable expenditure of effort and money.

Shakespear's cogent arguments were at least dignified with a reply from the highest level of the Indian Empire, the Secretary of State for India, who telegraphed the viceroy on 6 June 1913. The reply gave no ground to hope for an improvement to the conditions on offer. The British government, according to this telegraph, attached the greatest importance to Shaikh Mubarak's acceptance of the agreement without any further alteration. The concessions being asked from him were 'part of the price he must pay for the permanent establishment, on a treaty basis, of his position and the recognition of his ample claims'. The secretary of state particularly hoped that Mubarak would agree that the appointment of an Ottoman agent in Kuwait would be 'purely formal', as the Ottomans had undertaken not to interfere in the succession to the Shaikhdom or in Kuwait's external and internal affairs. A British agent would also continue to reside in Kuwait to provide British support. In order to sweeten this rather bleak message, the secretary of state authorised the viceroy to consider granting Shaikh Sir Mubarak al-Sabah KCIE (as he now was) another British decoration.[49]

With his long experience of the Ottoman government at very close quarters, Shaikh Mubarak must have laughed a little hollowly at Britain's readiness to trust Ottoman assurances not to interfere in Kuwait. The British government's assurances that the British agent could act as some kind of umpire between the ruler of Kuwait and the Ottoman Agent must also have sounded strange to an elderly Arab shaikh who had never benefited from team-games at an English Public School, and who had governed his state for 17 years by very different rules. However, Mubarak had realised by now that the Anglo–Ottoman convention would go ahead whether he liked it or not, and that his best hope was to try to secure a few modifications in detail.

His last attempt to influence the convention before it was signed came during a trip to Muhammarah in early July 1913 to see his old friend Shaikh Kha'zal. The British resident in Bushire came over to Muhammarah to reassure Mubarak again about the provisions of the convention. Mubarak professed complete agreement with Cox's statement that there was no difference between his own interests and those of the British government, but he did try to persuade Cox to change the wording of the Convention to specify that his sons (*awlad*) should be specified as his successors to the Shaikhdom: the proposed British wording simply made the provisions covering Kuwait applicable to Mubarak and his '*khalaf*', who, as he pointed out, could be anyone, his sons or someone else. As we shall see this concern for his succession was now Mubarak's dominant worry as he grew older and his limbs got stiffer. Once again, he was unable to move the British government, which refused to make the change he requested, and pointed out that the Ottoman government had promised not to interfere with the succession process. Although Mubarak had not had his last word on the subject, the Anglo–Ottoman Convention was signed on 29 July 1913, with none of the changes which he had wanted.

In the event, Mubarak never had to accept the humiliation of a Turkish agent in Kuwait or a surrender of his rights over his territories and succession. The Anglo–Ottoman convention had still not been ratified by the time that Turkey declared war on Europe in August 1914. When the guns fell silent over four years later, Mubarak was dead and the Ottomans had lost all ability to influence events in Mesopotamia and the Gulf. His successors would have to deal with a new and aggressive neighbour in Mesopotamia, and with a very different and challenging balance of power in Arabia as a whole. Mubarak would surely have been furious to see Sir Percy Cox in 1922 sitting with Ibn Sa'ud at the Ugair conference and giving Ibn Sa'ud a large part of the territory received for Kuwait under the 1913 Anglo–Ottoman Convention.

6

Mubarak's Last Years

The End of an Age and an Evaluation

Shaikh Mubarak died suddenly of a heart-attack on the evening of 28 November 1915. By then, Britain had been at war with the Ottoman Empire for just over a year. Even before the Ottoman Empire joined Germany in the war against Britain, Mubarak had in August 1914 placed 'all his efforts, his men and his ships' at the disposal of Britain. He was soon rewarded. On 3 November 1914 his old friend Major Knox, now installed as British resident in Bushire, issued the promise for which Mubarak had been waiting since 1897: Kuwait would be recognised at the end of the war as an independent principality under British protection. A few days later, British and Indian forces landed at Fao and moved quickly up the Shatt al-Arab to Basra.

Elsewhere, the pattern of power was changing in Arabia during late 1914 and 1915. At the start of 1915, Mubarak's friend Captain Shakespear met an unlikely but heroic death fighting with Ibn Sa'ud against the forces of Ibn Rashid at Jarrab. At the end of December 1915, less than a month after Mubarak died, Shakespear would secure his posthumous triumph: a treaty which established Ibn Sa'ud's Najd as an independent state under British protection.

In November 1915, Mubarak was succeeded by his eldest son, Shaikh Jabir. There had been fears that his second son, Shaikh Salim, might try to bid for power when Mubarak died. Sir Percy Cox therefore sent a British warship to Kuwait as soon as he heard of Mubarak's death. If Salim had really intended to challenge his brother, the British warship dissuaded him, and he promised to serve Shaikh Jabir faithfully.[1]

As far as we can see, Mubarak had avoided naming Shaikh Jabir as his successor until very soon before his death. Indeed, the information that Jabir was the nominated successor only comes in the form of a telegram from the Viceroy of India to the India Office a month after Mubarak died. As recently as April 1914, the situation was that most people in Kuwait expected that Jabir would indeed succeed his father, but that nothing had been said officially to this effect.[2]

The fact that Mubarak seemed reluctant to name a successor does not mean that he was indifferent to the question: quite the reverse. In his dealings with Britain, he had often tried to obtain a guarantee that the British government would support 'his heirs' as his successors, so as to formalise the al-Sabah dynasty. The best guess must be that he delayed naming a successor for so long because of his deep-rooted aversion to any form of power sharing, even with his closest relatives. Back in 1908, Lorimer had commented on the highly personal nature of his rule, and his unwillingness to grant any power to his sons. Lorimer's remarks suggest that Mubarak well remembered the circumstances of his own fratricidal seizure of power back in 1896, and did not want a repetition:

> In all Mubarak's political arrangements, precaution is a conspicuous feature. The heads of his departments are mostly slaves; his near relations are excluded from his counsels; even his sons wield no executive powers. The duty of interviewing foreigners is one which he never delegates to an agent, and without his consent no stranger can obtain information or facilities of any sort in Kuwait.

But, despite his hesitations about delegating powers to his sons, Mubarak very much wanted them to succeed him. His concern surfaced during the negotiations of 1907 for the lease of Bandar Shuwaikh to Britain. At the last moment, Mubarak insisted on a clause under which the 'precious Imperial English Government' promised that the town of Kuwait and its boundaries belonged to Shaikh Mubarak and his heirs after him.[3] The department at the head of the previous Imperial English Government, the India Office, was rightly worried that this clause came dangerously close to giving a British guarantee of the rule of the al-Sabah dynasty over Kuwait. The India Office only removed its objections after assurances from India that British officials in the Gulf did not think that Mubarak intended this interpretation.[4] Unfortunately, it became clear six years later that Mubarak meant exactly this interpretation. In his letter to Cox of 7 July 1913 to which we have already referred, he pointed out that the Arabic text of the 1907 Bandar Shuwaikh lease referred to British recognition that Kuwait belonged to him and his sons (*awlad*).

It seems likely that Mubarak's interest in assuring that his sons took over on his death intensified during the years after 1907. In his old age, he certainly became more suspicious of those around him, and more concerned about the future of his branch of the family. The dramatic flight of the *towashis* in 1910 upset him greatly, and for a short time he appeared unusually courteous to his subjects, but the interval of politeness did not last for long. In January 1912, his men arrested a number of Kuwaitis and charged them with involvement in a plot to assassinate him.

Some of Mubarak's closest associates tried to convince him that his fears were exaggerated, and the brother of his private secretary came over from Basra to deny the existence of the plot. However Mubarak could not be convinced, and refused to move anywhere in the town without a well-armed escort. He identified a prominent merchant, Saqr Ibn Ghanim, as the leader of the supposed plot. Shakespear could not believe that there was any truth in the charge: Saqr Ibn Ghanim had been one of the most trusted and successful of Mubarak's military leaders in the operations against Shaikh Sa'dun.

It could be that Ibn Ghanim's success in that campaign and his popularity in Kuwait were the cause of Shaikh Mubarak's suspicions, which reached the level of almost paranoid violence. Many had noted the tyrannical nature of Mubarak's rule in Kuwait, but he had never before behaved as he did now. Saqr Ibn Ghanim was horrifically tortured, and before he was released from prison his eyes were put out with red-hot needles.[5] Mubarak tried to keep the matter secret, but this proved impossible, and the British agent reported that when news of Saqr Ibn Ghanim's treatment became known to the public in Kuwait, it was 'received with execration by anyone who dare express an opinion'.[6]

Mubarak never offered an explanation of his barbaric action, or any evidence for the existence of the plot. We have to speculate that it was his increasing sensitivity about the succession, and his fear that a more popular family might bid to supplant the al-Sabah on his death, which prompted his violent reaction. If this was the case, another threat to his family's long-term future surfaced during 1913. This time it came from his two closest allies, Ibn Sa'ud and the British. In the spring of 1913, Captain Shakespear, while on a tour of the Kuwait hinterland, ran into Ibn Sa'ud in the desert. Shakespear had first met Ibn Sa'ud two years before, and was already among the Najdi ruler's circle of friends. He received a very warm and friendly welcome, and remained in Ibn Sa'ud's camp for two days. During this time, the British officer and the ruler of Najd discussed the Ottoman Empire's poor performance in the Balkan War, and Ibn Sa'ud began to think aloud about the future of Arabia. He thought that the Arabs could evict the Turkish troops from Hasa and Qatif, which had been under Ottoman occupation since 1871, with the greatest of ease. Indeed, there might never be a better chance to do this than now, with the Ottoman Army broken, the Empire's finances in ruin, and unrest in the Arab provinces of Syria and Mesopotamia. Would Britain be prepared to give some sign of friendship or support to this plan, even if this had to be disguised from the outside world ?[7]

Shakespear told Ibn Sa'ud that there was absolutely no chance of British support for his plan. Britain was on friendly terms with the Ottoman Empire, and could not give even tacit support to the rebellion of an Ottoman subject against the Porte, but Ibn Sa'ud was clearly not discouraged by Shakespear's negative reply. Ibn Sa'ud explained that his power had grown so much in recent years that he feared no-one in Arabia itself. The only danger to the Sa'udi state now came from the Ottomans, who still had the capability to mount a simultaneous assault on Najd from Hasa in the east and from the Hijaz in the west. A two-pronged attack of this kind was the one thing which Ibn Sa'ud could not resist, so he was anxious to secure his Eastern border by taking over Hasa and removing one of the threats. He would also gain economic benefits from the revenues of Hasa and its ports on the Gulf coast.

Shakespear could see that Ibn Sa'ud was intending to launch his attack on Hasa very soon, but he did not know that when he bumped into Ibn Sa'ud in the desert the latter was already on his way to reconquer Hasa and Qatif. Before the British officer finished writing his report of his meeting for Sir Percy Cox in Bushire, Ibn Sa'ud had struck. On 8 May 1913, news reached Bahrain that Ibn Sa'ud's forces had occupied Hasa without any fighting. The news reached Kuwait a few days later, and was received with great surprise. The Kuwaiti reaction was that the Sa'udi attack was the result of Shakespear's 'high diplomacy' during his recent desert tour. Shakespear was sufficiently worried about this reaction to place a copy of his dispatch recording his conversation with Ibn Sa'ud and his forecast of the likelihood of an attack on Hasa (which he had been about to destroy as having been overtaken by events) on the record, so as to prove that he had not in fact encouraged Ibn Sa'ud in his venture.[8]

We can easily guess that Shaikh Mubarak was far from pleased with the news of the reoccupation of Hasa. Relations between Mubarak and Ibn Sa'ud had become cooler as Ibn Sa'ud's power and prestige grew. When Shakespear met Ibn Sa'ud for the first time in March 1911, and Ibn Sa'ud entranced his British guest with his views on the future of Arabia, the Najdi ruler specifically requested Shakespear not to repeat anything he had told him to Shaikh Mubarak. What was Mubarak to make of the events of April and May 1913?

The British political agent goes on a tour which takes him 150 miles south of any place ever claimed as a part of Kuwait. There, he 'happens' to run into Ibn Sa'ud who 'happens' to be on his way to attack Hasa. The coincidences are striking to the modern student. For Mubarak, they must have been deeply worrying. His position in the desert had always depended on his ability to act as an intermediary between the tribes which happened to be in the ascendant at any given time in central Arabia and the foreign powers which wanted to influence events in the area. Now, it very much seemed that his trusted protectors, the British, were engineering secret deals by direct negotiation with the leading figure of Arabia, and that these deals were greatly boosting the position of Ibn Sa'ud on the Gulf as well as in the centre of Arabia.

Mubarak's growing suspicion of Ibn Sa'ud may help to explain his extraordinary action in the following year. While Ibn Sa'ud was trying to negotiate a settlement with the Ottomans of all his outstanding problems, Mubarak first promised Ibn Sa'ud that he would be present during the talks, and then at the last moment refused to have anything to do with the negotiations.[9] Shaikh Mubarak may have calculated that his sudden withdrawal from the talks would force Ibn Sa'ud to return to a more subordinate role in his dealings with the Ottomans. If so, this was a mistake. Ibn Sa'ud angrily changed the location of his meeting with the Ottomans, and kept the content of the talks secret from Mubarak. Whatever degree of influence Mubarak had retained in the affairs of Najd was now at an end.

Although events in Najd must have been displeasing to Mubarak, the main concern of the Kuwaiti ruler in 1913–14 was his relationship with his crucially important allies the British. By the middle of 1913, Kuwait's strategic position had significantly altered for the worse. In the south, Ibn Sa'ud had moved into Hasa and the Gulf coast. The lands to the West were already Sa'udi territory, and the north was still blocked by the Ottoman Empire. On the east, Kuwait's British friends controlled the waters of the Gulf, so there was no direct threat to Kuwait from any of its regional rivals. The British were negotiating an agreement with the Porte, which would probably lead to permission for the Ottoman Empire to station a permanent agent in Kuwait itself, and this was only the public aspect of the Anglo–Ottoman Convention. What other concessions might have been negotiated in secret? Shaikh Mubarak's inclination was always to suspect conspiracies against him. His suspicions would have been strengthened by the fact that his own agreements with the British in the past had either been secret or generally included some secret provisions. The only way to avoid losing all the achievements of his reign was to attach the British to the fortunes of his branch of the al-Sabah family after his demise.

We have already seen how Mubarak introduced the question of a guarantee of his succession into the talks about the 1913 Anglo–Ottoman agreement. In his letter to Sir Percy Cox of 7 July 1913, he argued strongly for the inclusion of a reference to his sons (*awlad*) as his successors, but had to be content with a reassurance from Cox that the Ottomans would be making a specific promise not to interfere in the succession to Kuwait. Mubarak was not happy with this answer, and continued to press for some British statement about the succession to Kuwait. In November 1913, he explained to Cox exactly what he wanted. He did not want to designate a successor at this time but was worried that, when the time came for him to go, some disappointed individual or individuals from his family or kinsmen might create discord in Kuwait, which could undo his life's work if Britain stood aloof. He did want to feel sure that Britain would 'stand by' if he died suddenly, and would intervene if necessary to 'regulate the situation'.[10] Cox forwarded the request to the Government of India on 9 November, and followed it up a month later with a long formula of his own devising which he hoped would 'set the mind of our venerable protégé at rest', while not causing any inconvenient commitments for the government. Cox's long draft formula referred in effusive terms to Mubarak's statesmanship and wise control, as well as his friendliness in cooperating with Britain to promote order and good government on the shores of the Gulf. On this basis, the formula suggested that Mubarak should keep the British confidentially informed during his lifetime of his wishes about the designation of his successor. As long as his nominee had British approval, Britain would give him moral support, and would try to avoid any dissension in Kuwait. Cox's draft stated that the assurance was being given personally to Mubarak, in recognition of his close relations with the British government. This statement was clearly meant to limit the application of the pledge to Mubarak's immediate successor only, and to avoid an open-ended commitment to backing an al-Sabah dynasty in Kuwait.[11]

It is not clear whether the resident in fact gave something like this assurance to Shaikh Mubarak in anticipation of the ratification of the Anglo–Ottoman Convention: we do know that the Foreign Office ruled against giving the full text of Cox's draft to Mubarak until after ratification of the convention with the Ottoman Empire. But whatever message was given to Mubarak, it was not enough to dissuade him from the last and in some ways the most extraordinary act of his reign.

Mubarak's Last Offer to Britain

In September 1915, just a few weeks before his death, Mubarak made one last effort to control events in Kuwait after his death. His proposal was one of the oddest made to a British officer in all the centuries of British involvement in the Gulf: in effect, Mubarak proposed to give Kuwait to Britain.

The offer was made during a meeting with the resident, Sir Percy Cox, in mid-September. Mubarak told the resident that he had now arrived at a great age, and could not hope to live for many years more. His own affairs and the Kuwaiti economy as a whole had prospered during the past few years, because of the support he had received from the British government, but he had several sons and relations, and while some were harmless, some were dangerous. He did not therefore want to see the 'edifice which he has taken so much pains to build up' torn into fragments by a family scramble for the inheritance when he died. His scheme was to turn all sources of revenue over to the British for them to manage with a British staff. These sources of revenue would include his private income from the al-Sabah family properties and all the public revenues of Kuwait, such as the customs revenues. In return, Mubarak would receive the income less the expenses of administration for the rest of his life. In his will, he would specify the amount of cash to be settled on his beneficiaries, and these sums would be paid out by the British on his death.

Cox reacted positively to the proposal, which he described as a 'wise scheme worthy of his fine old character'.[12] Perhaps fortunately for the future of Kuwait and the Gulf region, the Government of India was horrified. As the government pointed out, there would be direct expense to Britain from installing British officials, and the loss of employment would cause resentment and probable obstruction on the part of Kuwaiti officials. It was also reasonable to expect that Mubarak's successors would resent the arrangement as a weakening of their political position. India's objections were supported by the Secretary of State for India, Chamberlain, and the plan became another of the intriguing might-have-beens of the British Empire in India.

7

Shaikh Mubarak in History

'Kuwait and everything in it *belongs* to the al-Sabah'. This comment by Shaikh Mubarak could serve as his epitaph. In no other town along the Gulf coast was power so concentrated in the hands of one ruler. Even his closest relatives were kept away from real power of any kind. All revenues were treated by Shaikh Mubarak as part of his personal treasury, whether they came from his date gardens or from the duties on imports and exports or from the taxes on pearl fishers, butchers, shopkeepers or roaming bedouin. Any contact with foreigners was closely controlled by the shaikh himself, and his immediate family only acted as his subordinates in dealings with the outside world. If he could be summoned to answer us, Mubarak might dispute our conclusions, but he would certainly not try to duck any responsibility for his actions as ruler of Kuwait.

In his attempts to secure Kuwait's place in the Gulf region, we must give Mubarak credit for achieving his major life-objective: the defining of Kuwait's practical autonomy as a state. These words are carefully chosen. At the start of his reign, Mubarak was prepared to make concessions to the Ottoman Empire which looked very much like a confession of Ottoman sovereignty over Kuwait. He flew the Ottoman flag and angled as hard as he could for the Ottoman title of Qaimaqam of Kuwait. His energetic attempts to persuade his British friends that these concessions did not amount to an admission of Ottoman sovereignty are simply unconvincing. He knew very well that the title of *qaimaqam*, which he gladly accepted in December 1897, did indeed mean that he acknowledged some measure of Ottoman sovereignty. When he went to the telegraph office at Basra in November 1900 in the company of the Vali of Basra to express his loyalty to the sultan at a low point in his fortunes, he was only accepting the implications of his status as a *qaimaqam*. But titles and flags were always a relatively minor matter in his eyes. What mattered to him was the autonomy he enjoyed, in practical terms, as the ruler of Kuwait, and here he succeeded in keeping the Ottomans always at arms' length by frustrating all their attempts to base a permanent agent or representative in Kuwait.

Whenever this idea surfaced, Mubarak always acted very quickly indeed. In early 1897, when it seemed that the Ottomans were going to appoint a quarantine official, he at once turned to Britain for help. Nearly three years later, when the Vali of Basra in September 1899 sent a harbour-master and five soldiers to take up posts in Kuwait, Mubarak had them marched out of his Shaikhdom. For the rest of his reign, no Ottoman official set foot in Kuwait except as a short-stay visitor.

For some months in 1913–14, Mubarak must have thought that he was going to lose his long running battle to keep an Ottoman agent out of Kuwait since his British friends told him that he would have to accept the presence of this agent as a 'price' for the benefits which the Anglo–Ottoman Convention was supposed to bring him. Mubarak did not in fact have to accept this humiliation, and even if the worst had happened, the convention had been ratified and the agent had arrived in Kuwait, do we have to assume that Mubarak's more pessimistic expectations would have come to pass? His position in 1913 was far stronger than at the start of his reign, as he now had a solid relationship with the British government and particularly with the British Residency in Bushire. By 1913, after all, a British agent had been in Kuwait to act as a link between Mubarak and the resident for more than eight years. The British resident treated Mubarak as a valued friend and ally.

While we can understand that Mubarak was not happy with British assurances in 1913 that the British agent and the British resident could protect Kuwait against intrigues by the Ottoman agent, we can be sure that he would have held some strong cards in any subsequent confrontation with the Ottomans. An Ottoman official who was unlucky enough to be posted to Kuwait would have found the Mubarak of 1913, with his British friends behind him, a very tough proposition indeed.

The way in which Mubarak enticed Britain into a close political relationship with Kuwait is perhaps the major single achievement of his reign, and it is simply not fair to ascribe his success with Britain to luck. Of course, luck played a major role. The late 1890s happened to be a time when British officials were ready for the first time to consider changing their long-standing strategy of limiting their role on the Arab side of the Gulf to a line just north of Bahrain. Mubarak could not have known this in 1897. Neither could he have known that his request for British protection would soon be followed by Lord Curzon's appointment to a position in which he could influence events in the Gulf, or by the utterly false rumours that the Russian government was about to back a bid for a railway concession to the Gulf. All this was luck on a very large scale, but Mubarak exploited the opportunities that luck brought him. It was his pressure which led Lt Col. Meade, sitting on his boat in Kuwait Bay in January 1899, to take the astonishing decision to give Mubarak a letter promising the good offices of Britain. Once the letter was in his hands, Mubarak played a very clever game indeed. The British mandarins in Whitehall were clear in their own minds that Britain had not meant this letter to be taken as a commitment to protect Kuwait. They reckoned without the skill and persistence of their new friend. By boasting far and wide to his friends in Arabia that he was under the protection of the British government, Mubarak made his survival as ruler of Kuwait into an issue of British prestige in the Gulf. Then, by presenting British officials with the fact of his political weakness in the face of threats from the Ottomans and from Ibn Rashid, he pushed the British into acting exactly as if they were the protecting power in Kuwait. When Sir N. O'Conor in September 1899 warned the Ottoman foreign minister off any plans to create an Ottoman customs house in Kuwait, or when Captain Simmons on board HMS *Perseus* in December 1901 threatened to bombard Kuwait if the Ottomans placed a garrison in the town, the mighty ambassador and the senior naval officer in the Persian Gulf were both being manipulated by the shaikh, much as they would have hated to admit it. Mubarak, incomparably the weaker partner in the relationship with Britain, used his weakness to make Britain deliver in reality the protection which it refused in theory.

Once the British government was thoroughly enmeshed in Kuwait's affairs, Shaikh Mubarak could manoeuvre between Britain and the Ottoman Empire to achieve the best results for his small state. Of course, he faced the constant risk that the two great powers would negotiate over his head to reach a deal about the future of Kuwait and the Gulf region as a whole. In 1913, this was exactly what seemed to be about to happen, but the risk was unavoidable. Mubarak, as a very small player in the Gulf scene, cannot be criticised for taking it. In any event, Mubarak was saved by the collapse of the entire world order in 1914, and died with exactly the prize for which he had applied in January 1897: a written guarantee from Britain that Kuwait was now an independent state under British protection. Even the aborted Anglo–Ottoman Convention, to which the old ruler had objected so strongly in 1913, was in many ways a testimony to Shaikh Mubarak's success in establishing the practical independence of Kuwait. As the British government pointed out in June 1913 with some asperity, the planned convention did establish Mubarak's position on a treaty basis, and recognised a large proportion of his territorial claims. Thanks to Mubarak's exploitation of the diplomatic 'space' between Britain and the Ottoman Empire, Kuwait was by 1913 a much more solid diplomatic entity than had ever seemed likely at the start of the century, when the Ottomans and the Rashids appeared with monotonous frequency at its gates.

Mubarak therefore deserves to be considered the founder of modern Kuwait on the basis of his success in establishing the state's political independence and its diplomatic identity. When we turn to Mubarak's efforts to establish Kuwait as a power in Arabia, the verdict has to be more cautious. We have seen that Mubarak consistently over-estimated his importance in desert affairs and his ability to raise and lead desert armies. His great expedition into Najd in the spring of 1901 ended in military and political disaster when his army was routed at Sarif. His attempt to mobilise and maintain a second large army for a desert expedition in 1910 also strained his resources, and forced him to abandon his plans in a humiliating climb-down. His desert diplomacy did, of course, benefit from the success of his Sa'udi protégé in re-occupying Riyadh in January 1902. But even this success turned sour for Mubarak, as it became clear that the new Sa'udi state would overshadow Kuwait and deny Mubarak the role he had always wanted – that of arbiter of desert politics. By the end of Mubarak's reign, the new Sa'udi state encircled Kuwait on the west and the south. It had also managed to acquire the friendship and support of Captain Shakespear in developing direct links with Britain.

On 26 December 1915, less than a month after Mubarak died, Ibn Sa'ud got his own treaty with Britain, recognising him as the independent ruler of Najd and its dependencies under British protection. Kuwait had therefore lost its role as the channel of communication between the interior of Najd and the world outside. Ibn Sa'ud could develop his own diplomacy, and the size and strategic importance of Najd would make him an attractive partner for Britain. In 1916, British weapons and money started to arrive in Riyadh as Britain's regard to its new friend. A superficial observer might say that Mubarak was wrong to get involved in the desert, and that he would have been better advised to concentrate on building up the prosperity of Kuwait rather than spending so much on desert campaigns and diplomacy. This argument looks convincing at first sight. Kuwait was not well equipped for desert warfare, as Mubarak's townsmen and pearl-fishers were not at a level to constitute a reliable military force and his support among the desert tribes was always much less than he would have liked. Could Mubarak really afford to turn his back on the desert? The lesson of history was that Kuwait, as a small town with no natural defences, was permanently vulnerable to any desert confederation which could unite the tribes of the interior in raids on the Gulf coast. Kuwait was not Switzerland, secure behind mountains and able to turn its back on the surrounding region by pursuing a policy of armed neutrality. When Mubarak became ruler, the town did not even have a wall around it. So he had to pursue a 'forward' policy in the desert, forming alliances and balancing one tribe against another in order to preserve his own position. Inactivity was simply not an option for Mubarak.

However, the ways in which Mubarak tried to extend Kuwait's influence in Arabia are certainly open to serious objection, and much of the responsibility for this rests with Shaikh Mubarak himself. Two major mistakes can be identified.

First, immediately after concluding his agreement with Britain in January 1899, Mubarak seems to have become carried away by the vision of himself as a great Arabian leader, even as the arbiter of Arabian politics. For example, in 1901 he led a large army into the desert and was soundly defeated at the disastrous battle of Sarif by the forces of Ibn Rashid. Mubarak had presumably gambled that a victory over Ibn Rashid would have given the al-Sabah a commanding position in Arabia for years to come. The expedition, however, was doomed to failure from the start because, as the rout at Sarif demonstrated, Kuwait's levies of townsmen and pearl-fishers were no match for a true Najdi army such as the army of Ibn Rashid, and Mubarak's allies among the al-Sa'ud and the bedouin tribes were not sufficiently numerous to make up for this discrepancy. Mubarak should surely have appreciated this from the start, and should have concentrated on using Kuwait's one great asset – its financial strength relative to the poverty of Arabia – in order to buy and build up a network of bedouin support, and to weaken the Ibn Rashid through diplomacy. From the little evidence available to us in British reports and in Kuwaiti oral tradition, it seems that Mubarak was over-confident about his abilities as a desert warrior. His tendency to fantasise was apparent immediately after the battle at Sarif, when he tried to claim (against overwhelming evidence of the rout) that his forces had actually been victorious in the battle and conceded the fact that his brother had been killed.

Second, after the disaster at Sarif, Mubarak did eventually draw the obvious the conclusion that he was not cut out for a career as a military commander in the desert, and turned his attention to the use of financial resources in order to play a role in desert affairs. Again, the verdict on his conduct of diplomacy between 1901 and 1915 is rather a negative one. The two cornerstones of his desert diplomacy should surely have been his relationship with Shaikh Sa'dun of the Muntafiq, and his more complex relationship with his one-time protégé,

Abdulaziz bin Abdulrahman Ibn Sa'ud, who was the rising star in Arabia from January 1902 onwards. In both cases, Mubarak was unable to build a lasting relationship. His quarrel with Sa'dun degenerated after 1909 to the point where Mubarak was again prepared to risk crippling his small state's economy by mounting another expedition of untrained townsmen into the desert in the summer of 1910 – a very risky move from which he was effectively rescued by the discontent of his own people. In regard to Ibn Sa'ud, we may perhaps have to admit that there would always be scope for conflict between him and Mubarak once Ibn Sa'ud began to emerge as the most successful leader in Arabia. After all, the earlier rulers of Najd had threatened Kuwait and other towns of the Gulf coast many times during the past 150 years. While the Najdi–Kuwaiti relationship could never be a wholly comfortable one, Mubarak seems to have done much to make it worse. On a personal level, he showed signs of an intense jealousy of Ibn Sa'ud, which took the form of blackening his name in conversations with other desert leaders and with British officials. Mubarak's insults went beyond any political manoeuvres, and hinted at a feeling of intense personal rivalry, perhaps mixed with jealousy of Ibn Sa'ud's high personal standing in the desert, his charismatic appeal to the desert tribes, and that quality of 'aristocracy' to which Mubarak could not himself aspire.

Mubarak's jealousy of Ibn Sa'ud could give us a clue to the reasons for his excessive ambition and frequent disappointment in desert affairs. In dealings with the Ottomans and the British, he always seemed to know how to play his cards to the best advantage, and to turn weaknesses into strengths. In Arabian affairs he often comes across as an unrealistic bungler, who had to dig deep into the finances of Kuwait in order to rescue himself from his misjudgements. The heavy taxes imposed on Kuwaitis in their trade, in their housing and in the form of 'levies' of money and manpower gave them no reward except virtual isolation within Arabia, and an edgy and unsatisfactory relationship with the new Sa'udi state.

Mubarak had not in fact the character or military skills to play the part of an Arabian chieftain successfully, even if the resources and traditions of Kuwait had made this a realistic ambition. As the British consul in Basra remarked:

… some years … before Mobarek murdered his brothers and seized Kowait … it was a well established custom for the Shaikhs of Koweit and Mohammarah (Khalal) and nakib of Basra (Taleb Nakib) to combine in organizing armed attacks on the inhabitants … or in undertaking piratical enterprises … who employed their own servants and retainers for the purpose and shared the spoils among them. I think we should be incorrect in presuming that this custom has entirely died out.[1]

This was not at all the same thing as the desert raiding which Ibn Sa'ud conducted so successfully.

The Arabian dream seems to have enticed Mubarak for much of his reign. We have seen the cost to Kuwait as his taxation dug deeper into its revenues. For this reason, the place he occupies in Kuwaiti folk-memory is rather equivocal. Of course, he is remembered as the man who ensured that Kuwait would be an independent political entity, in order words, as the true 'father' of an independent Kuwait. At the same time, there is a strong note of bitterness in the recollections, especially of older Kuwaitis. 'Yes, he was a great man in many ways,' they agree, 'but we paid a heavy price in the form of extortions and personal cruelty.'

Running through their accounts is a belief that Mubarak simply went beyond what was acceptable in the way he handled his people. Of course, a measure of cruelty and arbitrariness was to be expected from any ruler in the region, but by concentrating power in his own hands and placing heavy financial demands on his subjects Mubarak, towards the end of his reign, crossed the line from firmness to tyranny. His extraordinary response to the 'plot' against him in 1912, when he blinded a prominent warrior merchant, was another blow to his reputation among his own people.

Some of this bitterness and doubt even penetrated to the British officials in Kuwait, who normally regarded Mubarak with affection and tolerance. In April 1912, the shaikh's great friend Captain Shakespear, who was always prepared to give him full credit for his friendship with Britain and his ability to keep his town 'well in hand', wrote a remarkable letter to the political resident in Bushire describing the tense and unhappy atmosphere of Mubarak's last years:

> The old system under the iron rule of Sheikh Mobarak is rapidly breaking down and the wheel turn rustily. The merchant Sheikhs are things of the past and the few old survivals dare not call their souls their own. This would signify if the Sheikh himself was beyond reproach. But a good year or two in the pearl trade and the sudden increase of revenue from the importation of arms have revealed in him a hitherto unsuspected taste for luxury and ostentatious display ... Extortionate demands have been levies on the people. Everything points to lean years to come, and it is problematical whether the Sheikh will have the strength of mind to economise ... At present, the people, who complain continually, look to us as their deliverers. It will be an unpleasant moment for us (i.e. for Britain) when the arrive at a juster view of the situation, and realise that it is our support chiefly that has enabled Sheikh Mobarak's despotism to flourish, and taught him that he need no longer rely on the affections of his people and their confidence in his strength, wealth and justice.

The letter reads well today, Mubarak could say that his achievement still endures, in that the Kuwaiti flag, though tattered by the Iraqi invasion of 1990–91, still flies over an independent Kuwait, while other towns such as Zubair and Muhammarah have disappeared into the territories of oppressive and unfriendly states. There was a price to be paid for this and the price has not by any means been forgotten.

Finally, how does Mubarak stand in comparison with the other commanding figure of early twentieth-century Arabia, Abdulaziz Ibn Sa'ud, who was first Mubarak's protégé and then his rival for dominance in the region ? Both men reflect to an amazing degree the different milieux from which they sprang. Mubarak, calculating and avaricious, suspicious and brusque in his dealings with his own people, is very much an archetype of the commercial seaward-looking mentality of the Utub families who had moved up the Gulf into Kuwait around 1700 AD. As we have mentioned, these families seem to have lost much of their original desert traditions and mentality during their long period of travelling around the Gulf. They became a hard-headed and apparently rather joyless group, successful within certain limits, but without much capacity to fire the imagination. By contrast, Ibn Sa'ud retained throughout his life the courtesy and charm of his long bedouin lineage, and with it a great ability to inspire enthusiasm and admiration among Arabs and foreigners alike. Even among British officials, the reactions to the two men varied accordingly. Captain Shakespear acknowledged Mubarak's strengths as an ally and as a ruler, who kept his town under a 'strong hand', but also pointed out, in the letter we have just quoted, the negative and oppressive nature of Mubarak's rule. By contrast Shakespear's records of his meetings with Ibn Sa'ud brim over with the excitement and inspiration which this extraordinary man generated. In the end, Shakespear was prepared to defy the orders of his superiors and lose his life fighting in Ibn Sa'ud's army in January 1915. It is impossible to imagine Shakespear making a similar grand gesture on behalf of Mubarak.

This does not mean that Ibn Sa'ud could not be capricious and mean on occasion. In the lean years of the early 1930s, just before the discovery of oil in Damman, the merchants of Jiddah and Najd learned to dread the visits of Ibn Sa'ud's financial adviser and 'fixer', Abdullah Sulaiman, demanding yet more 'voluntary' contributions to the coffers of the Sa'udi state. Even so, there was a quality of imagination and inspiration in Ibn Sa'ud's political life which simply did not exist in Mubarak's smaller political ambit.

To simplify a highly-complex picture, we could perhaps say that Mubarak had ambitions, which he pursued relentlessly and often with success, but these ambitions were focused above all on the interests of himself and his immediate family. Such wealth as Kuwait had was sucked out to build up Mubarak's personal estates and to finance his own family's agenda. Ibn Sa'ud also used his position and his treasury for the benefit of his family, but he had something larger than this in mind. His ambitions were fired by a vision of a resurgent and modernised Arabia, which Mubarak could never have shared and probably would not have been able to comprehend.

Notes

Chapter One

I.   It is perhaps appropriate here to point out that Muhammad and Jarrah were Mubarak's full brothers, not half-brothers, as is frequently stated: Alan Rush, *AL SABAH: History of Genealogy* (London 1988 and personal knowledge).

2.   R/15/1/471, ff 95–7, second note of Gaskin on his visit to Kuwait, 6 September 1897.

3.   FO.195/1935, nf., Extract from Basra Consulate Diary for week ending 18 May 1896.

4.   FO 78/5113, ff. 10–21b, Memorandum by Capt. J. F. Whyte, 22 March 1897.

5.   FO 195/2116, ff. 241–41b, Wratislaw to O'Connor, 13 June 1902.

6.   L/P&S/18/C.239, J. A. Saldana, *Precis of Kuwait Affairs* (1904) p. 1.

7.   For what can be gleaned from surviving sources, see the flawed, though useful, study by A. M. Abu-Hakima, *History of Eastern Arabia, 1750–1800* (Beirut, 1965).

8.   The latter tribe is not mentioned by Abu-Hakima, but was part of the original migrants and comprised of the al-Ghanim, Saqr, al-Qutami and al-Badr (from Banu Subai tribe).

9.   For this interesting tradition see A. M. Abu-Hakima, *The Modern History of Kuwait*, Luzac, 1983, p. 5.

10. J. B. Lorimer, *Gazeteer of the Persian Gulf, Oman, and Central Arabia* (Calcutta, 1914) Vol. l, Pt. 111, page 1073.

11. See *Selections from the Records of the Bombay Government*, New Series, Vol. XXIV, pp. 531b34, Capt. J. B. Brucks, 'Memoir Descriptive of the Navigation of the Gulf of Persia' 21 August 1829; See also p. 418, where the Shaikh ' … declared himself a vassal of the park … ', hereinafter referred to as *Bombay Selections*.

12. FO. I9S/577, ff. 336–76, marginal note on Kemball to Bulwar (No. 42), 30 August 1858. The note added that 'Custom dates anterior to the general suppression of Piracy in the Persian Gulf by the British Government'.

13. FO. 195/521, ff. 14042b, Kemball to de Redcliffe (No. 30), 30 September 1856.

14. FO 195/624, ff. 286–96, Richard Rogers to Kemball, 18 January 1899.

15. Unless otherwise noted, the following account of the dispute is based on the long despatch by the Basra Consult, Mr W. P. Johnston; FO 195/803A, ff. 487–89, Johnston to Kemball (No. 27), 4 April 1866.

16. FO 195/803A, ff. 487–9, Johnston to Kemball (No. 49), 14 May 1866.

17. Ibid.

18. Ibid.

19. Johnston to Kemball (No. 35), 18 August 1867: FO. 195/803A, ff. 613–14. He added that the Amir was trying to court favour with the Muhir and Sabeeh tribes ' ... by giving their permission to plunder anything they come across belonging to the Zobeyr people or the Zeheyrs ...'.

20. L/P&S/5/266, pp. 265–6, Herbert to Elliot (No. 10), 24 March 1871.

21. L/P&S/5/266, pp. 966–7, Herbert to Elliot (No. 11), 29 March 1871.

22. Major Smith reported from Bahrain that everyone from whom he has managed to collect information agreed that every Kuwaiti stated after Kalif their next move would be Bahrain. L/P&S/9/18, pp. 55–8, Smith to Pelly (No. 19), 8 June 1871.

23. L/P&S/5/268, p. 415, Herbert to Elliot (No. 28), 21 June 1871.

24. L/P&S/9/18, p. 143, Major Smith to Pelly, 17 July 1871. Shaikh Muhammad later explained to Major Smith that the Ottoman and the British were ' ... sultans, and we are poor people, and we are unable to dispute either their, or your orders – you are the Sultan of the Sea, and they of the Land'. L/P&S/9/18, p. 389, Shaikh Muhammed bin Thani to Smith, 29 July 1871.

25. L/P&S/9/18, pp. 463–5, 'News Gleanings' (Katif), 6 August 1871. The Agent was Mohammed bin Ali Nehaylee who posed as a minor trader or merchant. L/P&S/9/18, p. 913, Abdul Kassim to Pelly, 1 September 1871.

26. L/P&S/9/19, p. 208, Mohammed bin Ali to Abul Kassim, 29 September 1871, and L/P&S/9/19, p. 274, 'News Gleanings' (Bahrain), 6 October 1871.

27. L/P&S/9/19, pp. 299–307, Pelly to Govt. of India (No. 1255/369), 22 November 1871, and L/P&S/9/19, pp. 317–21, Pelly to Govt. of India (No. 1257/371), 23 November 1871.

28. L/P&S/9/20, pp. 149–50, News Reports, Abul Kassim, 18–24 December 1871 and L/P&S/9/20, pp. 155–7, 'News Gleanings', Captain Charles Grant, 21–31 December 1871.

29. L/P&S/9/19, pp. 491–5, Pelly to Govt. of India (No. 1332/400), 29 December 1871, enclosing pp. 497–501, 'Summary of Conversations between between His Excellency Midhat Pasha and an Arab which passed during the 12th and 13th December 1871. Fearing he would endanger the man's life, Pelly refused to disclose his name, describing him only as a wealthy pearl merchant whose information was 'invariably found accurate'.

30. L/P&S/9/18, pp. 575–9, Pelly to Govt. of India (No. 974/254), 28 August 1871.

31. L/P&S/9/19, pp. 87–91, Guthrie to Pelly (No. 7), 14 September 1871.

32. L/P&S/9/20, pp. 349–51, Extract from Pelly to Govt. of India (No. 157/41), 29 January 1872.
33. L/P&S/9/21, pp. 63941, Captain Grant 'News Gleanings', 13 to 24 August 1872.
34. L/P&S/9/21, pp. 645–7, 'News Collector's Diary', 13–17 August 1872.
35. L/P&S/9/22, pp. 781–5, Captain Grant, 'News Diary', 8 May–l June 1873.
36. Note: EC 98.16.565597. Trade Reports, Vol. 3.
37. The Persian Gulf: Administration Reports: Report on the Trade of Kuwait for the Year 1912–1913: Vol. 3, p. 3, 1905–1925.
38. Note: this report is an unsigned and undated memorandum, probably written by the political agent in Kuwait in the late 1930s, on file R/IS/S/179.
39. In the last year of the pearling industry, Alan Villiers compiled an account based on actual experience on the pearl banks. He commented that because of the element of gambling imposed by the credit system, many Kuwait merchants would have nothing to do with pearling: A. Villiers, 'Sons of Sinbad' (New York 1969) pp. 353–4.
40. L. E. Sweet, 'Pirates or Politics? Arab Societies of the Persian or Arabian Gulf. 18th Century' *Ethnohistory* Vol. II (1964) pp. 263–80.
41. Richard Le Baron Bowen, 'The Pearl Fisheries of the Persian Gulf'. *Middle East Journal*. Vol. 5 (Winter 1851), pp. 161–80.
42. al-Shamlan, Saif Marzuq, *Tarikh al-ghaws ala al-lulufi al-Kuwait wa al-Khalij al-Arabi* [History of Pearl Diving in Kuwait] (Kuwait, 1975). Vol. l, p. 134.
43. al-Mas'udi, *Muruj al-dhahab* (The Golden Meadows), edited Yusif Daghir. 4 vols. Beirut 1981. Vol. I, pp. 168–9.
44. Ibn Battutah, *Travels in Asia and Africa. 1325–1354* (London 1983) p. 121.
45. Persian Gulf Administration Reports. Vol. 1. 1873–78. Appendix A to Part II p. 40. Note by Capt. E. L. Durand, First Assistant Political Resident. Persian Gulf.
46. William G. Palgrave, *Personal Narrative of a Year's Journey through Central and Eastern Arabia. 1862–63.* 2 vols London 1865. Vol. II, p. 232.
47. Lorimer, *Gazetteer of the Persian Gulf.* Appendix C. pp. 37–40.
48. al-Khusri, *Studies in the History of Kuwait*, p. 223.
49. H. Dickson, *The Arab of the Desert*, p. 484.
50. Col. D. Wilson, 'Memorandum respecting the Pearl Fisheries in the Persian Gulf'. *Journal of the Royal Geographic Society.* 3 (1833) p. 285.
51. Hissah al Rifai, 'Sea Chanties of Kuwait' in R. B. Serjeant and R. D. Bidwell (eds), *Arabian Studies* Vol. 8, p. 87, 1985.
52. Lorimer, *Gazetteer* Appendix C. p. 8.
53. Report by political agent in Kuwait, dated 2 September 1910, R/15/5/18.
54. al-Khusri, *Dirasat fi tarikh al-Kuwait,* Studies in the History of Kuwait, p. 171.
55. Col. D. Wilson, 'Memorandum respecting the Pearl fisheries in tbe Persian Gulf. *Journal of the Royal Geographic Society,* 3 (1833) p. 285.
56. Lorimer, *Gazetteer*, Appendix C, p. 8.
58. Bushire Diary for week ending 13 October 1907: L/P&S/71208 (2078).

59. Gratham Geary, *Through Asiatic Turkey* (London 1878). Vol. 1, p. 43.
60. Source: *The Persian Gulf Administration Reports*. Vol. VI, 1905–1911. By S. G. Knox, Cpt., Political Agent Kuwait, p. 168.
61. D. Fromkin, *A Peace to End All Peace*, A. Deutsch, 1989, p. 35.
62. L. Pelly, 'Remarks on Tribes, Trade and Resources around the Shoreline of the Persian Gulf', *Transactions of the Bombay Geographical Society*, XVII (1863–64), p. 77.
63. F.O. 195/803A, ff. 487–9, Johnston to Kemball (No. 49), 14 May 1866.
64. L/P&S/3/355, File 805, Baker to Rear-Admiral E. C. Drummond, 4 August 1896, enclosed in Admiralty to India Office (No. M/0362), 15 October 1896.
65. F.O. 195/1978, nf., Whyte, Memorandum on Hamdi Pasha, nd., enclosed in Mockler to Cume, 6 January 1 897.
66. R/15/1/472, ff. 73–73b, Memo by M. Mark (Dragoman of Basra Consultate), 19 October 1896.
67. F.O. 195/1935, nf., Memorandum by Captain J. F. Whyte, 11 November 1896, enclosed in Mockler to Currie (No. 99), 24 November 1896.
68. F.O. 195/202, nf., Lieut. Forbes, 'Memorandum on the previous career of and administration of the Wilait of Basrah by HE Anf Pasha, Late Governor-General of Basrah', nd., enclosed in Loch to Currie (No. 29), 4 May 1898.
69. L/P&S/3/356, nf., undated and unsigned note in Lee Warner's hand on Cover of File 1722 containing Currie's (No. 11) of 3 February 1897.
70. L/P&S/7/90, File 225, Viceroy to Secretary of State, 12 February 1897.
71. Foreign Office memorandum respecting Kuwait, 30 October 1901, L/P and S/18/B133, recording a conversation of July 1901.

Chapter Two

1. British Memorandum on Kuwait of 30 October 1901, F.O. 195/7696, for an account of this correspondence.
2. Note: this remarkably frank document is quoted in a paper of January 1903 analysing Ottoman claims, file L/P&S/18/8141. The writer of 1903 commented: 'The objection in 1879 was not to Turkish rule to the North of Odeid, but to anarchy'.
3. R/15/1/471, f. 12b, Office Note, to First Assistant (Lt. C. T. Ducat) 1899.
4. R/15/1/471, ff. 10–11, Wilson to Government of India, 3 October 1896.
5. L/P&S/3/357, File 1812, Sanderson to Godley, 22 March 1897.
6. FO.78/5113, ff. 38–9, Sanderson to Salisbury, 7 April 1897.
7. L/P&S/3/357, File 1812, Marginal note by Salisbury on Sanderson to Salisbury, 7 April 1897.
8. R/15/1/471, ff. 24b–26b, Minute by Gaskin, 22 May 1897.
9. Husain Khalaf Shaikh Kha'zal, *Tarikh al-Kuwait al-siyasi* (The political history

of Kuwait). *The Reign of Sheikh Mubarak* (Beirut, 1962), Vol. II, p. 20.

10. R/15/1/471, f. 30, British Telegraph Office (Fao) to Resident, 5 July 1897.
11. FO. 78/5113, f. 46, Note by Lee Warner, 16 July 1897.
12. R/15/1/471, ff. 72–73b, Gaskin to Meade, 10 August 1897. In the course of time this remark would become more applicable to the Shaikh of Kuwait.
13. R/15/1/471, ff. 44–5, Government of India to Meade, nd. (received 26 July 1897).
14. R/15/1/471, f. 62–3b, Meade to Cunningham, 31 July 1897.
15. R/15/1/471, ff. 77–8, Gaskin to Meade, 18 August 1897.
16. R/15/1/471, ff. 91–3, F. Prideaux, 'Confidential Instructions given by Mr Gaskin Extra Assistant resident on his proceeding to Koweit on 3rd Sept. 97'.
17. Ibid.
18. R/15/1/471, ff. 93–4b, First Note by Gaskin on his visit to Kuwait, 5 September 1897.
19. R/15/1/471, ff. 95–7, Second Note by Gaskin on his visit to Kuwait, 6 September 1897.
20. R/15/1/471, ff. 99–100, Third Note by Gaskin on his visit to Kuwait, 6 September 1897.
21. R/15/1/471, f. 62–3b, Meade to Cunningham, 31 July 1897.
22. R/15/1/471, ff. 108–9, Meade to Government of India, 10 September 1897.
23. R/15/1/471, ff. 106–07b, Fagan to Meade, 10 September 1897.
24. R/15/1/471, ff. 114–20, Meade to Government of India, 25 September 1897.
25. Ibid.
26. L/P&S/3/360, file 2250, Sec. of State to Viceroy, 13 October 1897.
27. Husain Kalaf al-Shaikh Kha'zal, *Political History of Kuwait*, Vol. I, p. 25, (Beirut, 1962).
28. R/15/1/471, ff. 137–37b, Mohd. Rahim to Resident (No. 139), 5 October 1897.
29. Kha'zal, *op. cit.*, p. 25.
30. R/15/1/471, ff. 137–37b, Mohd. Rahim to Resident, (No. 139), 5 October 1897.
31. Kha'zal, *op.cit.*, p. 25.
32. R/15/1/471, ff. 168–69b, Mohd. Rahim to Prideaux (No. 163), 23 November 1897.
33. R/15/1/471, ff. 131–2b, Loch to Meade, 5 October 1897.
34. L/P&S/7/96, File 1069, Minute by Horace Walpole (nd., c. 17 November 1897).
35. Kha'zal, *op.cit.*, p. 16.
36. L/P&S/3/362, File 1746, Loch to Government of India, 22.
37. R/lS/l/471 ff. 192–95b, Forbes to Meade, 2 January 1898.
38. Ibid.
40. R/15/1/471, ff. 169–70b, Loch to Meade, 16 November 1897.
41. G. N. Curzon, *Russia in Central Asia in 1889 and the Anglo-Russian Question* (London, 1889) p. 378.
42. L/P&S/3/362, file 1746, Loch to Government of India (No. 659), 22 December 1897. H. Nicolson 'Curzon, the last phase', p. 73, Constable, 1934.

43. For this summary, I am indebted to Peter Hopkirk, *The Great Game: On Secret Service in High Asia*, John Murray, 1990.

44. FO. 78/5113, ff. 125–6, Curzon to Salisbury, 4 February 1898.

45. FO 78/5113, ff. 14142b, Meade to Curzon, 28 March 1898.

46. L/P&S/3/365, File 2067, Note on Kuwait by Lee Warner, 23 June 1868.

47. FO. 78/5102, ff. 29–29b, Note, 'Euphrates Valley Railway', by Curzon, 5 October 1898.

48. J. B. Kelly, 'Salisbury, Curzon and the Kuwait Agreement of 1899'. *Studies in International History*, Longman, Green and Co., 1967.

49. FO. 78/5102, ff. 139–48, Memorandum by Sir John Ardagh, 28 November 1898.

50. FO. 881.7067, 'Memorandum by Lord Curzon Respecting Persian Affairs', 19 November 1898.

51. L/P&S/3/367, File 2448, Sanderson to Godley, 5 December 1898.

52. L/P&S/3/367, File 2448, Lyall to Godley, 'Wednesday' (6 October 1898).

53. L/P&S/3/367, File 2448, emended draft telegram.

54. FO. 78/5113, ff. 151–3, O'Conor to Salisbury (No. 667), 22 December 1898.

55. R/15/1/472, ff. 6–7, Meade to Government of India, 30 December 1898.

56. L/P&S/3/367, File 2520, Note on File Cover by Lee Warner, nd.

57. L/P&S/3/368, File 1657, Sanderson to Lee Warner, 4 January 1899.

58. MSS.Eur.F.111/142, Godley to Curzon, 6 January 1899.

59. R/15/1/472, ff.l8–20b, Wratislaw to Meade, 13 January 1899.

60. L/P&S/7/111, File 155, Government of India to India Office, 14 January 1899. For agreement, see C. U. Aitchison, A *Collection of Treaties, Engagements and Sanads Relating to India and Neighbouring Countries*, Vol. XII, pp. 256–7 (Delhi, 1933).

61. L/P&S/3/11, File 155, Lee Warner to Lord George Hamilton, 16 January 1899.

62. For text see Aitchison, *op.cit.*, pp. 317–8.

63. L/P&S/3/11, O'Conor to Salisbury (No. 667), 22 December 1898.

64. L/P&S/3/368, File 168, Sanderson to Godley, 18 January 1899.

65. MSS.Eur.F.111/142, Hamilton to Curzon, 24 January 1899.

66. L/P&S/3/368, File 1681, Note on file cover by Lee Warner, January 1899.

67. L/P&S/7/111, File 155, Sanderson to Lee Warner, 16 January 1899.

68. L/P&S/3/111, File 155, Secretary of State to Viceroy, 17 January 1898.

69. MSS.Eur.D.S10/1, ff. 11–14, Curzon to Hamilton, 12 January 1899.

70. R/15/1/472, ff. 27–30, When Meade's instructions were communicated to London, Lee Warner noted that, 'The negotiations will now take their course. I hardly think that they will improve the Sheikh's relations with the Porte.' Lee Warner to Sanderson, 19 January 1899 (FO. 78/5113, f. 193).

71. The following discussion is, unless otherwise noted, based on Meade's account of his negotiations contained in his letter to the Government of India (No. 10) of 30 January 1899, enclosed in L/P&S/7/114, File 109, Foreign Secretary's letter (No. 35), 23 February 1899.

72. R/15/1/472, ff. 31–31b, 'Communication to the brother of Sheikh Mobarik on the 22nd of Janry 99'.
73. Ibid.
74. R/15/1/472, ff. 32–32b, Meade to Shaikh Mubarak bin Subah, 23 January 1899.
75. R/15/1/471, ff. 301–2, Kuwait News Agent to Moh. Khalil, 4 September 1899.
76. MSS.Eur.D510/1, ff. 43–44b, Curzon to Hamilton, 16 January 1899.
77. Ibid.
78. L/P&S/7/111, File 189, Secretary of State to Viceroy, 10 February 1899, and *op.cit.*,File 219, Viceroy to Secretary of State, 12 February 1899.
79. L/P&S/7/111, File 219, Minute by Lee Warner on Viceroy's telegram of 12 February 1899.
80. MSS.Eur.F.111/142, Hamilton to Curzon, 16 February 1899.
81. MSS.Eur.F. 102/6, f. 151, Sanderson to Godley, nd., enclosed in Godley to Hamilton, 23 March 1899.
82. MSS.Eur.F.111/142, Hamilton to Curzon, 16 February 1899.
83. L/P&S/3/368, File 1751, Sanderson to Godley, 14 February 1899, and ibid., India Office to Government of India, 14 February 1899.

Chapter Three

1. L/P&S/7/189, file 1153, Diary of the Persian Gulf Residency for the Week Ending 20 May 1906.
2. R/15/1/472, ff. 18–20b, Wratislaw to Meade, 13 January 1899. The British suspected that the Ottomans were using Ibn Rashid as a surrogate to bring pressure on Mubarak. There is a traditional story that on his death-bed Prince Muhammed ibn Rashid warned his nephew, ' ... do not be tempted by Turkish blandishments into hostilities with Kuwait ... ', Philby, *Arabian Jubilee*, (London 1948), p.8. However, it is unlikely that this was true as early as 1899.
3. The vicissitudes of the al-Sa'ud dynasty have been sketched in Ch. 1.
4. FO. 602/1, f. 24, Report of Dragoman of Basra Consulate, 14 April 1891, Philby, *Saudi Arabia*, (London 1955), p. 235.
5. Lorimer, *Gazetteer* p. 1141, R/15/1/473, ff. 82–82b, Report of Kuwait News Agent, 17 August 1900.
6. R/15/1/472, f. 119b, [Mubarak] to Meade, nd., enclosed in R/15/1/472, ff. 115–15b, Saffer to Meade, No. 35, 17 March 1899.
7. R/15/1/472, ff. 134–34b, Mubarak to Meade, nd., enclosed in R/15/1/472, f. 130, Saffer to Meade, No. 66, 9 April 1899.
8. R/15/1/472, ff. 155–55b, Buckley to Meade, 21 April 1899. R/15/1/472, ff. 156–56b, Meade to Government of India, No. 49.
9. R/15/1/472, ff. 163–67b, Meade to Government of India, No. 58, 7 May 1899.
10. R/15/1/472, ff. 208–10, Gaskin to Resident, 16 June 1899.

11. R/15/1/471, f. 356, Kuwait News Agent to Mohd. Khalil, 2 October 1899.
12. R/15/1/471, f. 363, Report of Kuwait News Agent, 28 November 1899.
13. FO. 19512055, nf., Wratislaw to O'Conor, No. 39, 25 August 1899.
14. R/15/1/471, ff. 308–9b, Kuwait News Agent to Moh. Khalil, 6 September 1899.
15. FO. 195/2041, nf., Salisbury to O'Conor, No. 87/T, 8 September 1899.
16. FO. 78/5114, f. 89, O'Conor to Salisbury, No. 41/T, 12 September 1899, and FO. 78/5114, ff. 11–13, same to same, No. 440, 13 September 1899.
17. FO. 195/2055, nf., Wratislaw to O'Conor, nn/T, 8 September 1899.
18. FO. 195/2055, nf., Wratislaw to O'Conor, No. 44, 16 September 1899.
19. FO. 195/2074, ff. 126–29b, Wratislaw to O'Conor, No. 3, 24 January 1900.
20. FO. 195/2074, ff. 200–3, Shipley to O'Conor, No. 20, 7 July 1900.
21. Ibid.
22. See Ebeizer Tauber's excellent article 'Sayyid Talib and the Young Turks in Basra'. *Middle Eastern Studies*, Volume 25, No. 1, January 1989.
23. R/15/1/473, ff. 75–75b, Report by Moh. Khalil (Dragoman of Residency), 10 August 1900.
24. R/15/1/473, f. 12, Report from Kuwait News Agent, nd., translated at Bushire on 4 June 1900.
25. R/15/1/473, ff. 82–82b, Report of Kuwait News Agent, 17 August 1900.
26. R/15/1/473, ff. 110–15, Shipley to Kemball, 5 October 1900.
27. R/15/1/473, f. 142, Wratislaw to Kemball, 8 November 1900.
28. R/15/1/473, ff. 165–7, Report of Kuwait News Agent, 20 November 1900.
29. FO. 195/2074, ff. 371–9, Wratislaw to de Bunsen, No. 44, 22 November 1900.
30. R/15/1/473, ff. 189–91, Kemball to Government of India, 3 December 1900.
31. R/15/1/473, ff. 204–04b, Kemball to Mubarak, 10 December 1900.
32. R/15/1/473, ff. 218–18b, Phillips to Kemball, 9 February 1901. These figures were given to Capt. H. A. Phillips (SNOPG) by Mubarak and are almost certainly greatly exaggerated. Wratislaw called them 'absolutely ludicrous'. FO. 195/2096, ff. 3941, Wratislaw to O'Conor, No. 8, 16 February 1901.
33. R. 15/1/473, ff. 225–26b, William McDouall (Vice-Consul Muhammarah 1890–1904) to Kemball, 23 February 1901.
34. R/15/1/473, ff. 230–30b, extract from private from McDouall, 11 March 1901.
35. Ibid.
36. R/15/1/473, f. 256, Wratislaw to Kemball, 29 March 1901.
37. The following details of the battle of al-Sarif are based on R/15/1/473, ff. 298–89, Report by Mohammed Khalil, 16 April 1901; ibid., ff. 332–7, 'Full information about the Occurrence'. This interesting account was written by an unknown Kuwaiti merchant, who was present at the battle, to his brother; ibid., pp. 323–4, Gaskin to Kemball, 21 September 1901; ibid., ff. 272–3, 274–75b, Gaskin to David, 2 and 6 April; ibid., ff. 282–4, 'Statement of Falah bin Chantam of the Beni Amer Section of the Subaie tribe', 7 April 1901.
38. Lorimer, *op. cit.*, p. 1029, fn.

39. R/15/1/473, ff. 269–71b, Gaskin to David, I April 1901. Gaskin wrote that the Shaikh of Bahrain's writer, who had just returned from Kuwait, had reported that no one dared to speak of the Shaikh's defeat, '... on account of the sons suppressing it and no one dared to allude to it', ibid.

40. R/15/1/473, ff. 303–11b, Kemball to Government of India, No. 77, 20 April 1901.

41. 'The Manners and Customs of the Rwala Bedouin' by Aloin Musil. American Geographical Society. *Oriental Explorations and Studies* No. 6, p.635, New York 1928.

42. FO. 195/2096, ff. 76, 83, Wratislaw to O'Conor, Nos 18/T and 19/T, 26 and 27 April 1901. The first contingent was only 250 men, but Wratislaw learnt a few days later that the government contractor had received orders to prepare bread rations for eight battalions. FO. l95/2096, f. 78, Wratislaw to O'Conor, No. 21/T, 21 April 1901.

43. R/15/1/473, f. 319, Wratislaw to Kemball, 26 April 1901.

44. FO. 78/5173, f. 134, Lansdowne to O'Conor, No. 31/T, 26 April 1901.

45. R/IS/1/474, ff. 6–6b, Government of India to Kemball, nd., received 30 April 1901.

46. R/15/1/474, ff. 10–llb, Wratislaw to Kemball, 30 April 1901.

47. R/IS/1/473, f. 339, Wratislaw to Kemball, No. 21, 29 April 1901; R/IS/1/474, f. 9, Wratislaw to Kemball, nn., 1 May 1901; FO. 195/2096, f. 96, Wratislaw to O'Conor [22]/T, 1 May 1901.

48. R/15/1/474, f. 21, Commander-in-Chief, Sixth Army Corps, to Mubarak, 2 May 1901.

49. R/15/1/474, ff. 24b–25, Mohsin Pasha to Mubarak, 2 May 1901.

50. FO. 195/2096, f. 84, Wratislaw to O'Conor, N. 20/T, 28 April 1901. Wratislaw's telegram refers to the Amir's nephew 'Sebshar' which was presumably a confusion for one of the al-Sabah nephews, see FO. 195/2096, ff. 18084, Wratislaw to O'Conor, No. 31, 3 June 1901.

51. R/15/1/474, ff. 15–18b, McDouall to Kemball, 4 May 1901.

52. R/15/1/474, ff. 61–61b, Capt. H. A. Phillips (HMS *Sphinx*) *to* Captain HMS *Marathon*, 29 May 1901, FO. 195/2096, ff. 177–79b, Wratislaw to O'Conor, No. 30, I June 1901.

53. Mss. Eue, F. 111/353, Capt. Phillips to Meade, 18 June 1901.

54. R/15/1/474, ff. 74–6, Report of Kuwait News Agent, 7 June 1901. With considerable hyperbole the Kuwait News Agent reported that, 'When Sheikh Mubarak and his sons saw what support they were getting from the British Govt. just when it was needed, they became very grateful and almost wished to become British subjects.'

55. FO. 78/5173, ff. 385–90, O'Conor to Lansdowne, No. 310, 20 August 1901.

56. FO. 78/5173, ff. 385–90, Capt. Phillips to Capt. Field (SNOPG, HMS *Marathon*), 29 May 1901.

57. *Loc. cit.*, Kemball to Government of India No. 107, 3 June 1901.

58. L/P&S/7/133, file 651, Government of India to India Office, 8 June 1901.
59. Ibid.
60. R/15/1/474, f. 92–2b, Gaskin to Kemball, No. 102, 29 June 1901. R/IS/1/474, ff. 93–4b. Report of Kuwait News Agent, 23 June 1901.
61. R/lS/1/474, ff. 103–04b, Report of Kuwait News Agent, 29 June 1901.
62. R/14/1/474, ff. 114–15b, Report of Kuwait News Agent, 16 July 1901.
63. R/IS/1/474, ff. 96–8, Report of Kuwait News Agent, 13 July 1901.
64. R/IS/1/474, ff. 154–54b, Mubarak to Kemball, 4 July 1901.
65. R/15/1/474, ff. 118–20, Phillips to Kemball, 31 July 1901.
66. FO. 195/2096, ff. 213–13b, Wratislaw to O'Conor, No. 43/T, 7 August 1901.
67. R/15/1/474, ff. 124–24b, J. C. Gaskin, 'The Conditions drawn up by Sheikh Mubarak on which he is prepared to make peace with the Amir of Nejd', 13 August 1901. There were in addition some minor points regarding the settlement of tribal disputes.
68. R/lS/1/474, ff. 125–25b, Government of India to Kemball, 14 August 1901.
69. ADM. 127/28, pp. 475–91: the following account is based on the report of the *Perseus* commanding officer; Phillips to Capt. Field, 25 August 1901.
70. R/15/1/474, ff. 148–48b, Kemball to Government of India, 20 August 1901.
71. Foreign Office Memorandum respecting Kuwait of 30 October 1901, F.O. 7596.
72. R/15/1/474, ff. 202–03, Mubarak to Kemball, 22 September 1901, *op. cit.*, ff. 204–04b, Fao, Telegraph Office to Bushire Residency, 24 September 1901; R/15/1/474, ff. 215–6, Capt. G. M. Field to Rear. Adm. Bosanquet (C-ln-C East Indies Station) nd., C25/26 September 1901.
73. FO. 78/5174, ff. 224, 225, Wratislaw to Kemball, 28 and 29 September 1901.
74. Ibid.
75. R/15/1/474, ff. 221–21b, Government of India to Kemball, 28 September 1901. 76 R/15/1/474, ff. 273–4, Abdul Latif to Mubarak, 16 October 1901.
76. R/15/1/474, ff.273–4, Abdul Latif to Mubarak, 16 October 1901.
77. R/15/1/474, ff. 305–05b, Bash Kateb el Hamdyuni to Vali, 29 September 1901.
78. R/15/1/474, ff. 293–5, Report by Kuwait News Agent, 11 November 1901.
79. R/15/1/474, ff. 324–6, Wratislaw to Kemball, 24 November 1901.
80. R/15/1/474, ff. 339–405, Mubarak to Kemball, 1 December 1901.
81. Admn. 127/28, pp. 557–75, Capt. Simmons to Rear. Adm. Bosqanquet, 'Reporting Proceedings taken in connection with the Nakib of Basrah to Koweit in *Zuhaf*, 14 December 1901. Unless otherwise indicated, the following account of the confrontation in Kuwait is based on Capt. Simmons' report.
82. R/15/1/474, ff. 359–60, Mubarak to Kemball, 3 December 1901.
83. R/15/1/474, ff. 351–52b, Simmons to Kemball, 4 December 1901.
84. R/15/1/474. ff. 375–6, Government of India to Kemball, 6 December 1901.
85. R/lS/1/474, ff. 403–03b, Report of Kuwait News Agent, 16 December 1901.
86. R/15/l/474, f. 402, Kemball to Government of India, l9 December 1901.
87. L/P&S/3/387, file 27 19, Lansdowne to O'Conor, No. 1 87/T, 27 December 1901,

enclosed in Foreign office to India Office, 27 December 1901.

88. Note on the Boundaries of Kuwait by Capt. Shakespear, 9 August 1912, R/15/5/65.
89. R/15/1/475, ff. 19–20b, Wratislaw to David, 18 January 1902.
90. FO. 195/2115, ff. 26–9, Wratislaw to O'Conor, No. 1, 10 January 1902.
91. FO. 195/2116, ff. 194–5, Wratislaw to O'Conor, No. 25, 27 May 1902.
92. FO. 195/2116, ff. 376–76b, Wratislaw to O'Conor, No. 47, 29 August 1902.
93. R/15/1/474, ff. 149–49b, Wratislaw to Kemball, 2 June 1902.
94. FO. 195/2116, ff. 237–39b, Wratislaw to O'Conor, No. 29, 13 June 1902.
95. FO. 78/5252, ff. 42–2b, de Bunsen to Lansdowne, No. 286, 18 June 1902, R/15/1/475, f. 193, Mubarak to Hunt, 25 July 1902.
96. FO. 195/2116, ff. 373–5b, Wratislaw to O'Conor, No. 46, 26 August 1902.
97. Ibid., FO. 195/2116, ff. 373–5b, Wratislaw to O'Conor, No. 46, 26 August 1902.
98. For a full account of the action see R/15/1/475, ff. 269–71, 'Reporting the Capture of Two Dhows' by the *Lapwing*'s commanding officer, Lt. Cmdr Armstrong.
99. FO. 7815252, ff. 313–14b, O'Conor to Lansdowne, No. 529, 2 December 1902.
100. FO. 195/2138, ff. 88–93, Wratislaw to O'Conor, No. 4, 8 January 1903.
101. FO. 195/2138, ff. 363–5, Crow to O'Conor, No. 26, 8 June 1903.
102. FO. 195/2139, ff. 121–24, Crow to O'Conor, No. 47, 11 September 1903.

Chapter Four

1. R/15/5/65 'Note on the boundaries of Kuwait Principality', dated 9 August 1912.
2. W. Facey, *Riyadh, the Old City*, Inmel Publishing, 1992, Chapter 15.
3. R/15/1/475, f. 257, Government of India to Kemball, 24 September 1902.
4. R/1511/475, ff. 257–576, Minute from Kemball to Hunt, 25 September 1902.
5. R/15/1/475, ff. 272–72b, Mubarak to Hunt, 13 October 1902.
6. R/15/1/475, ff. 216–17, Mubarak to Kemball, 26 August 1902.
7. R/15/1/475, ff. 305–05b, Kemball to Government Of India, No. 178, 22 December 1902.
8. In this context it is interesting to note that in the following summer Lt Col. Maunsell, the military attaché of the British Embassy in Constantinople, reported a conversation with the Ottoman minister of war in which the latter spoke as if Ibn Rashid's lands were Ottoman territory, including a reference to 'our territory Of Kassim', FO.195/2176, nf., Maunsell to O'Conor, No. 51, 9 August 1904.
9. R/15/1/476, f. 195, Crow to Cox, 27 April 1904.
10. FO.78/5385, f. 98, O'Conor to Lansdowne, No. 77, 29 April 1904
11. FO. 195/2163, ff. 236–38b, Crow to O'Conor, No. 22, 27 April 1904.
12. R/15/1/476, f. 207, Mubarak to Cox, 9 May 1904.
13. Philby, *Saudi Arabia*, pp. 245–57; FO. 195/2164, ff. 111–13, Monoham to O'Conor, No. 41, 19 August 1904.

No. 41, 19 August 1904.

14. FO. 195/2164, ff. 114–46, Newmarch to O'Conor, No. 44, 10 August 1904.

15. FO. 78/5336, nf., O'Conor to Lansdowne, No. 735, 20 September 1904.

16. Lorimer, *Gazetteer*, p. 1504, Credits Nuri Pasha's successor, Fakhri Pasha, with the opening of negotiations, but the chronology of events suggests the initial approach came during the administration of Mustafa Nuri.

17. R/15/1/476, ff. 231–34b, Knox to Cox, No. 18, 3 September 1904.

18. Ibid.

19. From Political Agent Kuwait to Political Resident Bushire 25 April 1930: R/15/5/126, ref. 375, Confidential.

20. R/15/1/477, ff. 7–7b, Knox to Cox, No. 179, 23 September 1905.

21. FO. 195/2176, nf., Maunsell to Townley, No. 68, 8 November 1904, enclosed in *loc. cit.*, Townley to Lansdowne, No. 682, 8 November 1904.

22. R/15/1/477, ff. 12–13b, Knox to Cox, No. 135, 4 January 1905.

23. It is significant that a week and a half after the second meeting the vali told the British consul that the Ottoman Officials for Qasim would soon follow as they had been accepted by Abdul Rahman. FO. 195/2188, ff. 113–21, Monahan to Townley, No. 8, 24 February 1905.

24. R/15/1/477, ff. 52–53b, Knox to Cox, 28 February 1905. This was Mubarak's account of the meeting and Knox noted that the sheikh ' ... was unusually profuse in professions of friendship and attachment Mubarak is not gushing as a rule, and I think that he is distinctly nervous as to the view the British may take of his Sefwan policy'.

25. R/15/1/477 ff. 52–3b. Knox to Cox, 28 February 1905. Mubarak's account to Knox was clearly presented as what he thought the British agent would want to hear, 'all the above was said slowly and steadily and was evidently the impression which Sheikh Mubarak wished to convey to the British Government of what had taken place at Sefwan. It had been, I should say, carefully studied and rehearsed.'

26. R/15/1/508, f. 96, Cox to Government of India, 28 December 1904.

27. FO. 195/2188, f. 643, Crow to O'Conor, No. 58/T, 30 November 1905, FO. 195/2214, ff. 6–8, Crow to O'Conor, No. 1, 4 January 1906.

28. This account of Najd affairs is based on R/15/5/24, ff. 91–3b, 'Sheikh Mubarak's Description of Present State of Political Situation in the Interior of Arabia' (October 1905).

29. R115111566, f. 6, Ibn Saud to Shaikh of Dubai, 22 August 1905.

30. R11515124, ff. 94–5, Cox to Knox, No. 97, 17 January 1906.

31. R115111556, ff. 19b–20, Knox to Cox, No. 1, 19 January 1906.

32. R115111556, f. 21, Knox to Cox, No. 4, 3 February 1906.

33. FO. 195/2224, ff. 111–12b, Moh. Hussain (Vice-Consul Jeddah) to O'Conor, No. 25, 13 May 1906.

34. R/15/1/446, f. 21, Cox to Government of India, No. 63, 2 February 1906.

35. L/P&S/7/189, File 1153, Diary of the Persian Residency for the week ending 20 May 1906.

36. L/P&S/7/191, File 1537, Diary of the Persian Gulf Residency for the Week Ending 5 August 1906. This was no idle bedouin boast, simply premature; it was to be another 15 years before the Ibn Sa'ud attempted to absorb Kuwait.

37. A member of a noble Najd family and a direct descendent of the original Muhammad al-Sa'ud, L/P&S.20/C.131, p.16, 'Personalities, Arabia', Intelligence Division, Admiralty War Staff, April 1917, and R/15/1/478, ff. 8–11, Prideaux to Cox, 9 February 1906.

38. R/15/1/478, ff. 19–19b, Cox to Government of India, No. 64, 23 February 1906, enclosing 'Translation of a telegram despatched in Romanized Arabic to His Majesty the Sultan, Constantinople, from Bushire by a Representative of Ibn Saood and Sheikh Jasim ibn Thani, on the 18th February 1906'. It is likely that the use of Shaikh Jasim's name was simply a manoeuvre on Ibn Sa'ud's part to avoid addressing the Porte directly and thereby implying his subservience; see R/15/1/478, ff. 60–60b, Prideaux to Cox, 9 March 1906.

39. Ibid., and L/P&S/7/190, file 1306, Diary of the Persian Gulf Residency for the Week Ending 17 June 1906.

40. *Loc. cit.*, 'Note of a Conversation between the Resident in the Persian Gulf and Sheikh Mubarak of Kuwait', by Capt. Knox, 7 March 1906.

41. Ibid.

42. Ibid.

43. L/P&S/7/194, File 1925, Diary of the Persian Residency for the week ending 14 October 1906.

44. R/15/1/479, f. 252, Shakespear to Assistant Resident (C–1), 4 January 1910.

45. L/P&S/7/203, File 1155, Bushire Residency Diary for week ending 26 May 1907.

46. R/15/1/479, ff. 113–13b, Knox to Cox, No. 481, 3 September 1907.

47. R/15/6/507, p. 105, Administration Report for Kuwait for the Year 1907–8.

48. R/15/1/477, ff. 19b–22, Mubarak to Cox, 26 January 1905.

49. R/15/1/476, ff. 231–4, Knox to Cox, No. 18,3 September 1904.

50. R/15/1/479,ff. 45–9, Knox to Cox, No. 223, 13 May 1907.

51. R/15/1/476, ff. 45b–47, Hunt to Kemball, 1 February 1904.

52. For an account of the introduction of the steam ship service and Mubarak's initial fears that the Ottomans would try to throttle the service by enforcing quarantine restrictions. F.O. Memorandum on Kuwait No. 7596 of 30 October 1901, p. 19.

53. R/15/6/505, p. 86, Administration Report of the Kuwait Political Agency for the year 1905–6.

54. R/15/6/513, p. 126, Administration Report of the Kuwait Agency for the year 1913.

55. R/15/6/507, p. 11, Administration Report of the Kuwait Agency for the year 1907–8.

56. L/P&S/7/198, File 339, Bushire Residency Diary for week ending 20 January 1907.

57. L/P&S/7198, File 339, Bushire Residency Diary for week ending 20 January 1907.

58. R/15/6/508, p. 102, Administration Report for Kuwait for the nine months ending 31 December 1908. In addition there were rumours in Kuwait of oppressive levies imposed on the workers on the shaikh's Fao estates.

59. R/15/S/18, ff. 99–100, Knox to Cox, No. 294, 8 July 1908.

60. Ibid.

61. Ibid.

62. R/15/1/479, ff. 263–4, Shakespear to Cox, C-14, 30 March 1910.

63. R/15/5/26, ff. 21–3, Extracts from Kuwait Diary No. 7 for the week ending 16 February 1910; ibid., ff. 24–6, Extracts from Kuwait Diary No. 9 for the week ending 2 March 1910; R/15/1/479, ff. 254–5, Shakespear to Cox, C-12, 9 March 1910.

64. R/15/5/25, ff. 18–19, Extracts from Kuwait Diary No. 5 for week ending 2 February 1910.

65. R/1/5/26, ff. 78–9, Extracts from Kuwait News for week ending 3 August 1910; R/15/5/25, f. 91, Confidential Memorandum by British Residency (Baghdad).

66. R/15/5/26, f. 58, Extracts from Diary No. 21 of the Kuwait Political Agency for the week ending 2 May 1910. R15/1/479, f. 209, Shakespear to Cox, C-30, 25 May 1910.

67. R/15/1/479, ff. 264b-5, Shakespear, 'Shaikh Mubarak's Military Arrangements,' 28 March 1910.

68. R/15/1/479, ff. 288–9, Extracts from Diary No. 17 of the Kuwait Political Agency for the week ending 27 April 1910, Ibid., Shakespear to Cox, 18 May 1910.

69. L/P&S/7/241, File 1031, Political Diary of the Persian Gulf Residency for the month of May 1910.

70. R/15/5/26, f. 82, Extracts from Kuwait News for week ending 31 August 1910.

71. There is discussion of 'tribal flight' in the Trucial States region in A. M. Khalifa, *The United Arab Emirates, Unity in Fragmentation*. Croom Helm 1979 pp. 98–9.

72. L/P&S/7/251, File 1540, Political Diary of the Persian Gulf Residency for the month of July 1911.

73. R/15/5/26, ff. 73–4, Shakespear to Cox, C-42, 12 July 1910.

74. R/15/1/479, ff. 301–02, Shakespear to Cox, C-l, 18 January 1911.

Chapter Six

1. R/15/1/513, ff. 21–2, Grey to Cox, No. C-14, 11 December 1915.

2. R/15/1/615, pp. 59, 59–60, Knox to Grey, D/O, 3 April 1914, and Grey to Cox, D/O 14 April 1914.

3. R/15/5/92, ff. 115–21, 'Translation of the Lease of the Shweikh Lands', Clause 9, 15 October 1907.

4. R/15/5/92, f. 145, *loc. cit.*, Government of India to Cox, No. 535–58, 22 November 1907. Knox to Cox, No. 636, 30 November 1907. L/P&S/10/48, f. 139, Viceroy to Secretary of State for India, 10 January 1908.

5. L/P&S/10/827, ff. 445–506, Political Diary of the Persian Gulf Residency for the Month of May 1912.

6. L/P&S/lO/827, ff. 478–85, Political Diary of the Persian Gulf Residency for the Month of May 1912, Vol. 4, p. 550.

7. R11515127, ff. 50–9, Shakespear to Cox, No. C–10, 15 May 1913.

8. R/15/5/27, ff. 64b, Shakespear to Cox, D/O nn., 20 May 1913.

9. L/P&S/10/387, ff. 626–64, Shakespear to Resident, No. 5–13, 4 January 1915.

10. L/P&S/11/70, File 135/14, Cox to Government of India, No. 3359, 9 November 1913.

11. L/P&S/11/70, File 135/14, Cox to Government of India, No. 3726, 7 December 1913.

12. L/P&S/11/72, File 618/14, Cox to Government of India, nn., 14 September 1915.

Chapter Seven

1. HBM's Consul F. E. Crow in Basra, l909. Quoted in Alan Rush, *Records of Kuwait 1899–1961*, Volume I p. 312, No. 17.

Bibliography

Unpublished Documents

Public Record Office

ADM. 127   Admiralty: East Indies Station Records, Correspondence, 1908–1930.
CAB. 28   Cabinet: copies of Minutes and Memoranda of the Committee of
            Imperial Defence, 1888–1914.
FO. 78   Foreign Office: General Correspondence before 1906: Turkey, 1780–
            1905.
FO. 195   Embassy and Consular Archives: Turkey Correspondence, 1808–1950.
FO. 371   Foreign Office: General Correspondence: Political, 1906–1941.
FO. 602   Embassy and Consular Archives: Basra, 1761–1914.
FO. 881   Foreign Office: Confidential Print: Numerical Series,1829–1914.
            India Office Library and Records.
L/P&S/3   Home Correspondence, 1807–1911.
L/P&S/7   Political and Secret Correspondence with India, 1875–1911.
L/P&S/5   Secret Correspondence with India, 1756–1874.
L/P&S/9   Correspondence relating to areas outside India, 1781–1911.
L/P&S/10   Departmental Papers: Political and Secret Files, 1902–1931.
L/P&S/ll   Departmental Papers: Political and Secret Annual Files, 1912–1930.
L/P&S/12   Political (External) Files and Collections, 1931–1950.
L/P&S/18   Political and Secret Memoranda, 1840–1947.
L/P&S/20   Political and Secret Library, 1800–1947.
R/15/1   Records of the British Political Residency, Bushire, 1763–1947.
R/15/2   Records of the British Political Agency, Bahrain, 1900–1947.
R/15/5   Records of the British Political Agency, Kuwait, 1904–1947.
R/15/6   Records of the British Political Agency, Muscat,1800–1947.

MSS Eur.

F. 102   Kilbracken Collections: Papers of Sir Arthur Godley, First Baron Kilbracken.

F. 111   Curzon Collection: Papers of George Nathaniel Curzon, Marquis of Kedleston.

F. 126   Pelly Collection: Papers of Lieut-General Sir Lewis Pelly.

D. 510   Hamilton Collection: Papers of Lord George Francis Hamilton.

Books

Abu Hakima, Ahmad Mustafa *Tarikh al–Kuwait* [History of Kuwait] 2 Vols (Kuwait, 1966).

Albaharna, Husain M., *The Arabian Gulf States: The Legal and Political Status and Their International Problems* (Beirut, reprinted 1978).

Anderson, M. S., *The Eastern Question 1774–1923: A Study in International Relations* (London, 1966).

Belgrave, Sir Charles, *The Pirate Coast* (London, 1966).

Beloff, Max, *Imperial Sunset*, Vol. I, 'Britain's Liberal Empire 1897–1921' (New York, 1970).

Blunt, Lady Anne, *Bedouin Tribes of the Euphrates*, 2 Vols (London, 1879).

Bourne, Kenneth and Watt, D. Cameron, *Studies in International History* (London, 1967).

Brent, Peter, *Far Arabia: Explorers of the Myth* (London, 1977).

Burton, Sir Richard F., *Personal Narrative of a Pilgrimage lo El–Medinah and Meccah*, 3 Vols (London, 1855).

Busch, B. C., *Britain and the Persian Gulf 1884–1914* (Berkeley, 1967).

Chapman, Maybelle Kennedy, *Great Britain and the Baghdad Railway 1888–1914* (Massachusetts, 1948).

Chatty, Dawn, *From Camel to Truck: The Bedouin the Modern World* (New York, 1986).

Chaudhuri, K. N., *Trade and Civilization in the Indian Ocean: An Economic History from the Rise of Islam to 1750* (Cambridge, 1985).

Churchill Semple, Ellen, *Influences of Geographic Environment* (London, 1911).

Clark, Edson L., *The Arabs and the Turks: Their Origin and History* (Boston, 1875).

Clements, Frank, A., *Kuwait*, Kuwait World Biographical Series (Oxford, 1985).

Cobbold, Lady Evelyn, *Pilgrimage of Mecca* (London, 1934).

Cole, Donald Rowell, *Nomads of the Nomads: The Al Murrah Bedouin of the Empty Quarter* (Chicago, 1975).

Conder, Josiah, *The Modern Traveller, a Description*, Vol. 4 of *Geographical, Historical and Topographical of the Various Countries of the Globe*, 30 Vols (London, 1830).

Cottrell, Alvin *et al.*, *The Persian Gulf States: A General Survey* (London and Baltimore, 1980).

Crichton, Andrew, *History of Arabia Ancient and Modern* (London and Edinburgh, 1833).

Curzon, George N., *Persia and the Persian Question*, 2 Vols (London 1892).

—*Russia in Central Asia in 1889* (new impression, London, 1967).

Daniel, Norman, *Islam and the West: The Making of an Image* (Edinburgh, 1960).

Daniels, John, *Kuwait Journey* (Luton, 1971).

Davis, David Brion, *Slavery and Human Progress* (Oxford, 1986).

Dawn, C. E., *From Ottomanisn to Arabism: Essays on the Origins of Arab Nationalism* (Urbana, 1973).

De Gaury, Gerald, *Arabia Phoenix* (London, 1946).

—*Arabian Journey and Other Desert Travels* (London, 1950).

—*Traces of Travel: Brought Home from Abroad* (London, 1983).

De Gaury, Gerald and Winstone, H. V. F., *Spirit of the East* (London, 1979).

De Laborde, M. Leon, *Journey through Arabia, Petraea to Mount Sinai, and the Excavated City of Petra.* 2nd edn (London, 1838).

Dickson, H. R., *The Arabs of the Desert* (London, 1949).

Djait, Hichem, *Europe and Islam* (tr. Peter Heinegg) (Berkeley, 1985).

Dodd, C. H., *Nations in the Ottoman Empire. A Caste Study in Devolution* (Hull, 1980).

Dougherty, Raymond Philip, *The Sealand of Ancient Arabia* (Oxford, 1932).

Doughty, Charles M., *Travels in Arabia's Deserts* (Cambridge, 1888).

—*Wanderings in Arabia* (an abridgement of *Travels in Arabia Desert* (London, 1908).

Dunn, Ross E., *The Adventures of Ibn Battuta: A Muslim Traveller of the 14th Century* (London, 1986).

El–Sheikh, Ibrahim A., van de Koppel, C. Aart, and Peter, Rudolph, *The Mysteries of the Oriental Mind. Some Remarks on the Development of Western Stereotypes of Arabs* (Amsterdam, 1982).

Eldridge, C. C., *British Imperialism in the Nineteenth Century* (London, 1984).

Farago, Ladislas, *The Riddle of Arabia* (London, *c.* 1940).

Fitzsimons, M. A., *Empire by Treaty: Britain and the Middle East in the Twentieth Century.*

Fleischer, Cornell H., *Bureaucrat and Intellectual in the Ottoman Empire: The Historian Mustapha Ali (1541–1610)* (Princeton, 1986).

Forster, Charles, *The Historical Geography of Arabia or the Patriarchal Evidences of Revealed Religion*, 2 Vols (London, 1844).

Fraser, David, *The Short–Cut to India. Record of a Journey along the Route of the Baghdad Railway* (Edinburgh and London, 1909).

Fraser, Lovat, *India under Curzon and After* (London, 1911).

Geary, Grattan, *Through Asiatic Turkey* (London, 1875).

Goldberg, Jacob, *The Foreign Policy of Saudi Arabia. The Formative Years 1902–1918* (Cambridge, Mass., 1986).

Graves, Philip, *The Life of Sir Percy Cox* (London, 1941).

Groom, Nigel, *Frankincense and Myrrh: A Study of the Arabian Incense Trade* (London, 1981).

Guarmani, Carlo, *Northern Najd: A Journey from Jerusalem to Anaiza in Qasim* (London, 1838).

Gulick, John, *The Middle East: An Anthropological Perspective* (Boston, 1983).

Hamilton, Angus, *Problems of the Middle East* (London, 1909).

Harrison, Paul W., *The Arab at Home* (New York, 1923).

—*Doctor in Arabia* (New York, 1942).

Heller, Joseph, *British Policy Toward the Ottoman Empire: 1908–1914* (London, 1983).

Henige, David, *Oram History* (London, 1982).

Hewing, Ralph, *A Golden Dream. The Miracle of Kuwait* (London, 1963).

Hoagland Brown, Edward, *The Saudi Arabian–Kuwait Neutral Zone* (Beirut, 1963).

Hoffman, Ruth and Helen, *Our Arabian Nights* (New York, 1940).

Hogarth, D. G., *Arabia* (Oxford, 1922).

—D. G., *Hejaz before World War I – A Handbook* (Cambridge, 1978; reprint of 2nd (1917) edition).

Holden, David and Johns, Richard, *The House of Saud* (London, 1981).

Hope, Stanton, *Arabian Adventurer The Story of Haji Abdullah Williamson* (London, 1951).

Hourani, Albert, *Europe and the Middle East* (London, 1980).

Hourani, George Gadlo, *Arab Seafaring in the Indian Ocean in Ancient and Early Medieval Times* (Princeton, 1951).

Howard, Harry N., *The Partition of Turkey. Diplomatic History 1912–1923* (Oklahoma, 1931).

Howarth, David, *The Desert King: The Life of Ibn Saud* (London, 1964).

Ibn Battuta, *Travels in Asia and Africa 1325–1354* (London, 1983).

Al–Ibrahim, Hassarl, *Kuwait: A Political Study* (Kuwait, 1975).

Ingram, Edward, *In Defence of British India: Great Britain in the Middle East 1775–1948* (London, 1984).

Irons, William, and Dyson–Hudson, Neville (eds), *Perspective on Nomadism* (Leiden, 1972).

Jastrow, Morris, *The War and the Baghdad Railway* (Philadelphia, 1917).

Kazemzadeh, Firuz, *Russia and Britain. A Study in Imperialism* (New Haven, 1968).

Kedourie, Elie, *The Chatham House Version and Other Middle Eastern Studies* (London, 1970).

—*Arabic Political Memoirs and Other Studies* (London, 1974).

—*England the Middle East: The Destruction of the Ottoman Empire 1914–1921* (London, 1956).

Kelly, J. B., *Eastern Arabian Frontier* (London, 1964).

—*Britain and the Persian Gulf 1795–1880* (Oxford, 1968).

—*The Arabian Gulf and the West* (London, 1980).

Kent, Marion, *The Great Powers and the End of the Ottoman Empire* (London, 1984).

al–Khusri, Badr al–Din, *Dirasat fi tarikh al–Kuwait* [Studies in the History of Kuwait] (Kuwait, 1983).

King, Peter, *Lord Curzon's Travels with a Superior Person* (London, 1985).

Kohn, H., *Nationalism and Imperialism in the Near East* (London, 1932).

Kumar, R., *India and the Persian Gulf 1858–1907, a Study of British Imperial Policy* (London, 1965).

Kunz, George F. and Stevenson, Charles H., *The Books of Pearl* (London, 1908).

Lackner, Helen, *A House Built on Sand: A Political Economy of Saudi Arabia* (Ithaca, 1978).

Lawless, R. I. (ed.), *The Gulf in the Early 20th Century* (Durham, 1986).

Lorimer, J. G., *Gazetteer of the Persian Gulf, Oman and Central Arabia*, printed from an original in the India Office Library (Calcutta, 1908–1915). The Gazetteer was reprinted in two volumes: Vol. I, Historical (in 3 parts), and Vol. II, Geographical and Statistical, in Parts A and B (reprinted Farnborough, 1970).

Malcolm, Sir John, *Political History of India from 1784–1823*, 2 Vols (London, 1 826).

al–Mas'udi, *Muruj al–Dhahab* [The Golden Meadows], ed. Yusif Dagher, 4 Vols (Beirut, 1981).

Meade Earle, Edward, *Turkey: The Great Powers and the Baghdad Railway. A Study in Imperialism* (New York, 1923).

Miles, S. B., *The Countries and Tribes of the Persian Gulf* (London, 1919).

Miller, J. Innes, *The Spice Trade of the Roman Empire 29 BC to AD 641* (Oxford, 1969).

Monroe, Elizabeth, *Philby of Arabia* (London, 1973).

Moss Helms, Christine *The Cohesion of Saudi Arabia* (London, 1981).

Musil, Alois, *The Northern Hegaz. A Topographical Itinerary* (New York, 1926).

—*The Middle Euphrates* (New York, 1927).

—*The Manners and Customs of the Rwala Bedouins* (New York, 1928).

Netton, Ian Richard (ed.), *Arabia and the Gulf From Traditional Society to Modern States* (London, 1986).

Niebuhr, Carsten, *Travels through Arabia and Other Countries in the East* (tr. Robert Heron), 2 Vols (Edinburgh, 1792).

Nugent, Jeffrey B. and Thomes, Theodore H., *Bahrain and the Gulf* (London, 1988).

Palgrave, William Gifford, *Narrative of a Year's Journey through Central and Eastern Arabia 1826–1863* (London, 1865).

Phelps Grant, Christina, *The Syrian Desert* (London, 1937).

Philby, H. St. J., *The Heart of Arabia*, 2 Vols (London, 1925).

—*Arabia of the Wahhabis* (London, 1928).

—*Arabia* (1932).

—*A Pilgrim in Arabia* (London, 1943).

—*Arabian Days, an Autobiography* (London, 1948).

—*Forty Years in the Wilderness* (London, 1957).

—*Saudi Arabia* (London, 1955).

Porter, Bernard, *Britain, Europe and the World 1850–1986: Delusions of Grandeur* (London, 1987).

Prasad, Yuvaraj Deva, *The Indian Muslims and World War I (A phase of disillusionment with British rule 1914–1918)* (New Delhi, 1985).

Praunkiaer, Barclay, *Through Wahhbiland on Camelback* (tr. Gerald de Gaury) (London, 1969).

Pridham, B. R. (ed.), *The Arab Gulf and the Arab World* (London, 1988).

—*The Arab Gulf and the West* (London, 1985).

Rathbone Low, Charles, *History of the Indian Navy* (London, 1877).

Rawan, Carl R., *Black Tents of Arabia* (Boston, 1935).

al-Rifa'i, Hissah, *Min tarikh al–Kuwait* [From the History of Kuwait] (Cairo, 1959).

Rihani, Ameen, *Ibn Sa'oud of Arabia. His People and his Land* (London, 1928).

—*Around the Coasts of Arabia* (London, 1930, reprinted New York, 1983).

Ronaldshay, Earl of, *The Life of Lord Curzon* (London, 1928).

Rosenthal, Erwin I. J., *Islam in the Modern National State* (Cambridge, 1965).

Royal Intelligence Division, *Western Arabia and the Red Sea* (Oxford, 1946).

Rumaihi, Muhammad, *Beyond Oil* (tr. James Dickins) (London, 1986).

Rush, Alan, *Al–Sabah: History and Genealogy of Kuwait's Ruling Family 1752–1987*(London, 1987).

al-Rushaid, Abdul Aziz, *Tarikh al–Kuwait* [History of Kuwait] (Dar Maktabat, al–Hayat, 1978).

Sadleir, George Forster, *Diary of Journey across Arabia 1819* (Reprint, 1977).

Schoff, Z., (tr.), *The Periplus of the Erythrean Sea by a Greek Merchant (AD 60)* (London, 1912).

Serjeant, R. B. and Bidwell, R. L., *Arabian Studies* (London, 1975).

al-Shaikh Kha'zal, Husain Kalaf, *Tarikh al–Kuwait al–siyasi* [Political History of Kuwait], 5 Vols (1817–1950) (Beirut, 1962).

al-Shamlan, Saif Marzuq, *Tarikh al–ghaws ala al–lulufi al–Kuwait wa al–Khalij al–Arabi* [History of Pearl Diving in Kuwait] (Kuwait, 1975).

Sitwell, N. H. H., *Outside the Empire: The World the Romans Knew* (London, 1986).

Steiner, Z., *The Foreign Office and Foreign Policy 1898–1914* (Cambridge, 1969).

Sweet, Louise E. (ed.), *The Central Middle East: A Handbook of Anthropology*, Vol. II (Connecticut, 1968).

—*Peoples and Cultures of the Middle East*, Vol. I (New York, 1970).

Taylor, A. J. P., *The Trouble–Makers: Dissent over Foreign Policy 1792–1939* (Harmondsworth, 1985).

Teixera, Pedro (tr. William F. Sinclair), *The Travels of Pedro Teixera* (London, 1802).

Thomas, Bertram, *The Arabs* (London, 1937).

Tibbetts, G. R., *Arab Navigation in the Indian Ocean before the Coming of the Portuguese* (London, 1971).

Trench, Richard, *Arabian Travellers* (London, 1986).

Troeller, Gary, *The Birth of Saudi Arabia. Britain and the Rise of the House of Saud* (London, 1976).

Tauber, Ebeizer, 'Sayyid Talib and the Young Turks in Basra'. *Middle Eastern Studies*, Vol. 25, No. 1, January 1989.

Tweedie, W., *The Arabian Horse. His Country and People* (Beirut, 1894).

Varthema, L. de (tr. from original Italian edition of 1510 by George Percy Badger), *The Travels of Ludovico di Vartherna in Egypt, Syria, Arabia Deserts and Arabia Felix, in Persia, India and Ehtiopia AD 1503 to 1508* (London, 1863).

Villiers, Alan, *Sons of Sinbad* (New York, 1940).

Wahba, Hafiz, *Arabian Days* (London, 1964).

Wallin, Gerg August, *Travels in Arabia (1845 and 1848)* (Reprint, 1979).

Wellsted, James Raymond, *Travels to the City of the Caliphs, along the Shores of the Persian Gulf and the Mediterranean: Including a Voyage to the Coast of Arabia, and a Tour on the Island of Socotra* (London, 1840).

—*Travels in Arabia*, 2 Vols (London, 1838 (reprinted 1932).

Wilson, Sir Arnold T., *The Persian Gulf* (Oxford, 1928).

—*Loyalties Mesopotamia, 1914–1917* (London, 1930).

Winstone, H. V. F., *Captain Shakespear: A Portrait* (London, 1978).

—*The Illicit Adventure: The Story of Political and Military Intelligence in the Middle East from 1898 to 1926* (London, 1982).

Zaki, Saleh, *Mesopotamia 1600–1914* (London, 1957).

Zeine, Z. N., *The Emergence of Arab Nationalism* (Beirut, 1958).

Zwemer, S. M., *Arabia: The Cradle of Islam* (Edinburgh, 1900).

Articles and Dissertations.

Abbott, A. G. F. 'A Revolt of Islam?', *The Quarterly Review*, Vol. 223, No. 442, Part I, January–April 1915, pp. 66–67.

ABC 'British Foreign Policy', *National Review*, XXXVIII, November 1901, pp. 343–58.

Abu–Manneh, B. 'Sultan Abdul Hamid II and Shaikh Abulhuda Al-Sayyadi', *Middle Eastern Studies*, Vol. 15, No. 2, May 1979, pp. 131–48.

Ahmad, F. 'Great Britain's Relations with the Young Turks 1908–1914', *Middle Eastern Studies*, Vol. 2, No. 4, July 1966, pp. 302–29.

Anon. 'Memorandum of the Proceedings of the Expedition against the Pirates of the Gulf of Persia AD 1819–20', *Blackwood's Edinburgh Magazine*, Vol. 10, September 1821, pp. 151–8.

Anon. 'Baghdad Railway Negotiation', *The Quarterly Review*, Vol. 228, No. 453, October 1917, pp. 487–528.

Ashkenazi, T. 'The Anazah Tribes', *Southwestern Journal of Anthropology*, Vol. 4, No. 2, Summer 1948, pp. 222–39.

'Asiaticus' 'India – What has become of the Anglo–German Agreement?', *National Review*, Vol. 65, March–August 1915, pp. 148–56.

Axelson, Eric 'Prince Henry the Navigator and the Discovery of the Sea Route to India', *Geographical Journal*, Vol. 127, Part II, June 1961, pp. 145–58.

Belgrave, C. 'Persian Gulf – Past and Present', *Journal of the Royal Central Asian Society*,

Vol. LV, 1968, pp. 28–34.

Belhaven ad Stenton 'Abd–el–Aziz Ibn Saud', *Nineteenth Century and After*, Vol. 95, April 1924, pp. 587–91.

Bell, H. T. M. 'Great Britain and the Persian Gulf', *United Empire*, Vol. 6, 1915, pp. 274–78.

Bennett, T. J. 'The Past and Present Connection of England with the Persian Gulf', *Journal of the Society of Art*, Vol. L, 13 June 1902, pp. 634–51.

Bent, Theodore 'Exploration of the Frankincense Country, Southern Arabia', *The Geographical Journal*, Vol. 6, No. 2, August 1895, pp. 109–34.

Blunt, Wilfred Scawen 'A Visit to Jebel Shammer (nejd)', *Proceedings of the Royal Geographical Society*, Vol. II, No. 2, February 1880, pp. 81–102.

Bowen, R. Le B., jr. 'The Pearl Fisheries of the Persian Gulf', *Middle East Journal*, Vol. 5, No. 2, Winter 1951, pp. 161–80.

Buckingham, C. F. 'Some Early European Travellers in Arabia', in R. B. Serjeant and R. L. Bidwell (eds), *Arabian Studies*, Vol. 9, 1976, pp. 1–4.

Busch, B. C. 'Britain and the states of Kuwayt 1896–1899', *Middle East Journal*, Vol. 21, No. 2, Spring 1967, pp. 187–98.

Caskel, W. 'The Bedouinization of Arabia', in G. E. von Grunebaum (ed.), *The American Anthropological Association*, Vol. 56, No. 2, April 1954, pp. 37–46.

Chirol, V. 'Turkey in the Grip of Germany', *The Quarterly Review*, Vol. 223, January 1915, No. 442, Part I, pp. 231–51.

—'Storm Waves in the Mohammedan World', *Journal of the Royal Central Asian Society*, Vol. IX, 1922, Pt I, pp. 193–223.

—'The Downfall of the Ottoman Khalifat', *Journal of the Royal Central Asian Society*, Vol. XI, 1924, Pt III, pp. 229–43.

Chowdhury, D. A. 'The Mohammadans of Bengal', *Muslim World*, Vol. 15, April 1925, No. 2, pp. 135–9.

Cohen, S. A. 'The Genesis of the British Campaign in Mesopotamia, 1914', *Middle Eastern Studies*, Vol. 12, No. 2, May 1976, pp. 119–32.

Cole, Juan R. I. 'Indian Money and the Shi'i Shrine Cities of Iraq', *Middle Eastern Studies*, Vol. 22, No. 4, October 1986, pp. 461–80.

Coleridge, G. 'Great Britain and the Persian Gulf', *Nineteenth Century and After*, Vol. 100, December 1926, pp. 828–36.

Cunningham, A. 'The Sick Man and the British Physician', *Middle Eastern Studies*, Vol. 17, No. 2, April 1981, pp. 147–73.

—'Dragomania – The Dragoman of the British Embassy in Turkey', *St Antony's Papers*, Oxford, No. 11, 1961, pp. 81–100.

—'The Wrong Horse? A Study of Anglo–Turkish Relations before the First World War', *St Antony's Papers*, Oxford, No. 17, 1965, pp. 56–76.

Dalyell, G. 'The Persian Gulf', *Journal of the Royal Central Asian Society*, Vol. 25, Pt III, pp. 349–64.

Danvers, F. G. 'Persian Gulf Route and Commerce', *Asiatic Quarterly Review*, Vol. 10,

No. 10, April 1888.

Doughty, Charles M. 'Travels in Nejd', *Proceedings of the Royal Geographical Society*, Vol. 6, No. 71, 1884, pp. 382–99.

Dubuisson, P. 'Qasimi Piracy and the General Treaty of Peace 1820', in R. B. Serjeant and R. L. Bidwell (eds), *Arabian Studies*, Vol. 4, 1978, pp. 47–57.

Earle, E. M. 'The Secret Anglo–German Convention of 1914 Regarding Asiatic Turkey', *Political Science Quarterly*, XXXVIII, March 1923, pp. 24–33.

van Ess, J. 'Why the Holy War Failed', *Muslim World*, Vol. 8, April 1918, No. 2, pp. l89–90.

Field, Arthur 'A Turco–British Entente', *The Asiatic Quarterly Review*, new series, Vol. II, Nos 3 and 4, July–October 1913, pp. 249–55.

Fraser, L. 'Some Problems in the Persian Gulf', *Proceedings of the Royal Central Asian Society*, Vol. 33, 1911.

—'Gun–running in the Persian Gulf', *Proceedings of the Royal Central Asian Society*, Vol. 33, 1911, pp. 1–23.

—'Position in the Persian Gulf', *National Review*, Vol. 50, No. 298, December 1907, pp. 624–36.

Geddes, Patrick 'The Influence of Geographical Conditions of Social Development', *Geographical Journal*, Vol. 12, No. 6, December 1898, pp. 580–7.

Gleig, G. R. Review of J. Malcolm's *Political History of India, 1784–1823*, *Blackwood's Edinburgh Magazine*, Vol. XX, July–December 1826, pp. 689–709.

Goldberg, J. 'Saudi Ottoman Treaty Myth or Reality', *Journal of Contemporary History* 19, 1984, pp. 289–314.

—'Philby as a Source for Early 20th Century Saudi History: A Critical Examination', *Middle Eastern Studies*, Vol. 21, No. 2, April 1985, pp. 223–43.

—'Captain Shakespear and Ibn Saud: A balanced reappraisal', *Middle Eastern Studies*, Vol. 22, No. 1, January 1986, pp. 74–88.

Gopal, K. 'The Caliphate Movement in India: The First Phase', *Journal of the Royal Asiatic Society of Great Britain and Ireland* (new series), Vol. 1967–68, Pts 1 and 2, pp. 37–53.

Gouldrup, Lawrence 'The Ikhwan Movement of Central Arabia', *Arabian Studies*, Vol. VI, pp. 161–9.

Groom, N. 'Eastern Arabia in Ptolemy's Map', in R. D. Serjeant and R. L. Bidwell (eds), *Arabian Studies*, Vol. 16, 1986, pp. 65–75.

Hardford, F. D. 'An Old Route to India', *Journal of the Royal Central Asian Society*, Vol. VI, 1919, Pts III and IV, pp. 99–118.

Harlow, S. Ralph et al. 'The War and Islam', *Muslim World*, Vol. 5, January 1915, No. l, pp. 4–19.

Heller, Joseph 'Sir Louis Mallet and the Ottoman Empire: The Road to War', *Middle Eastern Studies*, Vol. 12, January 1976, No. 1, pp. 3–44.

Hinsley, F. H. 'British Foreign Policy and the Colonial Question 1895–1904', in E. A. Berians et al. (eds), *Cambridge History of the British Empire*, Vol. III (Cambridge,

1959), pp. 490–537.

—'Great Britain and the Powers 1904–1914', *The Empire Commonwealth*, Vol. III, 1959, pp. 538–62.

Hogarth, D. G. 'The Nearer East: British policy in Persia and Asiatic Turkey', *Edinburgh Review*, Vol. 195, April 1902, pp. 398–428.

Holme, Frederick 'Travels of Ebn Batuta', *Blackwood's Edinburgh Magazine*, Vol. 49, May 1841, pp. 597–615.

Hoskins, H. L. 'Background of the British Position in Arabia', *Middle East Journal*, Vol. 1, No. 2, April 1947, pp. 137–47.

Hunter, F. Fraser 'Reminiscences of the Map of Arabia and Persian Gulf', *The Geographical Journal*, Vol. 54, No. 6, December 1919, pp. 355–63.

Ingram, E. 'From Trade to Empire in the Near East', Part I, 'The end of the spectre of the overland trade, 1775–1801', *Middle Eastern Studies*, Vol. 14, No. 1, January 1978, pp. 3–21.

—'From Trade to Empire in the Near East', Part II, 'The repercussions of the incident at Nakhilu in 1803', *Middle Eastern Studies*, Vol. 14, No. 2, May 1978, pp. 183–204.

—'From Trade to Empire in the Near East', Part III, 'The uses of the Residency at Baghdad, 1794–1804', *Middle Eastern Studies*, Vol. 14, No. 3, October 1978, pp. 278–306.

Iseminger, G. L. 'The Old Turkish Hands: The British Levantine Consuls 1856–76', *Middle East Journal*, Vol. 22, No. 3, September 1968, pp. 297–316.

Kedourie, E. 'Egypt and the Caliphate, 1915–1946', *Journal of the Royal Asiatic Society of Great Britain and Ireland* (new series), Vol. 1963–64, Pts 3 and 4, pp. 208–48.

Kelly, J. B. 'Mehmet Ali's Expedition to the Persian Gulf, 1837–1840', Pts 1 and 2, *Middle Eastern Studies*, Vol. l, No. 4, July 1965, pp. 350–81, and Vol. 2, No. 1, October 1965, pp. 31–65.

—'History of Eastern Arabia', *Bulletin of School of Oriental and African Studies*, No. 31, 1968, pp. 152–3.

—'The Legal and Historical Basis of the British Position in the Persian Gulf', *St Antony's Papers*, Oxford, No. 4, 1958, pp. 119–60.

Kempthorne, G. B. 'Notes Made on a Survey along the Eastern Shores of the Persian Gulf in 1828', *Journal of the Royal Geographical Society*, Vol. V, 1835, pp. 263–82.

Kumar, R. 'Abdul Aziz Al–Saud and the Genesis of Saudi Arabia 1900–1907', Pts I and II, *Bengal: Past and Present*, Vols 79–89 (1960–61), Pt I – January–June, pp. 60–6, Pt II – July–December, pp. 83–9.

Lancaster, Halford 'Background of the British Position in Arabia', *Middle East Journal*, Vol. I, No. 2, April 1947, pp. l37–47.

Leachman, G. 'A Journey through Central Arabia', *Geographical Journal*, Vol. 43, May 1914, pp. 500–20.

Leitner, G. W. 'The Khalifa Question and the Sultan of Turkey', *The Imperial and Asiatic Quarterly Review*, 3rd series, Vol. I, Nos l and 2, January–April 1896, pp. 65–74.

Levine, I. D. 'Arab versus Turks', *The American Review of Reviews*, Vol. 54, November

1916, pp. 527–32.

Lewis, C. C. 'Ibn Saud and the Future of Arabia', *International Affairs*, Vol. 12, No. 4, July 1933, pp. 518–34.

Lynch, H. F. B. 'The Persian Gulf and International Relations', *International Review*, pp. 27–45.

—'The Persian Gulf', *Imperial and Asiatic Quarterly Review and Oriental Review and Oriental and Colonial Record* , 3rd series, XIII, April 1902, pp. 225–34.

—'Railways in the Middle East', *Imperial and Asiatic Quarterly Review and Oriental Review and Oriental and Colonial Record* , Vol. 31, Nos 61–2, 3rd series, April 1911, pp. 225–49.

Mahan, A. T. 'The Persian Gulf and International Relations', *National Review*, Vol. XL, September 1902, pp. 27–45.

Maltzan, Baron von 'Geography of Southern Arabia', *Proceedings of the Royal Geographical Society*, Vol. 16, No. 2, 27 February 1872, pp. 115–23.

Miles, S. B. 'Notes on Pliny's Geography of the East Coast of Arabia', *Journal of the Royal Asiatic Society of Great Britain and Ireland*, Vol. 10 (new series), 1878, pp. 157–72.

Moreland, W. H. 'The Ships of the Arabian Sea about AD1500', Pts I and II, *Journal of the Royal Asiatic Society of Great Britain and Ireland*, Pt I – January 1939, p. 63: Pt II – April 1939, p. 173.

Moore, A. 'Notes on Dhows', *Mariner's Mirror*, Vol. 26, 1940, pp. 203–13.

Mylrea, S. G. 'Kuwait, Arabia', *Muslim World*, Vol. 7, April 1917, No. 2, pp. 118–26.

—'Mediaevalism in Arabia', *Muslim World*, Vol. 22, No. 2, April 1932.

Nadvi, Saiyed Sulyman 'The Commercial Relations of India with Arabia', *Islamic Culture*, Vol. 7, April 1933, pp. 281–308.

—'Arab Navigation', *Islamic Culture*, Vol. 15, No. 4, October 1941, pp. 435–48; Vol. 16, No. 1, January 1942, pp. 72–86; Vol. 16, No. 2, April 1942, pp. 182–98; Vol. 16, No. 4, October 1942, pp. 404–22.

Naimatullah, S. M. 'Recent Turkish Events and Moslem India', *Asiatic Quarterly Review*, October 1913, pp. 241–8, Vol. 11, Nos 3 and 4.

Newcombe, S. F., and J. P. S. Grieg 'The Baghdad Railway', *Geographical Journal*, Vol. 44, No. 1, July 1914, pp. 577–80.

Ormsby Gore, W. 'The Organisation of British Responsibilities in the Middle East', *Journal of the Royal Central Asian Society*, Vol. VII, 1920, Pts II and III, pp. 83–105.

Palgrave, Gifford 'Notes of a Journey from Gaza, through the Interior of Arabia, to El Khatif on the Persian Gulf, and thence to Oman, in 1862–3', *Proceedings of the Royal Geographical Society*, Vol. 8, No. 3, Session 1863–64, pp. 63–82.

Pastner, S. 'Desert and Coast: Population flux between pastoral and maritime adaptation in the Old World arid zone', *International Union of Anthropological and Ethnological Sciences*, No. 6, June 1980.

Pelly, L. 'Persian Gulf as an Area of Trade, 1863–1864', *Proceedings of the Royal Geographical Society*, Vol. 8, pp. 18–21.

—'Account of a Recent Tour round the Northern Position of the Persian Gulf'. *Transactions of the Bombay Geographic Society*, Vol. 17, January 1863 to December 1864, pp. 113–40.

—'Remarks on the Tribes, Trade and Resources around the Shoreline of the Persian Gulf', *Transactions of the Bombay Geographic Society*, Vol. 17, January 1863 to December 1864, pp. 62–112.

—'Remarks on the Pearl Oyster Beds in the Persian Gulf', *Transactions of the Bombay Geographic Society*, Vol. 18, from January 1865 to December 1867, pp. 32–5.

—'Visit to the Wahabee Capital of Central Arabia', *Proceedings of the Royal Geographical Society*, Vol. 9, Series 1864–5, pp. 293–6.

Peterson, J. E. 'Tribes and Policies in Eastern Arabia', *Middle East Journal*, Vol. 31, No. 3, Summer 1977, pp. 297–312.

Philby, H. St. John 'The Highway of Central Arabia', *Journal of the Royal Central Asian Society*, Vol. VI, 1920, Pt IV, pp. 112–25.

—'The Recent History of the Hijaz', *Journal of the Central Asian Society*, Vol. XII, Pt 4, 1925, pp. 332–51.

—'The Triumph of the Wahhabis', *Journal of the Royal Central Asian Society*, Vol. XIII, 1926, Pt IV, pp. 293–319.

Pilla, R. V., and M. Kumar 'The Political and Legal Status of Kuwait', *International and Comparative Law Quarterly*, Vol. II, 1962, pp. 108–30.

Rawlinson, H. C. 'Notes on Extracts from Report on the Islands and Antiquities of Bahrain by Captain Durand', *Journal of the Royal Asiatic Society of Great Britain and Ireland*, Vol. 12 (new series), 1880, pp. 189–227.

—'Notes on Moham'roh and the Choab Arabs, etc. ', *Proceedings of the Royal Geographical Society*, Vol. I, No. 9, April and May 1857, pp. 351–64.

al-Rifai, H. 'Sea Chanties of Kuwait', in R. B. Serjeant and R. L. Bidwell (eds), *Arabian Studies*, Vol. VII, 1985, p. 89.

Roff, W. R. 'Sanitation and Security: The Imperial Powers and the 19th-century Hajj', in R. B. Serjeant and R. L. Bidwell (eds), *Arabian Studies*, Vol. VI, pp. 143–60.

Salibi, K. 'Middle East Parallel: Syria, Iraq, Arabic in Ottoman Tune', *Middle Eastern Studies*, Vol. 15, No. 1, January 1979, pp. 70–81.

Silverfarb, D. 'The Anglo–Najd Treaty of December 1915', *Middle Eastern Studies*, Vol. 16, No. 3, October 1980, pp. 167–77.

Smith, T. F. A. 'German War Literature on the Near and Middle East', *The Quarterly Review*, Vol. 227, January–April 1917, pp. 144–59.

Standish, J. F. 'British Maritime Policy in the Persian Gulf', *Middle Eastern Studies*, Vol. 3, No. 4, July 1967, pp. 324–54.

Stiff, Arthur W. 'Ancient Trading Centres of the Persian Gulf: I - Sitaf', *Geographical Journal*, Vol. 6, No. 8, August 1895, pp. 166–73.

—'Ancient Trading Centres of the Persian Gulf: Kais, or al Kais', *Geographical Journal*, Vol. 7, No. 6, June 1896, pp. 644–49.

—'Ancient Trading Centres of the Persian Gulf: pre-Mohammedan Settlements',

Geographical Journal, Vol. 9, No. 3, March 1897, pp. 309–14.

—'Ancient Trading Centres of the Persian Gulf: IV—Maskat', *Geographical Journal*, Vol. 10, No. 6, December 1897, pp. 608–18.

Strunk, William Theodore, 'The Reign of Shaykh Khazal Ibn Jabir and the Suppression of the Principality of Arabistan: A Study in British Imperialism in Southwestern Iran, 1897–1925', unpublished Ph.D. thesis, Indiana University, 1977.

Sweet, L. E. 'Pirates or Politics? Arab Societies of the Persian or Arabian Gulf in the 18th Century', *Ethnohistory*, Vol. 11, 1964, pp. 263–80.

Tibbetts, G. R. 'Arabia in the Fifteenth–century Navigational Texts', *Arabian Studies*, Vol. I, pp. 86–101.

Toynbee, A. 'The Turks in the Near and Middle East', *Journal of the Royal Asiatic Society of Great Britain and Ireland* (new series), Vol. 1961–2, Pts 3 and 4, pp. 77–99.

Trowbridge, S. van R. S., *et al.* 'The Moslem Press and the War', *Muslim World*, Vol. 5, January 1915, No. l, pp. 413–25.

Vickery, C. E. 'Arabia and the Hedjaz', *Journal of the Royal Central Asian Society*, Vol. X, 1923, Pt I, pp. 46–67.

Villiers, A. 'Dhow Builders of Kuwait', *Geographical Magazine*, Vol. XX, No. 9, January 1948, pp. 345–49.

—'The Astonishing Port of Kuwait', 171e *Trident*, Vol. 12, No. 131, March 1950, pp. 96–9.

—'Some Aspects of the Arab Dhow Trade', *Middle East Journal*, Vol. 2, No. 4, October 1948, pp. 399–416.

—'Some Aspects of the Arab Dhow Trade', in L. E. Sweet (ed.), *Peoples and Cultures of the Middle East*, Vol. I, The Natural History Press, 1970, New York, pp. 155–72.

Waddell, L. A. 'Speculations on New Near Eastern Frontiers after the War', *The Arabic Review*, Vols 9 and 10, July–November 1916, Nos 25–28, pp. 405–11.

Wilson, A. T. 'Persian Gulf', *Edinburgh Review*, Vol. 240, October 1924, pp. 284–95.

—'Some Early Travellers in Persia and the Persian Gulf', *Journal of the Royal Central Asian Society*, Vol. 12, Part I, 1925, pp. 68–82.

Woods, C. H. 'The Baghdad Railway and its Tributaries' *Geographical Journal*, Vol. 40, No. 1, July 1917, pp. 32–56.

Wylie, MacLeod 'The Arabian Empire', *Blackwood's Edinburgh Magazine*, Vol. 43, May 1838, pp. 661–76.

'X' 'The Focus of Asiatic Policy', *National Review*, Vol. 37, March–August 1901, pp. 624–37.

Zwemer, S. M. 'Islam: its Worth and its Failure', *Muslim World*, Vol. 10, April 1920, pp. 144–56.

—'Islam in India', *Muslim World*, Vol. 15, April 1925, No. 2, pp. 109–14.

Index